The Temple with the Chrysanthemums

Copyright © 2018 Ineke van der Wal

ISBN: 9781790557769

Ineke van der Wal

The Temple with the Chrysanthemums

Dutch Prisoners of War in Tokyo

INEKE VAN DER WAL

A so-called 'convalescent kit' as distributed by the American Red Cross to prisoners of war. The contents exist of small items which you so terribly miss during captivity such as a toothbrush and toothpaste, a comb, flea powder, soap, writing paper with a pencil, a shaving kit and a book to read. This kit was sponsored by the Red Cross in Houston.

Ineke van der Wal

Introduction

Beb Einthoven-Zeeman, the main character of this book, is my grandmother. She has led an eventful life, part of which takes place during World War II. Beb and her family fled The Netherlands in May 1940 after the German invasion and were liberated in Japan in August 1945 as part of a group of 22 Dutch prisoners of war. This group was transported from the Dutch East Indies (now Indonesia) to Japan, and this time it was not just the men who went, but the women and children were forced to go along too.

During the five years of war, there was no contact between Beb and her family in The Netherlands. After the liberation, Beb wrote 23 letters to explain what had happened to her. These letters are the basis of this book.

This fairly complete report is supplemented with the diary of one of the other prisoners of war together with interviews with members of this particular group. Chapters were added about the history of the main characters with some background information on Dutch East Indies, the work there and finally a description of the journey back.

Why embark on such a project? Because I realized one day that my mother was deeply impacted by events from her past, which she did not want to discuss with her children. My mother did not, for example, display a flag on May 5 (Dutch liberation day); a flag was flown on August 15 (Japanese surrender day, her liberation day). As a child, I felt embarrassed because our house was the only house with a flag in August.

Most Dutch people living in the Dutch East Indies were imprisoned during the Japanese occupation in a camp, often a point of recognition in later encounters. My mother was not in a camp, where was she then?

At the home of friends I heard parents talk about the war in The Netherlands. Funny stories sometimes about sending the occupier in the wrong direction or other small acts of resistance. Cousins told me that their parents were unresponsive as well. The war was an inaccessible part of their life.

One day I found a blue cotton bag at my mother's house with the words: 'Convalescent Kit' and the emblem of the Red Cross. 'I never want to part with that,' she said, 'That was my only possession after the war.'

What had happened during that war?

Eventually, I met with George Levenbach, one of the Dutch prisoners who was willing to share his experiences. A family friend, who was listening in, urged me to write up the whole story. Many years later and with much research, Beb's story is now available. Almost eighty years after the beginning of the war in The Netherlands! What a deep impression is left behind by such an event.

The letters from my grandmother already show a certain distance from her experiences. She wrote them after the war. The isolation of the group becomes only apparent in Beb's first letter to her family. The last line reads: 'It was so lonely.'

Ineke van der Wal

I believe it was this isolation that made the internment so difficult. Fifteen months of house arrest in the middle of Tokyo without contact with the outside world. The adults taught the children and seized every opportunity to organize something, to keep busy and to keep alive the spirit to survive. The death of her husband Wim pushed Beb further into complete loneliness.

A prisoner yearns for liberation, but that does not automatically mean the end of one's problems. Not being able to return to the Dutch East Indies and the loss of all property is an unexpected disappointment after the end of the war, which one must deal with at a moment when one no longer expects it.

As a grandchild I did not know this story; Beb was for me just grandma Haarlem, where she lived. She was tall and had an impressive head of gray hair. She walked upright and was neatly dressed in a suit with a colorful silk blouse, always decorated with some jewelry. Even in her old age she walked briskly saying 'Hurry on, we can catch the green light' and she would. Beb wanted to live on despite all adversities, and she did just that in her own way.

Ineke van der Wal

Contents

Ineke van der Wal

CHAPTER I

Beb

'Yes, sir,' says Kate de Bruyn to Piet Zeeman, a friend of her father and the man who asks her to marry him. The wedding is on April 5, 1894. Piet is 42 and Kate is 22 years old and they decide to live in Vrijenban near Delft, where Piet has been a professor at the Delft University of Technology since 1879. On April 13, 1895, at half past ten in the evening on the Saturday before Easter, their first child is born, a daughter. They name her Elisabeth Cornelia, the names of her mother, but in reverse. However, the baby is soon called Beb and that will remain so for a lifetime.

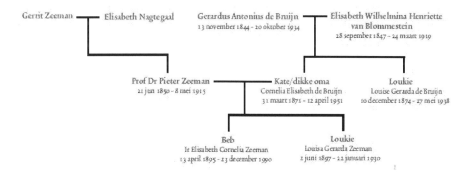

Pedigree of Beb Zeeman.

Mother Kate keeps a diary during the first years of Beb's life. Many names of acquaintances are mentioned, engagements and deaths, the ups and downs, people who come to visit or where they visit. Family comes to stay (sister, parents, sister-in-law) and they also go there regularly and they enjoy trips to the *Grand Hotel Kurhaus* in Scheveningen. They have household staff: Cor, a girl who comes daily and sometimes babysits, and Jansje who helps in the kitchen. However, the major part of the diaries is filled with the wonderful holidays. In the summer Piet has a long vacation, and then they travel through Europe. Beb then stays with her maternal grandparents in Bergen op Zoom. In 1896 they take a trip to Brussels: dining at the *Laiterie* in the *Bois* and looking at the *Cortège Militaire*. They travel via Luxembourg to Trier, Manderscheid ('second-class hotel, fairly good bread, bad coffee'), Wiesbaden (dinner at the *Nassauer Hof*), Frankfurt (where they visit the opera and the *Bauer Palmgarten*). In every city they visit friends or meet acquaintances. Via Cologne and Arnhem they travel back to Bergen op Zoom, where they stay for another three weeks. There they can walk in the *Wouwse Plantage* and swim every day. On September 1, they return to their home in Delft, where mother Kate has to get used to the household routine again.

During the holidays of 1897 Kate and Piet stay in The Netherlands because Kate is pregnant. A large part of the summer is spent in Bergen op Zoom with the grandparents, among other things to avoid the smelly Delft canals. Kate tries to wean Beb from the bottle and toilet train her. This would make life easier when the second child arrives, but she does not cooperate. Beb remains in Bergen op Zoom at the end of the summer while Kate goes back to Delft. Mrs. Eijk van Voorthuyzen, a nurse, moves in per September 1, to help with the birth. The nurse checks the baby outfit together with Kate that day, and Kate goes into labor soon after. On September 2, 1897, at one thirty in the morning, Beb's sister is born: a large baby with a big bunch of black hair. They call her Louise (after Kate's sister) Gerarda (after Kate's father), and give her the nickname Loukie.

The summer of 1898 is filled with the 5-year anniversary celebrations in Delft and the coronation festivals in The Hague. Beb comes home to see the large party for which all members of the university dress up

Ineke van der Wal

according to the theme of the festivities. The parents are busy attending three balls starting at 10 pm and finishing at 5 am. 'Piet had been taking exams for 7 weeks and therefore needed some distraction.'

Mother Cornelia Elizabeth Zeeman-De Bruyn with her 13 months old daughter Elizabeth Cornelia Zeeman.

Piet Zeeman, Beb's father, holds a PhD in mathematics with a dissertation entitled *The Curved Lines of the Third Order in Space* and works as a professor of theoretical mechanics. Father Zeeman is much appreciated in Delft:

'At that time, theoretical mechanics was virtually the only purely theoretical exam of the engineering course, and the study of this often resulted in great difficulties for the more practical students. Professor Zeeman succeeded by his excellent teachings to remove these difficulties to a large extent. His perfectly clear and detailed lectures were followed by an always numerous audience with special attention and appreciation, and many engineers remember their former teacher with large gratitude.'

Father Zeeman is also active as a scientist, supervises many a student's work for his doctor's degree, is a member of the Mathematical Society and works as editor of the *Revue Semestrielle des Publications Mathématiques*. (The twice yearly review of mathematical publications)

The house of grandparents De Bruyn in the Biltstraat 194 in Utrecht, The Netherlands, where granddaughter Beb stays regularly.

Kate's parents give a lot of help to the young family. They regularly come by to do some chores or they let the girls stay with grandma and grandpa, so that mother Kate can recover. It is not only a close-knit family, but thanks to the military career of Kate's father there is a lot of help in the household of the grandparents and they live in large houses. First in Bergen op Zoom, then in the Celebesstraat in The Hague, which is again exchanged for the Oosterpark in Amsterdam.

Beb Zeeman (right) with her little sister Loukie in 1898.

After Grandpa's appointment to General, the grandparents live in Utrecht at Biltstraat 194, near the Maliebaan where the army practices. Soldiers come to the house to sharpen the knives and Beb and Loukie are allowed to ride a horse with Grandpa on the Maliebaan. The De Bruyn family is a family of distinction. Uncle Johan even becomes mayor of Kampen. Around 1900 belonging to a respected family is a great support and you try to keep your family in good standing. At that time, the five million people in The Netherlands live in a strongly segregated society. Approximately five percent of the population belongs to the social elite, the highest level: factory directors, city administrators and nobility. This group is in charge. Forty-five percent belong to the middle class, shopkeepers, artisans, ordinary citizens. The other fifty percent is known as laborers, usually without any education and with nothing more than a few hands to make a living. (*Woud, Koninkrijk vol sloppen*)

Mother Zeeman with her two daughters in 1902.

Ineke van der Wal

For a long time Kate and Piet keep their schedule of summer vacations that are filled with travel through Europe while the children stay with Grandpa and Grandma. They take all these journeys by train. At that time, almost no one has a car. In 1899 they take a trip to the Teutoburg Forest in Germany where they stay for 14 days in Hotel Kaiserhof, complete room and board for 10 marks per day. Afterwards they enjoy a few more days at the Victoria Hotel in Amsterdam, where they eat at *Kras* and *Americain*. In October 1900, mother Kate writes that all four of them are well, 'so well, so well. The children are both our pride and joy and sometimes also my despair.' Kate and Piet Zeeman do their best to give Beb and Loukie the best possible upbringing. In the summer at the Wouwse *Plantage* they learn about the importance of working on a farm: harvesting potatoes, bringing in the hay, feeding the cows and a calf, and picking berries and raspberries, but they also play with the girls from the castle: Germaine and Hélène Emsens. Despite a lot of practice, the children keep pronouncing these names with an accent, writes their mother. Beb gets physical therapy because one shoulder is slightly higher than the other and there are regular visits to the dentist to make sure that their teeth come in correctly. The children go to kindergarten on Saturday and Wednesday afternoon for a kind of handicraft. When Beb turns six, in 1901, she starts to visit Miss Pont's school, from 9 to 12 in the morning and from 2 to 4 in the afternoon. It is a 20-minute walk from home. Finally, mother thinks it is very important that the daughters look good. As there are no store bought clothes available, this task is time consuming. It means consultation with the seamstress, but often you have to make clothes yourself.

After having worked in Delft for twenty years, father Piet accepts a professorship in Leiden in the geometric sciences and in analytical mechanics. He accepts his office on October 8, 1902 with an inaugural speech entitled 'Pure and Applied Mathematics'. In this speech he discusses the dangers of a one-sided development of mathematical science and he insists on the maintenance of a close link between the actual mathematics and its applications as auxiliary science in the practice of physics and technology.

Beb's father always aims first and foremost to develop a thorough knowledge of the principles of mathematics, convinced as he is, 'that there is little to be achieved from advanced study if the foundations are not carefully established.' This conviction leads him to become a member and later chairman of the Supervisory Committee on the Secondary Education. This work means that a group of math professors ('math artists') travel through the country to examine future mathematics teachers at the so called *acte exam*.

Portrait of Prof. Dr. P. Zeeman, the father of Beb
made in 1902 by Frits Grips.

These examiners are a close knit group who also become friends with each other. Father Piet sends letters almost every day when he is on the road. 'Dearest Kate' he writes, he tells about his day and always says that he misses his family. He also sends home some local specialties such as Frisian butter cakes from the Grand Hotel Wapen van Friesland, 'a first-class house'. In addition to the examinations, he also strives for better salaries for the teaching staff. This task as a member of the board was actually already on the horizon when he included as the nineteenth thesis of his dissertation: 'It is unjust to bestow the authority to teach geography to those who hold the degree of Doctor in Dutch literature.

The father of Beb is a member of an examining-board for which he travels throughout the country. He sends letters home to his wife and children. This one dates from June 1907.

The family moves to the Rijnsburgerweg 24 in Leiden, a neighborhood where many professors live. One of them, Professor Einthoven, has a daughter, Koosje, who has the same age as Loukie. The Einthoven family invites the Zeeman family to get acquainted and the daughters bake pancakes in the conservatory. Afterwards, older brother Wim also shares in the eating of the pancakes, but that brother leaves no special impression.

Mother Kate describes many diseases and ailments and the worries that go along with them. The general practitioner Dr. Scheltema is called to give advice several times. The girls get all the common children's illnesses and there is always some risk involved. Beb's friend Geertje dies of an illness when she is 13.

In August 1902 Loukie, then five years old, appears seriously ill. She has problems with her kidneys and is put on a strict diet: no meat or anything with eggs. She can have milk and all its varieties, rusk, bread and fruits. Twice a week she has to take a hot bath and then remain seated for an hour, wrapped up in a warm blanket to make her perspire, and of course she has to take lots of rest in bed. They consult Professor Rosenstein. Piet has already been there to bring a urine sample and to talk about Loukie's illness. They start experimenting with more time out of bed, meat, proteins and they keep checking her urine. Protein is sometimes present, but it is random and has nothing to do with her diet or bed rest.

To give Loukie healthier air, mother and child decide to go to Wiesbaden, a well-known spa. They are picked up from the station by an ambulance. In Wiesbaden they stay with aunt Lee de Bruyn, who runs the *Pension De Bruyn* at Wilhelmstrasse 38. The first goal is treatment for Loukie, but father Piet urges mother Kate to enjoy herself a little and visit the *Opera* and the *Comedy*. 'Here in Leiden you are not spoiled in this respect.' He sends money so she can really act upon his suggestion. Father thinks it's important that they both relax. He also sends a letter from yet another professor with a recommendation for a doctor in Wiesbaden. Mother and daughter get a visit from Louise, Kate's sister, who recently married Adriaan van der Chijs, a neurologist from Amsterdam. They are on their honeymoon and go to Heidelberg and Baden-Baden to study the 'local

　　　　　　　　　　　　　　　　Ineke van der Wal

music relations'. It sounds as though Kate has not lost her sense of humor, but she is worried for her youngest child, who may never get out of bed again. However, the cures work well for Loukie and in the autumn of 1904 she can start school for half-a-day, which is then gradually increased to full days.

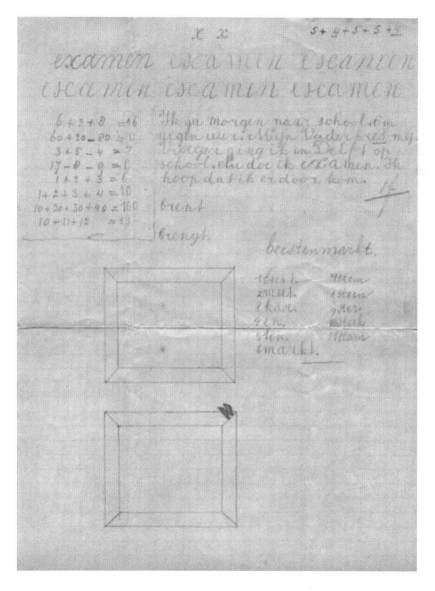

Beb's father makes small exams for Beb.

It is not surprising that Beb tries her best to attract some extra attention from her mother during this time. When Mother goes out and doesn't have time to come upstairs to help Beb get dressed, Beb says: 'Your hair is untidy, you have to come upstairs again', so that Beb has some time with her mother. Kate interprets it as a sign of social intelligence.

In this period Beb and her father spend a lot of time together. Beb's father is already older and that determines their relationship. There are no wild physical games, but simple math practices which are followed by small exams and they write to mother twice a day. Beb writes beautiful phrases and draws rectangles using a ruler. A favorite game is 'narrow dinner': you have to push your elbows into your ribs and still eat properly.

The family Zeeman-De Bruyn is financially well off, but they sometimes dream about an unknown uncle from the Dutch East Indies with a surprise inheritance. In the diary of Beb's mother money is mentioned several times. They decide to take out a life insurance policy on the life of Piet Zeeman for 3000 guilders. When Kate receives money from her parents for the grandchildren such as a rijksdaalder (a coin worth 2½ guilders) or a golden cent, she brings it to the bank right away. 'No matter how hard it rains, I will bring the money to the Savings bank in the afternoon.' The gifts they exchange for birthdays or on St. Nicholas day are always practical gifts: a chair for Beb, a light for Kate, a cash box, and stationery with initials in the letterhead. Kate makes nightgowns for the children out of old bed curtains. Stationery is re-used by writing a reply vertically over the original letter. When both daughters go to primary school, it is decided to dismiss Cor and Rika so that only Janke remains as help. They think that they can manage with only one girl as a maid in their small house, but it is not easy. In winter, a part of the house is closed; only father's study is heated and in the spring the room-en-suite with sitting and dining room is prepared for use again. In 1905 they decide to stay on the Rijnsburgerweg 24, although they think this house small. As compensation, they take a long vacation.

Grandpa and Grandma welcome the two little ones for a stay again and they re-hire Cor, who has not found a new position yet, to come and help. Piet and Kate travel via Frankfurt to Munich and on to Garmisch. These are places where Piet has been before. 'Does Dad stay in the same hotel, where he left his hiking boots?' Beb writes. They eat *Kaiserschmarren* (sugared pancakes with raisins), without napkins, accompanied by zither music and singing. The crowds in Munich and the trip are a bit much; The grandparents send migraine powders from Utrecht. They speak of 'a sudden indisposition that has affected your nervous system.' When they leave Munich, they visit the castles Neuschwanstein and Hohenschwangau, and then travel back to Utrecht via Innsbruck and Wiesbaden, where they have a few more pleasasant days. They are just in time to experience the birth of a yellow canary.

Kate has doubts about herself as a mother. Other mothers are more efficient, she thinks. For example, her friend Thilde, is already outside with her twins at 9 o'clock in the morning. Kate also thinks that she spoils the children too much:

'I do not know how it happens, because I am probably the cause of it, but our children are very demanding and if something is not allowed right away, they are angry and feel they're being punished. Nor are they obedient, which is my fault, but also Piet's, who lets me handle everything that has to do with the children's upbringing. Piet never intervenes, even if it would be helpful for him to say something.'

Later in 1945 she writes in a letter to Beb: 'I comfort myself with the thought that I was just the wife your father needed, as he has assured me thousands of times.' Kate describes a good marriage with interludes

This picture of father and daughters is the one that Beb's mother
kept at her desk. Beb stands at the left hand side.

Ineke van der Wal

such as Piet's periods of silence. She regrets it that she is sometimes hot-tempered and since Beb can be hot-tempered too, the emotions run high every once in a while. As an example, Kate quotes from the book *Gösta Berling* by Selma Lagerlöf: 'She is sensible and wise. Her eyes, like the sun, bless everything they irradiate. She controls and guards the house. Wherever she is, everything has to grow and thrive. She carries happiness with her.'

Beb on her fourteenth birthday together with her girlfriends.
April 13, 1909

Beb is intelligent and the parents decide to send her to the HBS, the five-year high school. Officially, this is a boys' school, but they do allow some girls. The well-educated citizens of Leiden send their children there. After school, there is time for piano lessons, singing, embroidery, watercolors and especially writing thank-you notes which must be written within 24 hours after a visit. Beb also signs up for dance lessons and at the Christmas ball Wim Einthoven writes Beb

Zeeman's name twice in his dance card, once for the Polonaise-Polka and another time for the *Cotillon*. The family goes on holiday for the first time with their daughters. They go to Nunspeet together with the Wijsman (wise man) family, whom they know from Leiden where Father Wijsman is also a professor. They talk about the Wise man (a 'Wijsman') and the Sea man (a 'Zeeman').

Willem Einthoven's dance card

Ineke van der Wal

Mother Kate's sister Louise gives birth to a daughter in 1909 and they name her Louise Adriana van der Chijs, nicknamed Loukie. The couple had to wait a long time for this daughter and they are very happy. They celebrate this occasion with a photo in the garden of the grandparents' house where the whole family is present with the new offspring on her mother's lap. Beb is fourteen years older than her niece and Loukie is twelve years older, but it is their only first cousin, so they are very interested in her.

The proud De Bruyn Family with their youngest granddaughter. De Bilt, The Netherlands, 1909. Standing from left: Adriaan van der Chijs, Beb Zeeman, Loukie Zeeman, Piet Zeeman. Seated from left: Loukie van der Chijs-De Bruyn with her daughter Loukie van der Chijs, Opa De Bruyn, Oma De Bruyn en Kate Zeeman-De Bruyn.

Beb's father continues to emphasize the importance of languages, so Beb goes to Oxford in the autumn of 1912 after her graduation to improve her English. She stays at Mrs. Lake's home at 19 Park Crescent in Oxford, a house where 'proper' girls live. Beb wants a camera so she can take pictures of her stay in Oxford, but that is considered too expensive. Father and mother and her sister, Loukie, take her to Oxford. They sail with the Batavier IV and visit London extensively. Beb is surprised that people in Hyde Park are sitting or lying on the grass. They travel on to Oxford: 'Then the carriage came and we rode to the station. There was Mrs. Lake and we both waited for the train to leave. We went to her house and 'the new life started.'

Beb starts a busy correspondence with her parents. With her mother she talks about what she wears, which clothes match well together, which cardigan keeps her warm and elegant, and how she has to hide valuable things. Mother advises her: 'Have a good and cozy time and spread a lot of love around you'

Beb's parents write regularly during Beb's stay in Oxford, UK. This envelope is from October 30, 1912.

Beb obviously writes a lot about her excursions, knows so many people that there is always someone she recognizes. The correspondence with her father is mainly about her choice of profession. What does she want to do in life? Beb proposes an accounting course, but her father thinks that she needs to raise her ambitions. They decide on architecture. In preparation, Beb asks her father about 'interesting

Ineke van der Wal

questions about geometry' but instead she gets the fatherly advice to particularly enjoy her time in Oxford.

After her return, she registers at Delft Technical University in the autumn of 1913. She decides, however, to follow mathematics classes in Leiden with her father. At that time sixty women study in Delft, about 4% of the total student population and the men don't make it easy for these women. The professors and male fellow students do not regard these daughters of professors (which they usually are) as serious students: the lectures are seen as a pastime for these women to obtain some cultural background. Vocational training is not the goal but to 'snag an attractive partner in their nets'.

Inauguration dinner of DVSV-Delft female students association on September 26, 1913. Beb stands on the hindmost row as number twelve from the left.

Many female students become members of *DVSV* - Delft Female Student Association, which provides fellowship, friends and housing and Beb also takes advantage of that. Beb does not succeed in her first year, but after that she adapts and applies herself. Beb's sister Loukie chooses a different path in 1914. She goes to the home economics school in Amsterdam, at that time mainly a school for well-to-do girls to learn how to run a household.

It looks like 1914 will be a good year: both Zeeman daughters have started their advanced education and their parents enjoy some rest. However, this image is disrupted by the start of the First World War and Beb's father suffering a brain hemorrhage. He does not have to go to the hospital; he can stay in his own unheated bedroom, and he is allowed to take a ride every day in a wheelchair with rubber tires.

Father in a wheelchair after his stroke.

Ineke van der Wal

However, he has a second hemorrhage which is fatal and he dies on May 8, 1915. Father Piet is buried in the cemetery next to the *Groene Kerkje* ('Green Church') in Oegstgeest. There is no family income now and it is uncertain whether Beb can continue studying. Luckily, an anonymous friend of the family decides to pay the tuition fees, 200 guilders in those days, for Beb; Beb's mother takes in some girl students to pay for their daily expenses.

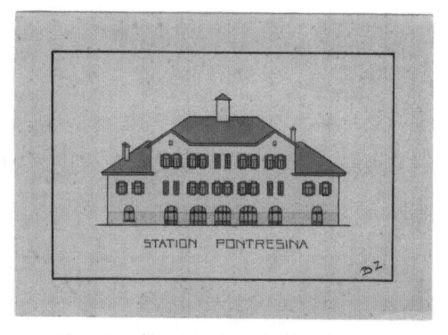

The station of Pontresina, Switzerland by Beb Zeeman.

During her college years Beb learns to make detailed drawings and she searches for an important architectural structure in every city, which she then draws in minute detail. She becomes a member of a Society of Architects called *Kwim Kwam Kwepele*. They become good friends with whom she maintains contact over her lifetime. The building industry is busy at that time: the *Jaarbeurs* building in Utrecht, the building of the School of Philosophy in Amersfoort, the *Hirsch* building in Amsterdam, and the *Rietveld-Schröder* house in Utrecht. Foreign architectural movements are the *Modernista* in Spain with

Gaudi as the main architect and Frank Lloyd Wright's concrete-frame construction in the United States.

The Engineering Society *Kwim Kwam Kwepele* in May 1930.

For her internship Beb goes to Rotterdam where she contributes to the antechamber of the mayor. A temporary workshop has been set up in the post office next to the town hall. Beb is staying with her mother's sister, aunt Louise, her husband Adriaan and daughter Loukie at the Mathenesserlaan in Rotterdam. Louise writes to her sister Kate:

'I cannot tell you how nice we all feel about having her here. She is so easy-going and has a wonderful zest for life.' In the condolence letter after Beb's death, daughter Loukie writes: 'I remember the years when I was still at school. Beb often came to our house to sing along at our regular music evenings where an opera - usually Mozart - was rehearsed in concert form. She also found time to help me with mathematics, which I only understood when she explained it to me. I could easily talk to her. I was an only child

Ineke van der Wal

and I have always looked up to Beb as an older sister. It was nice when she was there. I will often think back to Beb, because she was a great support in my childhood.'

Besides studying there is also time to have fun. In July 1915, the lustrum (fifth anniversary) of the *DSC* ('Delft Male Student Society') is celebrated in an elaborate way: a procession through the city of Delft, visits to the decorated party grounds, various balls to attend in Persian costumes, *reveille* (early wake up with a trumpet concert), fighting with the old members, a mime performance and tea at the Phoenix club. 'The ball is very lively, our supper table is filled with excitement and ice is thrown around, ice is passed along and ice is put down the neck, the ball bouquets are put in the champagne bucket.' Beb writes to her mother. Here Beb meets Willem Einthoven again, her former neighbor.

In 1916, the second lustrum of the *DVSV* ('Delft Female Student Association') is celebrated with an official reception in the town hall followed by a dinner. Beb is a member of the board of the *DVSV* at that time, together with Ms. H.J. Kruseman and Ms. M.F.H. Snethlage. They pose in large, white, solemn dresses for *Pak Me Mee,* an illustrated weekly.

In the summer the Zeeman sisters are invited to spend time with different families. They go to *Heiduin* of the Wijsman family in Huis ter Heide, to the De Lint family in Scheveningen and the Rahusen family. The house of the Coldewey family, *De Parkeler* in Twello, becomes Beb's favorite. Mart Coldewey is a fellow student and her father Piet has designed the garden around the house himself as a beautiful English landscaped park. In this garden however, it is not the house itself which is the center, but the view over the open surrounding lowland. Beb enjoys reading the many volumes of *Country Life* magazine where she learns about outdoor life, plants, animals, beautiful country houses and nice gardens. There are colourful books

DVSV-Delft students association celebrates its second lustrum in 1916. Beb is a member of the governing board and she is the one on the left of the upper photograph.

Ineke van der Wal

about borders, complete with detailed maps, which Piet uses for his designs in wintertime. The garden has an abundance of flowers that Piet uses for his paintings. An old avenue of trees connects the estate with Twello, which has a train station. The proximity of this station ensures a constant flow of visitors. There is rowing, picnicking, playing tennis at *Jagtlust* and walking to the *Oldenbroek* army camp. They set up the dance club *FIG* ('Flirting Is Healthy') and the tennis club *VIOS* ('Courting Is Our Strife').

Villa Leyenstein, Soestdijkseweg 276, De Bilt, The Netherlands, where the grandparents of Beb live. You see the staff together with Loukie van der Chijs. March 1913.

Beb also regularly visits her Grandparents, who after Grandpa's retirement, went to live at *Leyenstein* on the Soestdijkseweg 276 in Station de Bilt. They use the large rose hedge to make many bouquets which they bring along as a gift when they go visiting. *Leyenstein* is also the place where Christmas is celebrated with the whole De Bruyn family and where they perform operas together with the Wijsman family. Early in the fall they start practicing and choosing costumes. Beb usually sings, but can also play the piano very well.

Sister Loukie becomes engaged on September 21, 1917 to Albert Carpentier Alting. Albert has not even passed his bachelors exam yet and mother thinks it is a bit early for an engagement, also because Loukie is just twenty. To celebrate the engagement, they drink champagne with mother Kate, daughters Beb and Loukie and Albert. The three girls who board, are coincidentally out so they have the house just for themselves.

Albert en Loukie on their wedding day.

Ineke van der Wal

Albert and Loukie marry four years later on September 21, 1921 and move to Tegal in Java, where Albert will work as an engineer at the Semarang-Cheribon steam train company.

Beb graduates in 1920. At that time, she is the second female architectural engineer in The Netherlands (Grada Wolffensperger was the first in 1917) and she starts to work. She moves to Baarn to live with her grandfather, who became an enthusiastic painter after his retirement and where her mother Kate lives as well. In Baarn she finds

A portrait of Beb probably commissioned on the occasion of her graduation in 1920.

work at the private office of Engineer Leliman and she is part of the team that works on *Posbank*, the national monument close to Rheden at the national Veluwe park. When this agency ceases to exist, she accepts a job at the Public Works of Amsterdam, the City Architect Bureau.

Beb's sister soon gives birth to a son, Tip. This is actually a lonely period for Beb. She follows the tradition of her parents; she travels a lot through Europe and faithfully sends postcards to her mother and grandfather. In her reports of visits to friends, who are married and have children, a certain sadness is palpable. A letter about the reunion of the architectural group Kwim Kwam Kwepele is mainly about the children of the group. She is in her late twenties and not married yet.

Years later, when King Baudouin of Belgium marries Queen Fabiola, who was already in her thirties, Beb makes the remark 'Yes, she must have given up on the idea of a marriage in her life.' Beb starts to realize that there is a chance that she might stay single.

CHAPTER II

Wim

I n chapter 1, Wim Einthoven is already mentioned as a brother of a friend. Wim also grew up in Leiden, and also in an academic environment. His father, Willem Einthoven, is a professor of Physiology and Histology in Leiden since 1886. When he was asked to accept this professorship at the end of 1885, he had already obtained his PhD, but was not yet a practicing doctor. On January 9, 1886 he obtains his doctor's diploma, after which he is accepted as a professor in Leiden at the age of 25.

Willem comes from a family of doctors: Willem's grandfather, Salomon Jurdan Einthoven, was a surgeon in the English army, son Jacob (Willem's father) studied medicine in Groningen and Willem himself studied medicine in Utrecht.

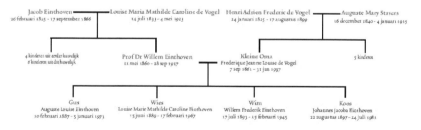

Pedigree of Wim Einthoven which shows clearly how interwoven the De Vogel and Einthoven families are.

Professor Willem Einthoven decides in July 1892 to travel to the zoological station in Naples to do research there. After completing his task, Willem returns to Leiden at the end of the summer, to be with his wife, Fréderique Jeanne Louise de Vogel, nicknamed Loukie. The couple is happy to be united again, as evidenced by the fact that nine months after Willem's return, on July 17, 1893, a son is born: Willem Frederik Einthoven. He is the third child in the Einthoven family. He has two older sisters: Gus, born February 10, 1887, and Wies, born on June 15, 1889. The younger sister Koos, is born later on August 22, 1897. Wim's father is 33 years old and his mother 32 years old at the time of the birth of their only son, who is soon called Wim.

Father Willem comes from a family of ten children, his wife from a family of six children and they are a close-knit family; in other words, they stay in regular contact with each family member, which is time consuming. Every morning Wim's father rides his bicycle to the university. Periodically he travels abroad for his work. He works on the string galvanometer, with which he wants to observe the activity of the human heart and the electrocardiogram, with which he can record the observations and make them interpretable. On Saturdays, he attends meetings of the Council of Sciences and the board of the university. Willem is a hard, disciplined worker; he lectures several times a week, conducts research, publishes regularly and maintains contacts with colleagues abroad. International visitors regularly come home for dinner. Of course he also supervises PhD students, such as W.Th. de Vogel, who is both a brother-in-law and a cousin of Willem.

In 1924 Professor Willem is praised as an example for younger colleagues by the Board of the Medical Faculty because he did not miss any of the ten faculty meetings and the sixteen graduations. In his last thesis of his dissertation, Willem uses a quote from the last line of Horace's 18th letter to his friend Lollius: 'He who wants to go through life in a balanced manner and wants to achieve something in life, with his gifts and abilities, as they are properly rewarded, has to proliferate, trying to make the best of it.' This has been a model of his own convictions, which he also instills in his family. However, all these activities mean that son Wim sees little of his father, Willem.

Ineke van der Wal

Wim as a small boy portrayed by photographer J. Goedeljee in Leiden. Date unknown.

Wim's mother Loukie runs the household and turns out to be economical. The income of a professor at that time is 4,000 guilders per year. The young couple must also use this not-so-generous salary to pay off father Willem's student debt because they have chosen a scientific career instead of the doctor's career in the Dutch East Indies, which was paid for by the government. He tries to increase his salary by selling his inventions commercially. He earns 10,000 guilders in royalties through Siemens with the rights he has on compasses that are used by the German Navy. He earns approximately 3500 guilders by selling 140 string galvanometers via CSI (Cambridge Scientific Instruments). The family first lives on the Rhijngeesterstraatweg in Oegstgeest, and later they move to the Rijnsburgerweg. In 1916 the family moves again and this time to Groenhovenstraat 5 in Leiden, which is closer to the university.

In 1921, the extra income gives the parents the opportunity to move to the idyllic *Bloemlust* house at the Galgewater. 'A pleasant and well maintained country estate, consisting of a mansion with a beautiful view of the Rhine, ten rooms, attic, kitchen, and cellar, a coach and boat house, stables, hothouses, barn, large garden with fine fruit trees, located close to Leiden at *den Hoogen Morsch* in the municipality of Oegstgeest and measures in size: 40 rods by 85 cubits.'

The 'Bloemlust' house at the Morschweg 66 in Leiden, The Netherlands where Wim's parents move to in 1921. Source: Baar, P.J.M. de, *Wonen aan het Galgewater.*

According to Hoogerwerf, the biographer of Willem Einthoven, Wim's mother commits her life to taking care of her family:

'I would shortchange the character of Einthoven if I did not mention that he had a life companion, whose aim was entirely devoted to creating a comfortable home-life, which enabled him to develop his inherent gifts unhindered. In that respect she had an important share in the scientific results achieved by her husband.

Ineke van der Wal

Those who had the privilege of being admitted into Einthoven's home immediately felt comfortable and welcome in their presence in every respect. After becoming acquainted with Mrs. Einthoven-De Vogel, one knew that she had created that atmosphere because of her peaceful, tranquil manner.'

The Einthoven family with from left to right: Gus, Wim, mother Einthoven, father Einthoven, Koos and Wies. Date unknown.

Leiden in those days, is a small village, there are hardly any cars. A horse-drawn tram connects East and West Leiden and there is a steam tram along the Rijnsburgerweg with a view over the meadows to the castle Poelgeest. In 1886, there are 290 medical students in Leiden, of which about eighty are studying under Professor Einthoven. Albert Einstein, who regularly gives guest lectures in Leiden and later escapes to America via Leiden, calls Leiden 'that delightful spot of land on this dry earth'.

In 1905 the Leiden University celebrates a 'lustrum' - a five year anniversary celebration - and HM Queen Wilhelmina visits the university together with HRH Prince Hendrik. Willem Einthoven is then Secretary of the Senate and hosts the visit, together with the Chancellor J. van Leeuwen. It is the job of Willem to accompany Prince Hendrik. While walking to the academy building, the royal couple is photographed with their escorts. Prince Hendrik walks next to the red carpet, while Willem Einthoven walks on the red carpet. This is amusing to the family and subsequently becomes the subject of a Sint Nicholas poem. In 1905 Willem Einthoven himself becomes Chancellor of the University Senate.

Willem is always busy with his work and that is sometimes difficult for his family. When he appears at a dinner in his function as Chancellor, He is still wearing his lab coat and his regular suit, even though an evening suit is required. His wife sends him home to change into the evening suit she has hung out for him. Willem does indeed return after some time, but still with his white lab coat on. He walks to his wife and hands her a clean handkerchief with the words: 'I do not remember why I was sent home, but I brought a clean handkerchief for you.'

Son Wim loves sports: he fences, rows, ice-skates and sails. At 'Arie' in Warmond a sailboat is moored and the family is a member of the sailing club *De Kaag*. Through these sports he can separate himself from the women in the family, who mother him too much. It soon turns out that Wim has a talent for technology. He lives at the right time; he experiences the conversion from gas light to electric light, W.C. Röntgen wins the Nobel Prize for his discovery of X-rays, he sees cars with gasoline engines and the first attempts at flying that are successful. The Einthoven family already has electric light, but the neighbors do not yet have it. Wim helps the neighbors obtain electric light, but he installs it in such a way that he can turn the light off if, to his taste, his neighbor sits on the toilet too long.

He also builds a camera by himself. With this he photographs his 3 sisters, but as often happens, he is more interested in the construction of the object than in using it. He takes the picture too quickly with the

result that only Koos, the youngest and the shortest, is complete, the He also builds a camera by himself. With this he photographs his 3 sisters, but as often happens, he is more interested in the construction of the object than in using it. He takes the picture too quickly with the result that only Koos, the youngest and the shortest, is complete, the heads of the two older, taller sisters are cut off. Wim's talent for technology combined with his sense of humor and his lively nature characterize him.

Wim's sisters attend the 5-year HBS (high school) and Wim follows in their footsteps. After graduating from the HBS, Gus visits the Conservatory and Wies studies Dutch Language and Literature; Koos will study medicine later. Beb Zeeman attends the same HBS, but she is two grades lower than Wim, at least at the beginning of her school days. Wim has a talent for technology, but his talent for languages lags behind. The HBS final exam includes compulsory pass of the languages Dutch, German, English and French, and it turns out that he has to take the final exam three times because his marks for the languages are always too low. To avoid boredom during the last HBS-years, he is often found in his father's laboratory, where he can actually help and come up with clever suggestions. Guests in the lab are surprised about that. What is that kid doing here? The next day the guest has the answer: that kid knows the purpose of every screw in the lab. Eventually, Wim passes his final exams in 1912, the same year as Beb Zeeman.

Father Willem Einthoven (sitting, first left) and son Wim Einthoven (standing, first left) in the Physiology Laboratory, Zonneveldstraat 18a, Leiden, The Netherlands.

Wim decides to study electrical engineering in Delft. He lives at the 'Brabantse Turfmarkt' with the Frebé family and hands over his tuition fee to the Chancellor, Professor J. Bosscha. He becomes a member of *DSC* ('Delft Male Student Society'), and his parents write during the orientation days: 'Keep your head up! Write to us on the enclosed postcard in a few words: e.g. 'all is well' or 'am rather tired''. Wim buys a casual suit, a dress coat, a tuxedo and an overcoat from the tailor Samuel Brothers. From the weekly correspondence between parents and son, it becomes clear that the parents worry about Wim's health. He often has a cold and his airways bother him. Wim asks for advice about club matters. 'Emancipation: the students who emancipates you gives you the right and privilege to call them by their first name.'

Ineke van der Wal

During his time in Delft, Wim has an accident while fencing which results in a large scar on his upper lip. From then on he decides to grow a mustache. Because of his interest in film and photography he becomes a board member of the *DSAFV* ('Delft Student Amateur Photographers Association'), together with two cousins of the Julius family. Another of Wim's cousins, Han de Voogt, arrives in Delft at the same time as Wim. Han de Voogt has already bought a piece of land at the river Spaarne to build a boatyard there, not far from the rowing and sailing club in Haarlem. It has seventy meters water frontage and it *only* cost seven thousand guilders. During his studies, Wim remains interested in his father's string galvanometer and is still often found at the laboratory in Leiden, because Wim sees possibilities to use the string galvanometer in an adapted form - the vacuum model - for wireless telegraphy, a hot topic of those days. He has contact with professor Bosscha, Ir. C.J. de Groot and Ir. N. Koomans about this subject.

Sister Wies marries Arnold Terlet in Leiden on November 6, 1913 and she ends her Dutch studies. Arnold is a minister and his first appointment is in Zuid-Scharwoude, followed by Drempt close to Doesburg. Doesburg is beautifully situated along the IJssel river, but the residents suffer from high water and the parsonage only has petroleum lighting. The farmers take up a collection in the community to buy petroleum for the Christmas and New Year services. The whole Einthoven family helps Wies regularly and then stay overnight in the large parsonage.

At the end of 1914 the First World War breaks out. The Netherlands remains neutral, but there is a lack of food and refugees from Belgium are taken in by The Netherlands. Wim's parents ask cousin Tony van Vloten - a real practical farmer - to plant fruit trees on a piece of land that they rent. 'For our part, this is a precaution against a coming food shortage. We still have enough to eat, but the poorer people suffer.'

DSC (Delft male student society) is not discouraged by the war and celebrates a lustrum in 1915. Wim, of course, takes part in the celebrations. Here he meets Beb Zeeman again. Shortly afterwards, Wim interrupts his studies because he has to serve in the military. Although The Netherlands is not involved in the war, it has to be prepared. Father and son correspond about a 40 km march, about experiments with produced and delivered parts for the string galvanometer, and discuss the sergeant's exam. 'Take care of your health and be strong, then you will have a good future,' writes father.

In 1916, engineer C.J. de Groot obtains his PhD with honors at the Technical University in Delft with a thesis on *Radiotelegraphy in the Tropics*. With this thesis, he establishes his name as a pioneer of radiotelegraphy in the Dutch East Indies. His main thesis is: 'A radio connection between The Netherlands and its colonies, without the use of intermediate stations, is a political necessity and is technically feasible.' The Dutch government would like nothing more and asks Dr. Ir. De Groot to build a wireless radio telegraph connection to send Morse code. (No one dares to think of wireless voice connection over the enormous distance of 11,500 km.) The cables, which until now have been used for radiotelegraphy, are partly owned by other countries and are expensive to maintain. A wireless connection is cheaper and can work without the intervention of countries that can delay or withhold information. The Ministries of Colonies, War and Navy make huge sums available to achieve this goal; five million guilders for a station in The Netherlands alone.

Not everyone agrees: Dr. Nicolaas Koomans for example, working for the Dutch PTT (Post, Telephone and Telegraph), is against it. Koomans obtained his PhD with the same professor as De Groot and they represent differing opinions: Koomans wants to work with a Telefunken machine transmitter while De Groot wants to work with a high-power long-wave bow transmitter by Poulsen. De Groot wants to combine this type of bow transmitter with the string galvanometer from Einthoven to create a long-wave radio receiver for Morse code, which is insensitive to the heavy tropical atmospheric disturbances in the East. The Italian Dr. Marconi and other radio professionals are also working on this problem, but have not succeeded so far.

Ir. C.J. de Groot

To operate and develop the string galvanometer, De Groot hires Wim Einthoven and asks to borrow the only existing vacuum string galvanometer from Professor Einthoven, who agrees with this, as does the Ministry of Colonies. The Ministry of War grants Wim a license to stay in the Dutch East Indies. Some consider it wise to hire Wim Einthoven to operate the vacuum string galvanometer, others see it as an agreement between De Groot and father Einthoven to keep Wim out of military service. Wim will be conducting tests, led by De Groot. Wim has to report monthly to the Ministry of Colonies. If the tests succeed within two years, Willem 'the inventor' Einthoven will receive an amount of 100,000 guilders from the Governor General, but any patents will be issued in the name of the Dutch East Indies PTT. Father and son Einthoven agree that they will share the compensation.

In the jungle of the Malabar Mountains, Dutch East Indies. Wim is number four from right. Photograph taken in 1917.

The Ministry of War provides transport to the Dutch East Indies. Wim leaves at the end of 1916 with the naval ship *Seven Provinces* via northern Scotland, New York, the Panama Canal and Honolulu to Java. The Suez Canal is blocked, so this is the only possible route. As soon as he arrives in the Dutch East Indies, there is big news: on December 15, 1916 a telegraph operator in Sabang (the most northwestern point of the colony) has received Morse code signals coming from Nauen, Germany (the test station of Telefunken) while using a normal antenna and an ill-suited receiver.

De Groot is thus confirmed in his belief that such a long distance connection is possible on a regular basis and gets to work with a borrowed Telefunken receiver, the string galvanometer from the Einthovens, and a Poulsen bow transmitter, which will be delivered in the summer of 1917. The request is to make haste and De Groot therefore decides not to build towers to hang an antenna, but to use a mountain gorge for this purpose. The Topographic Service looks for a place with sufficient height and the best possible direction for the radio connection and eventually finds it in the Malabar Mountains. However, this gorge lies entirely outside the civilized world, 34 kilometers from Bandung and nine kilometers from the nearest road. A narrow footpath leads the way into this jungle-covered area of old crater walls, where panthers and wild boars are still living undisturbed. The elevation change of the footpath to the gorge is about 700 meters, while the gorge itself is 1250 meters above sea level. De Groot's life motto is: 'Attempt the impossible, in order to achieve the possible'. De Groot desperately needs this optimism to succeed with this project. Third-year student Wim becomes part of this adventure.

The war fuels fear for a blockade of telegraph transmissions. That is why everybody works at a feverish pace and in November 1917 they have progressed so far that they can start transmitting. However, The Netherlands is not ready to receive the Dutch East Indies broadcasts and does not even make the effort to set up a temporary reception facility. The Malabar station is left to call for months on end. This is unfortunate, because the expected telegraph blockade becomes real in November 1917 and the one way connection could have been of great use.

The activities don't always go as planned. This picture shows a transformer that sank in the mud and fell over.

The Telefunken test receiver is installed in Tjililin, so that both the receiver and the transmitter are located on Java. Soon, Morse code signals are picked up at night from European stations. A direct contact between The Netherlands and the Dutch East Indies cannot be established, however, as long as The Netherlands do not receive the Malabar. De Groot, at his wits' end, decides to build a receiver installation which he sends to The Netherlands with the H.M.S. The Seven Provinces in the last half of 1918 via the Panama Canal. Tests with this receiver during the trip show that transmissions from Malabar can be heard until Honolulu. That is about the same distance as from Malabar to The Netherlands. After the arrival of the man of war in The Netherlands in February 1919, the Indies' receiver is placed at a station in Blaricum. On June 5, 1919, the Malabar transmitter is heard for the first time in The Netherlands. The one sided connection is a reality at

Ineke van der Wal

last, fully established by East Indies' means and East Indies' initiative. Now that the test set-up has proven itself, De Groot wants to move on to a reliable installation that can serve the United States during the day and Europe at night. The Dutch government makes money available, but - on the advice of Dr. Ir. Koomans - demands that the transmitter will be a German Telefunken machine transmitter. De Groot prefers an American Poulsen bow lamp transmitter because it has a faster wavelength manipulation than the Telefunken transmitter. De Groot is at the losing end of this argument, and the conflict between De Groot and Koomans flares up again. The Netherlands PTT decide to set up a transmitting station in Kootwijk on the Veluwe and a receiving station in Sambeek, Noord-Brabant.

The Dutch PTT-Service does not agree with the advice of De Groot, but the Dutch East Indies PTT thinks otherwise. Immediately, money is made available to build a large (2400-3600 KW) bow lamp transmitter in Malabar. The transmitter is placed in a hall of 40 meters long, 14 meters wide, and 22 meters high. This would be nothing

Radio-station Malabar in its full glory.

special if it were not for the fact that the entire roof construction has to be made in wood in order to keep radio high-frequency losses to a minimum. It is also thought that a wooden building is more resistant to earthquakes. Furthermore, two cooling ponds are needed, one of which is located high at the spring and the other in front of the building to give it a 'rustic appearance'. The white-and-black framework hall is surrounded by wooded mountains that rise sky high on both sides and in the back. The antenna is made of five nearly two kilometer long cables, which are stretched at an 800 meters height between the two mountain peaks.

From the moment the test set-up works, the messages from several large European countries are collected and passed on to the government and the press. Often two to three thousand words of text are recorded per night, directly from the telephone to the typewriter. In the winter of 1918-1919, the reception is fairly good and a true enthusiasm arises for the radio service, when they appear to be capable of passing on news of the big events in Europe without any delay. The Dutch East Indies PTT Service is presumably the first one in the entire Far East, that on November 11, 1918 receives the radio telegram about the armistice. This means that the joyful news is received 20 hours earlier than via the usual route via Leafield, Alexandria, Sudan, Aden and Colombo.

In order to obtain a good, regular and reliable reception of the European transmitters, the extremely annoying tropical atmospheric disturbances will have to be eliminated. De Groot and Wim are trying to use the vacuum string galvanometer for this purpose. First, the entire string galvanometer is placed in a vacuum (an idea from Bosscha), then later only the string (Wim's idea). Their efforts, however, do not lead to success, but they persist. Father Willem writes: 'That's how it often goes with experiments: on and off.'

Mail from The Netherlands to the Dutch East Indies is sent via the United Kingdom and is subjected to Censure. Postmark: July 9, 1918.

On Java, Wim stays with his uncle Emile (one of his father's brothers) who lives in Bandung with his wife Jane. They keep an eye on Wim. Officially, they are not allowed to know what Wim is doing, that is why father Willem is upset when a telegram for Wim is delivered to Emile, because this could reveal the secret.

Emile and Jane regularly write to Willem Einthoven about Wim's ups and downs, because Wim doesn't write very often. It is a complaint that is regularly repeated in the letters that father Willem writes to son Wim. Of course, much of the correspondence between father and son is about the task that they have taken upon themselves. Wim writes the agreed upon monthly reports and Willem also sees them, but he is not satisfied:

> *'I recommend that you improve the reports about your work. Don't think - and especially do not say - that they seem crazy in Batavia. Imagine being in their place, of people who must govern and rule; later on you might find yourself in a similar position. They are now dealing with a student who is doing his utmost, but whose tests nevertheless still have a real chance to fail. As a father, I must be grateful to the Board, that they monitor you and do not leave you to your own devices.'*

The correspondence is not only about work, but also about the war and family matters such as the engagement of cousin Han de Voogt to Madeleine Aberson. 'To propose to a girl was worse than taking an exam,' says Han. Father exerts subtle pressure when he writes: 'All of the members of Han's club are engaged except for one.' In April 1918, charcoal is on ration, there is no more tea available and chocolate only for a few weeks. Koos is not well prepared for her exam, but will try anyway. Wim drives a lot through the Dutch East Indies' countryside on his motorcycle and saves money so his parents can travel to the Dutch East Indies - they were both born there but have never been back - but the parents advise him to use the money to buy a sailboat. Father and mother Einthoven long to see their son again, but they especially want him to come back to finish his studies. In December 1919, the father writes to his son:

'I think your request for an increase in salary is an excellent move. Did De Groot give you the idea? Do not let yourself be tempted by that money, to stay longer than is strictly necessary, because without an engineering diploma in your pocket, you will not be able to receive the position in society that you ultimately want to achieve, so that the money you earn now will be very disadvantageous to you in the long run.'

Willem is not sure that his words will convince Wim and he asks his brother Emile and De Groot to help him and they agree. When all engineers receive a bonus at the laboratory, Wim does not receive anything 'because he has worked hard, but he is not an engineer', after which Wim decides to resign and return to The Netherlands. Just before the ship leaves the Dutch East Indies quay, a messenger brings Wim a package. It is the bonus that was withheld.

Before Wim returns to his studies in Delft, he tries one more time to make the vacuum string galvanometer suitable for wireless telegraphy, this time together with his father. Willem asks and receives leave from his professorship and a few days later some sailors install a receiving

Mother and father Einthoven at 'Bloemlust'

antenna between two church towers, the *Lodewijkskerk* and *St. Petruskerk*, across from the side wing of the laboratory. The end of this antenna is connected to the string galvanometer and now the Morse signals from Malabar should be received by the galvanometer. But it does not work. Malabar sends at a wavelength of 7.5 km. The frequency then corresponds to 40,000 vibrations/second (a frequency of 40 kHz). The technique of the experiment is, that the string is stretched so tightly that it resonates with the frequency of the transmitter. The experiment apparently fails because the resonance point cannot be achieved.

Professor Einthoven calculates the conditions the string must meet in order to be tuned to the transmitter. It appears that the difficulty lies in the tension of the string. The laboratory chief produces the newly designed string . When it is ready and placed in the galvanometer, the calculation and the clever construction prove correct, because after some searching the Malabar signal is received. In the end, two vacuum string galvanometers (per De Groot's idea) are linked together: one adjusted to the transmission frequency, the other to the opposite frequency. The result is a double long-wave telegraph receiver, which is just as sensitive as a headphone. Moreover, this receiver can receive 30 times as fast as a good telegraph operator and due to its extremely low bandwidth, it barely suffers from tropical, atmospheric disturbances. By recording both active and inactive waves, the chance of successful reconstruction of faulty signals, is greater than with a single receiver.

The vacuum string galvanometer as used for wireless telegraphy. Source: Waart, A. de, Het levenswerk van Willem Einthoven.

Now the time starts to give some publicity to this invention. On October 31, 1920, Wim gives a lecture for the Electrotechnical Society in Delft on the success of the vacuum string galvanometer in radiotelegraphy. He describes the operation of the machine, but he also gives some background stories. He discusses the receiving tests of the Malabar transmitter on Wim's home journey with SS Patria - tests taken every hour - and also the climatic conditions in the Malabar gorge. Bright tropical sun, cold fog clouds, hail storms and heavy thunderstorms all make great demands on the material, which also suffers from high voltages: 150,000 to 200,000 volts. The isolators need to be replaced regularly, which means that the antennas must be lowered. These are exciting adventures.

On March 24, 1923, Father Willem gives a lecture at the KHMW ('Royal Holland Academy of Sciences') entitled 'The string galvanometer at the service of radio telegraphy' in which he advertises the many advantages of reception by galvanometer versus by telephone. First he speaks about the sensitivity of the galvanometer that can be increased to that of the best telephone. Then he talks about the larger number of words per minute that can be sent. If one sends signals by hand and listens with the ear, the maximum is 25 words per minute. A machine transmitter easily gets 225 words/minute and Malabar can even get to 600 words/minute, which cannot be noted by the human ear. By means of lamp amplifiers, the signal is made so powerful that it can scratch itself into a wax roll like that of an earlier phonograph. This wax roll can later be translated by a telegraph operator. In this way the best transmission times - at night for both sending and receiving - can be used. Wim gives this lecture himself at the Physiological Laboratory in Leiden on October 22, 1923.

In addition to the lectures, father and son also publish various articles about the vacuum string galvanometer and Wim, as agreed with the Ministry, applies for a patent in The Netherlands, Germany, Canada, England, the US and Japan. The patents are in the name of The Netherlands Indies. On November 22, 1921, 100,000 guilders is paid to Professor W. Einthoven by the Department of Colonies, following the final report issued by De Groot. As agreed, father and son share this amount. Wim invests his share in London, but affords himself one luxury: the purchase of a sailing boat, the Tineke, a gaff rigged, cabin Yacht, which is docked with Arie in Warmond.

Wim Einthoven (left) with his sister Koos (right) on Wim's sailing boat the 'Tineke'.

Now that the matters around the string galvanometer in the service of the radio-telegraphy have been settled, Wim returns to Delft to finish his studies, as he had promised his father. He doesn't delay and on

June 21, 1923 he passes his bachelor's exam in electrical engineering and on July 10, 1924 he finishes his master's exam, 12 years after starting, 31 years old. This intervening period, however, was not just about studying: he joins the board of the 'Electronical Society', first as a librarian, then as its president. In June 1922, he becomes a member of the verification committee of the male student society and in September 1924 he becomes an honorary member of the male student society. In 1917 he already became an honorary member of the 'Delft Student Amateur Photographers Union'. And he is active in the Radio Society. On September 27, 1922, Wim receives a transmitting license from the Ministry of Transport, Department of Post & Telegraph, so that he can continue to work as an amateur radio operator.

The wireless telegraphy naturally develops further during Wim's studies and on May 5, 1923 there is an official opening of the bilateral

Ineke van der Wal

wireless radio-telegraph connection by Queen Wilhelmina. Because of all kinds of misunderstandings, it is impossible to establish a connection, and the radio pioneers are being roasted by the press. An investigation is demanded and for this a research committee of Dutch radio experts is established. This committee concludes that Malabar is not to blame. In Holland, with the best of intentions, the decision was made to start with a new receiving method that day. Despite this failure, The *New York Times* publishes the following on the front page on May 7, 1923:

'It is undoubtedly due to Holland's far distant colonies, which were completely cut off from the motherland during the recent war, that service from the most powerful wireless station in the world, carrying messages 7,500 miles between The Netherlands and the Dutch East Indies, was begun today by a message to Queen Wilhelmina from the Dutch East Indian Government.'

For the radio pioneer De Groot, this unsuccessful opening is, of course, not good news and he therefore decides to make a series of speeches to counter the criticism and convince everyone of the usefulness of the invention and the corresponding large investments. This charm offensive starts in Bandung on April 16, 1924 at the Catholic Social Association. During this period, the Malabar transmitter sends 7500 words per day in open language and 4500 words in code to The Netherlands. This is more words per day than the total daily telegraph traffic with The Netherlands. The telegraph cable is available 24 hours a day and wireless only a few hours, but wireless is faster and with fewer mistakes. In this speech De Groot elaborates on the wonderful invention of Einthoven. On September 9, 1924, a lecture is also given at the meeting of the Department of Electrical Engineering of the Royal Institute of Engineers. The favorable results with the Malabar antenna so appeal to the imagination that the Telefunken company decides to also place its station on Malabar, and the mountain antenna is copied in Bavaria and in the French Pyrenees. After all these successes, however, something unexpected happens: a change from long-wave to short-wave radio communication. Radio amateurs, the Philips Laboratories and the PTT Laboratories in The Hague and Bandung develop small short-wave transmitters that fit on a large table with a simple antenna suspended from a church tower. These new transmitters appear to perform as well as the long-wave giants in Kootwijk and Malabar with their enormous antennas and extensive power stations, and also at a fraction of the construction and operating costs.

The first short wave signals reach Java on April 23, 1925. This change is actually a tragic moment in the Malabar history: now that the life work of De Groot is finally ready and meets all expectations, after many setbacks, something intervenes through which the long-wave bow lamp system is considered outdated and doomed to disappear.

For Wim, this means that he has worked for ten years on the string galvanometer for use in radiotelegraphy, but that there is no longer a need for it. It has become a technical masterpiece only to be used in laboratories. Wim decides to turn his back on radiotelegraphy for a while.

Ineke van der Wal

CHAPTER III

Beb and Wim

The winter from 1923 to 1924 is cold, and the ice on the canals and rivers is good enough for skating. Beb goes, and on one of her skating trips she meets Wim Einthoven again. Wim decides to send an invitation to Beb for a sailing trip on his boat *Tineke* in the spring of 1924. Beb visits her mother that Saturday and does not see the invitation until Monday. She immediately writes a note in return because she is sorry to have missed this outing. They set a new date and many sailing trips follow which give them the opportunity to get to know each other better. Beb is 30 and Wim 32, old to be single for that time, and she earns more than he does, which is unconventional in those days. Wim proposes marriage to Beb on the *Tineke* and they decide to marry in the spring of 1925.

During their engagement period they meet each other's family again and are very much in love, as evidenced by a letter from Wim to Beb: 'Lots of love and a kiss (cannot do it yet!! can only imagine it)'. He also writes: 'No news about going to the Dutch East Indies yet.' In the meantime, he works in Hilversum and stays with the Dubois family. Mr. Dubois is the director of The Netherlands Signal Transmitter Factory and they sail together on the Loosdrecht lakes. He writes how much he likes the family. After his stay there Wim goes to Delft for a while. Beb and Wim decide to meet over the weekend in Warmond, which Beb can reach by train. He continues: 'Father and Mother are going to America on Saturday' and 'I do not spend too much time on wireless systems, because it will probably be completely different a year from now.' Beb resigns from the Amsterdam Bureau City Architect in November 1924 because married women are not allowed to continue working.

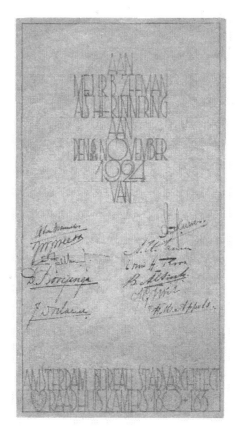

Beb resigns from the Amsterdam City Architect Office November 6, 1924. Married women are not allowed to continue paid work.

In October 1924, while he is in the United States, Professor Einthoven receives news that he has been awarded the Nobel Prize in Medicine. He collects the award a year later in Stockholm on December 10, 1925. In his acceptance speech he mentions his son: 'Engineer W.F.

Ineke van der Wal

Einthoven has made a model in which the string lies in a vacuum and this is specially suitable for the use of very thin strings' and so testifies about the long collaboration between father and son.

Wim looks for a job to support his future wife and finds one with Professor Van Houten in Leiden, where he designs an instrument for the treatment of patients with respiratory diseases. A friend later remembers how she stayed with Beb and Wim and how Beb was a guinea pig for tests that Wim did for fighting the common cold. It had something to do with chlorine, she recalls.

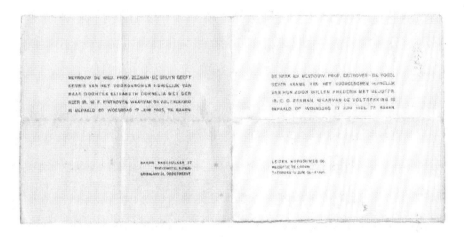

The wedding announcement of Beb and Wim.

On June 17, 1925 the wedding ceremony is held in Baarn, then the home of Beb's mother, who lives with her father, the retired General de Bruyn. It is General De Bruyn, Beb's grandfather, who gives away the bride and stands in for Beb's father. A reception is held at the Zeiler hotel. The wedding photo shows many flowers, and among the guests Professor Lorentz. Beb thus becomes part of the Einthoven family: 'A wonderful woman who fits in with your wonderful family,' a friend writes much later.

The radiant couple in the garden of hotel restaurant Zeiler, the current villa Amalia in Baarn, The Netherlands.

The first page of the 'Wedding Newspaper'.

Ineke van der Wal

In the 'Wedding Newspaper', a comical edition of the local newspaper, Wim's three sisters place an ad in which they ask for a new brother, with whom they can go sailing and who can play the gramophone for them. The couple will live in Oegstgeest, at Emmalaan 51, where they plant a chestnut tree in the garden. The trunk is still very thin - only one and a half centimeters thick. That is why the 'Wedding Newspaper' makes fun of the ambitious plan of a round bench to be placed around the foot of the tree.

Quite soon Beb gets pregnant and she busies herself with making an outfit for the baby. She designs, among other things, a cradle with large wheels and a separate wicker basket with handles, which can easily be picked up to carry the baby. Wim takes some internships abroad, but is home just in time for the birth of his first child on June 14, 1926 in Leiden - a daughter with a mop of dark hair. They name her Kate Lizbeth, after Beb's mother. Beb spends her first days with her new-born daughter in *Bloemlust* where she is well cared for by her in-laws, who have been looking forward to their first grandchild.

BEB

1. Er woonde eens in Leiden
   Een meiske jong en blij;
   Zij droeg in 't haar een grooten strik
   En was steeds duchtig in haar schik,
   Ja in haar schik, steeds in haar schik,
   Dat meiske jong en blij.

2. Zij had een kleine zuster
   Die net zoo was als zij,
   En samen ging zoo menig jaar
   Naar school dat aardig zusterpaar,
   Dat zusterpaar, dat zusterpaar,
   Zij gingen zij aan zij.

3. En toen de school ten einde was
   Toen zei Beb „geen gezeur,
   Ha, 'k heb mijn hoofd vol studiezin
   En maak daarmee een goed begin,
   Een goed begin, een goed begin
   En ik word ingenieur".

4. En Albert die vroeg Loekie,
   En Loekie zei niet neen,
   En toen haar zuster trouwen ging
   Was dat voor Beb een vreeselijk ding,
   Een vreeselijk ding, een vreeselijk ding,
   Want toen ging Loekie heen.

5. En Loekie trok naar Indië
   De wijde wereld in.
   Daar leefde zij met man en kind
   En alles ging er voor den wind,
   Ging voor den wind, ging voor den wind,
   Met haar en haar gezin.

6. Nu afloop van haar studie
   Kwam Beb op een bureau,
   En onze Beb die dacht toen stil:
   „Nu doe ik alles wat ik wil,
   Al wat ik wil, al wat ik wil,
   Nu ben ik vrij, ziezoo".

7. Maar eensklaps daar kwam Wimpie
   En toen was het gedaan,
   En met haar vrijheid is het uit
   Want nu is onze Beb de bruid,
   Is Beb de bruid, is Beb de bruid,
   Nu zal zij trouwen gaan.

8. En Beb haar moeder zei toen:
   „Kom gauw van het bureau,
   „Mijn beste kind ik zegen jou,
   „Heb veel geluk als Wim zijn vrouw,
   „Als Wim zijn vrouw, als Wim zijn vrouw,
   „Het is veel mooier zoo".

9. Nu Beb en Wim gaan trouwen,
   Wensch' iedereen met mij,
   Dat steeds zij zeggen moog' dit woord:
   „Wij hebben veel geluk aan boord,
   Geluk aan boord, geluk aan boord,
   Geluk, dat hebben wij".

The wedding song for Beb as a bride.

Ineke van der Wal

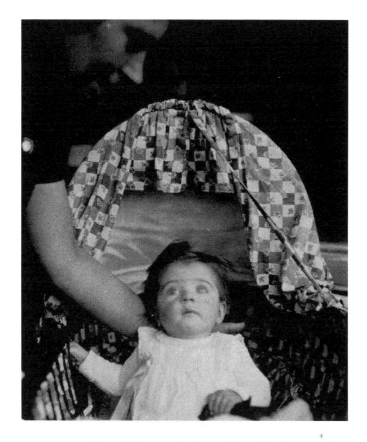

The two part cradle which was designed by Beb for her firstborn and is still used by the family.

One of Wim's sisters, Gus, who is a violin teacher in Leiden, in 1926 marries Rikkert Clevering, a lecturer in mathematics and physics at the technical school in Amsterdam. They too are 'older': Gus is 39 and Rik is 43. Rik is one of Wim's sailing friends, who Wim brought home one evening. Gus prepares dinner for Wim and his friend and so Wim accidentally became the marriage broker.

Father Einthoven undergoes surgery for colon cancer in May 1927 after which he stays bedridden for a long time. On June 21 he says goodbye to Wies and Arnold, who move to the Dutch East Indies; he is skinny then and in a lot of pain. The parents are allowed to travel along on the ship till it reaches the North Sea. Then they wave to Wies and Arnold from the quay. Koos is on vacation and she travels to Genoa to say goodbye to Wies and Arnold there. The parents are not rich but generous. 'We do not understand how you expect to live on 10 lire per day. We are sending you some extra money,' they write to Koos. On September 28, 1927 Wim's father passes away. He is buried at the *Green Church* in Oegstgeest, where the family graves of the De Vogel and Einthoven families are located.

For Wim this means that he loses both his mentors in two months' time, because on August 1, 1927 Dr. Ir. C.J. de Groot dies unexpectedly. De Groot was to attend an International Radio Conference in Washington and was on board the SS *J.P. Coen* sailing from the Dutch East Indies via The Netherlands to the United States. During the trip he suffers a heart attack. Several days before his death, De Groot visited the freighter *Bintang*, which carried the remains of his recently deceased wife. This ship was only a few kilometers ahead of the *J.P. Coen*. According to sailors (who are often superstitious) one should never do such a thing, because disaster will strike after such an act. The chief engineer of the *J.P. Coen* is able to make a lead box which

Ineke van der Wal

means that De Groot's body can travel to The Netherlands instead of being committed to the waves, as is customary. On August 22, Mr. and Mrs. De Groot are both buried in The Hague.

Already a few years before his death, De Groot had mentioned that Wim Einthoven should be his scientific successor. 'When I'm gone,' he once told the Chief of Radio Malabar, 'you must take this man, because he is the most suitable person to continue my work.' Few will have suspected then, and perhaps least of all De Groot, that his vision would become reality in such a short time.

On October 3, 1927 Wim's appointment is confirmed:

> 'The AID *learns that W.F. Einthoven, the son of the great scientist whose death was recently reported to us, is being deployed to the Dutch East Indies. Ir. Einthoven will be placed in Bandung at the radio service. He is known to have already made a name for himself in the field of radio-telegraphy, namely with testing rapid radio signaling, carried out with the application of the string galvanometer invented by his father. Because short wave radio has replaced this method, it is unlikely that the application of the string galvanometer will find much use.'*

On November 16, 1927, Beb, Wim and Kate start the journey to Bandung on the SS *Tabanan*, a mail ship from the *Rotterdamsche Lloyd*. Beb is pregnant and is often seasick, that is why she enjoys disembarking in the various ports. The two competing companies *Rotterdamsche Lloyd* and the *Stoomvaart Maatschappij Nederland* not only brag about their luxurious ships but also about the festive atmosphere on board. The journey takes more than four weeks and much is done to entertain the passengers by offering nights of dancing on the deck, fancy dress parties, cabaret, soapbox races, chess games, and bridge. Everything is done to keep boredom at bay. The ships also offers all kind of services, such as shops, a hairdresser and a medical ward.

The *Tabanan* departs from Rotterdam and sails past the chalk cliffs of Dover to Southampton. Here, English tourists come aboard; they will stay until Marseilles and then travel back over land. From Southampton they travel to the Bay of Biscay, which is notorious for its fog and storms with waves. When there is fog, speed is reduced and the foghorn is used. When it is stormy, speed is also reduced and all the portholes have to be closed to prevent water from entering. Everyone is happy when they pass Gibraltar, and then moor at Algiers where they take in supplies. After crossing the Mediterranean, where they see the lights of Monaco at night, they stop in Marseilles.

The English tourists disembark and they are replaced by Dutch passengers, who have traveled with the boat train to Marseilles. This way they have fewer days on board. The ship travels to Genoa, where you can make a trip to a cemetery with beautiful sculptures, the *Camposanto di Staglieno*, or to Rapallo that has a beautiful castle and to Nervi, a fishing village.

The main building of the cemetery close to Genoa, Italy, the *Camposanto di Staglieno*.

Via the Strait of Messina, between Italy and Sicily, the ship continues its journey to Port Said. Port Said is the first entry into a foreign continent. It caters to the passengers with a large department store on the *Rue du Commerce,* a statue of Ferdinand de Lesseps, the founder of

Geef den bediende het nummer van den gewenschten schotel op

Geef den bediende het nummer van den gewenschten schotel op

Heden Muziek van:
11 tot 12 uur V.M.
7 tot 8 uur N.M.
8,30 tot 10,30 N.M.

ONTBIJT 1e KLASSE

van 7 tot 9,30

MELKSPIJZEN

1-Havermout – 2-Gort – 3-Karnemelk met Gort

WARME GERECHTEN
(10 minuten).

4-Spiegeleieren met Spek – 5-Gekookte eieren
6-Roereieren met Tomaten – 7-Oeufs à la Tripe
8-Gebakken Ham – 9-Gebakken Tong
10-Toast

KOUDE GERECHTEN

11-Roastbeef – 12-Ham
13-Rookvleesch – 14-Thüringer Jachtworst
15-Makreel filets - 16-Hollandsche Haring

Fransche en Weenerbroodjes – Wit en Bruinbrood
Roggebrood – Ontbijtkoek

Hollandsche kaas – Jams – Honig – Marmelade
Koffie – Koffie HAG – Thee – Chocolade – Melk

Sinaasappelen

P.T.O.

„KONINGIN DER NEDERLANDEN" Dinsdag,27 November 1928.

The breakfast menu of the first class dining room of a ship on its way
to the Dutch East Indies. On the rear the menu is repeated in English.

the Suez Canal and trips through Egypt. A train will take you to Luxor, a ship will take you along the Nile to Cairo and then back by train to Port Said. The Suez Canal starts at Port Said, it is 161 km long, and ships have to sail slowly. Signal stations control the passage because the ships cannot pass each other, except at fixed exchange points. You see desert and a few Arabs on camels; you pass *Lake Timsah* near Ismailia, where a large monument has been erected in memory of the First World War, and you pass the *Great Bitter Lake*, after which you reach Suez.

Here the longest part of the journey begins without stopping at a port: ten days at sea. During those days, several parties are organized: the captain's dinner, the children's party, the Neptune party is prepared, and everything comes with a variety of foods. The passengers organize bridge games and people exchange books. In the Gulf of Suez, near Aden, at Cape Guardafui (the extreme tip of the African continent) and at the island of Socotra, there is land to be seen from the ship but the ship remains at sea. The whole journey can be followed on a small atlas, that Lloyd hands out to all the passengers. On the Red Sea, it can be very hot so the passengers start wearing their tropical clothes and sleep on deck to take advantage of the breeze. They enjoy watching the dolphins swimming next to the ship and the view of the beautiful island called Minicoy. This island looks like a tropical paradise with an opal blue sea, small boats with white sails, butterflies and green vegetation.

Then finally the ship moors at Colombo, Ceylon and Beb writes:

There is something beautiful to see here. The old church with Dutch tombstones (how brave those old Dutch sailors were, who traveled on all the seas dressed in their thick woolen slickers and still made it this far without mail ships and the Suez canal), and Mount Lavinia (cynical people remark - what is the point of it? For 10 days you have seen nothing but the sea, now finally here is land again and you rush off in cars to a spot where you can see the sea), and a beautiful native church, that you are not allowed to enter with your shoes on, and where prayers are written on palm leaves.

In Colombo the passengers can receive mail, because this is one of the cities with air mail. The timing of letters is therefore important. The journey continues across the Indian Ocean, where it is less hot, to Sabang, the first port in the Dutch East Indies, located on one of the 13,000 islands of the Dutch East Indies' archipelago. The harbor sits in a beautiful green valley and has a social club with a perfect view; it is Dutch East Indies at its best. Sabang is a free port, so there is good shopping. On the quay, toilet water and perfume are on display and the Alberti store is full of bargains; then, through the Strait of Malacca to Medan, Beb considers this the most beautiful part of the journey.

They dock in Singapore, the last port before they reach Batavia. Singapore has an endless Chinese neighborhood and a beautiful botanical garden, where lots of tame monkeys are very busy running around with their youngsters in their arms. At *John Little* (a large department store) you can buy some extra tropical clothing. The last party on the ship is the Neptune feast, and after crossing the equator the passengers start saying their goodbyes. During the voyage at sea you share companionship, but after arrival in the Dutch East Indies the passengers spread out all over the archipelago.

After a sea voyage of 10,000 miles, Beb and Wim arrive in the port of Batavia called *Tandjong Priok* at the end of December 1927. They disembark and first stay at the *Hotel des Indes* and later with Kitty van Lennep-de Voogt, a member of Wim's family. Here Beb receives her first impressions of the Dutch East Indies after hearing so many stories from her husband and sister. It is lively and busy with native women in traditional clothing, carrying a whole basket of bananas or coconuts on their heads, without holding on to it. Many women chew betel and the men smoke clove cigarettes, so there is always an exotic smell. She sees the rickshaws and notices that women walk three meters behind their husbands as is customary for Islamic people.

The train takes them to Bandung and along the way she sees simple houses with lots of palm trees, banana trees and cascading rice fields with intricate water irrigation systems. In Bandung, they can again stay at family members of Wim: Walther and Louise van Alphen de Veer-Brooshooft. He is head of the material research laboratory of the department of Civil Public Works and also a professor at the technical university in Bandung. Years later Beb writes: 'Wim has such a large family and knows so many people, that there is always someone around who can help you,'

From Bandung they travel to Semarang. This is a 12-hour train journey that costs 30 guilders. Wim's sister Wies lives there together with her husband Arnold Terlet, who is a minister and they celebrate Christmas together. For New Year's Eve they go to Ungaran, where Beb's sister Loukie lives with her husband Albert Carpentier-Alting and their son Hans, nicknamed Tip. Albert works as an engineer at the Railways.

Loukie writes to her mother that Beb glows with happiness: 'My brother-in-law is so alive and open, just so warm and friendly. He immediately fits in. How lucky these people are and what a success their marriage has become.' Beb confides in Loukie how clever it was of Wim to be so persistent. Loukie mentions this, of course, in her letter to her mother when she writes about the reunion of: 'Two sisters, two sons-in-law and two grandchildren'.

Ineke van der Wal

New Year's Eve 1927-28 in Oengaran near Semarang, Dutch East
Indies, where Beb's sister lives. From left to right: Hans Carpentier-
Alting, Loukie Carpentier-Alting-Zeeman, Albert Carpentier-Alting,
Kate Einthoven and pregnant Beb Einthoven-Zeeman. Wim
Einthoven is not in the picture, because he is the photographer.

Drawing of the house at Pasteurweg 21, Bandung by Beb Einthoven –
Zeeman.

Back in Bandung they rent a house at the Louis Pasteurweg 21, for 120 guilders per month. This road is named after the local Louis Pasteur Institute, famous for its vaccinations against all kinds of evil such as diseases, rabies and snake bites. The institute keeps snakes to produce antidote and one can go and view these snakes. They are kept in terrariums but are quite active. If you tap the glass with a large object, they immediately stand up and spray the window with their poison. Creepy fun for the little kids.

Beb hires a *kokki* (cook), a *babu* (nanny) and two *djongos* (male assistants) and spends time decorating the house with the items that they brought from The Netherlands. The paintings of Grandfather De Bruyn are hung, together with drawings of Harm Kamerlingh Onnes, Willem Hofker and Han van Meegeren and finally a portrait of Father and pictures of the in-laws. Beb's desk chair, the bedroom furniture with the nice dressing table, the cuddly basket with the parfait glasses, the Delft plates, the silverware and the cradle with the handles and the big wheels; everything gets a place. The cradle is filled again on March 23, 1928 by the arrival of a second daughter: Louise Joanne, nicknamed Loukie, after Beb's sister.

Wim goes to work at the *PTT* (Post, Telegraph, Telephone) in Bandung. There is an office in Bandung, but he also travels to Malabar and the other transmitting stations in Java. He is therefore regularly away from the family for long periods of time. It was De Groot's wish that Wim would succeed him, but there are some engineers who feel that they are being passed over. Wim is considered to be too young but he is determined to show that De Groot was not mistaken.

Beb finds Bandung to be a vibrant city, which is rapidly expanding and encourages many architects to produce beautiful work. Bandung is located in West Java in the Preanger area. This is a plateau (715 meters above sea level) surrounded by volcanoes, where the climate is nicer and healthier than in Batavia. After the completion of the Batavia-Bandung railway in 1894, Bandung positions itself as a better location

Ineke van der Wal

than Batavia, the capital. The government soon decides to move various government services to Bandung.

The army headquarters and the war department had already moved in 1914. This move was prompted by the need for a 'defensible stronghold' in the event of a foreign attack. The Department of Interior Affairs moves in 1921, with services such as railroads and tramways, salt regulation, *PTT* and mining services. After a battle between Batavia and Bandung, the Technical University is also based in Bandung.

It is especially the move of the headquarters of the *KNIL* (Royal Dutch Indies Army) to Bandung which convinces many suppliers to move to Bandung: machine and construction workshops, the Javanese canning factory, ammunition industry, a quinine factory and the Goodyear Rubber works that produces car tires. There is even a dairy factory: 'Do not forget that in The Netherlands East Indies there is only one milk factory and that is the Bandung milk factory.' Many large conferences are organized in the trade fair building: in 1922 the Natural Science congress and in 1929 the Fourth Pacific Science congress.

The railways open a central workshop, the Department of Civil Public Works moves from Batavia, the department of Agriculture, Industry and Trade establishes several laboratories, followed by the Dutch East Indies pension funds, banks and trading centers. Schools are established in order to train all the employees. In 1931 there are 116 schools with 22,072 pupils and students, many of whom live at the schools.

In 1922 the *Andir* airport opens with a direct connection to Batavia. In 1928 one can fly from Batavia to Amsterdam in 11 days. That is a huge improvement over the four to six weeks travel by ship. In 1927 the first flight with *De Postduif* from KLM is worldwide news.

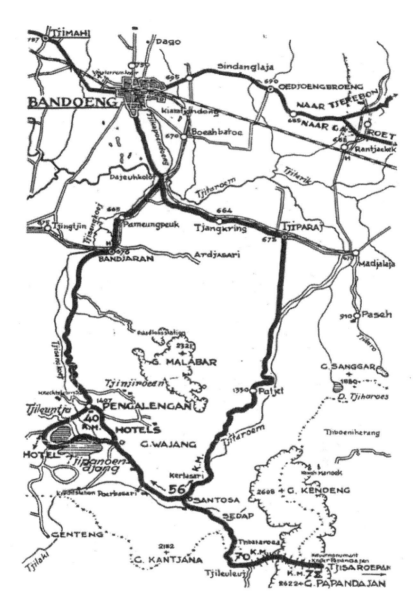

The surroundings of Bandung, Dutch East Indies, with Dago, Dajeuh
Kolot, Malabar, Pengalengan, Tjangkring and Rantja Ekek.
Source: Preangerbode, April 13, 1931.

Ineke van der Wal

All this activity brings highly qualified employment to the city and that means strengthening of the European element. A European middle class is emerging, together with a busy shopping street, the *Braga* road, with a variety of shops and Bandung quickly becomes the third most important city in the Dutch East Indies, following Batavia and Surabaya. In 1890 there were 340 Europeans in Bandung, in 1940 there are almost 27,000 and the total population has grown from 40,000 to 216,000. The number of academics among Europeans is unprecedentedly high, ten times as many as in The Netherlands. The Dutch East Indies rely on technical knowledge and performance, which gives technicians a remarkably important social status. The goal of the Dutch government is to develop the East Indies so that it can contribute to the Dutch economy. In 1930, the Dutch East Indies contributed 8% to the national income of The Netherlands.

The Dutch East Indies society is quite hierarchical with three populations that live separately from each other: Europeans, foreign Orientals (Chinese, Arab, British Indian), and indigenous people. The Europeans live mainly in the large, newly built residential areas north of the railway line, the Chinese mainly live in *Pasar Baru*, southwest of the railway line. Due to the rapid growth and expansion of Bandung, the *kampongs*, the residential areas of the indigenous population, shrink down to one third of their original size.

Living conditions for Europeans can be characterized as excellent. The club life is well organized, five cinemas show the latest films, and the music, theater and dance hall on the *Groote Postweg* accommodates a thousand people. Many artists want to perform in Bandung, which is also called the 'Paris of Java'.

The department of *BOW* (Civil Public Works) is responsible for the construction of government buildings. In 1909 the first construction engineer was hired by BOW, in 1912 the second one followed. In department of *BOW* is responsible for the construction of government buildings. In 1909 the first construction engineer was hired by *BOW*, in 1912 the second one followed. In addition, many private architects settle in Bandung, where they often combine their office with a construction agency. They build using the instruction books from The Netherlands or by inspiration from America. The villas are very similar to the type of villa built in The Netherlands and the neighborhoods for Europeans built in the 1920s and 30s have a completely European appearance. The houses are often covered with plaster because there is no good brick or good masons, but famous Dutch architect Berlage sighs during a visit to the Indies that he also could have been in Baarn or Hilversum in The Netherlands.

The Bragaweg in the 1930's (Source: Tropenmuseum) and Jalan Braga in recent times (Source: Fadey Jevera).

The *Braga* shopping street is a copy of a Dutch shopping street with many buildings in Art Deco style that one can also find in Europe. The new building style with concrete is also used: the extravagant Villa Isola, built for press magnate D.W. Berretty by architect Wolff Schoemaker, is an example of this style.

Ineke van der Wal

Villa Isola in Lembang, close to Bandung.

These building styles, however, do not provide much cooling. Architects aim to create a building style that is better adapted to the tropical conditions. In 1920 J. Gerber designs the Department of Interior Affairs and this building serves as an example of the search for an original Indies style.

The head office of the Semarang Cheribon Steam Tram Company in Tegal, designed by H. Maclaine Pont, applies a second façade that creates shade and due to the east-west orientation there is minimal heating and maximal ventilation. However, this building is still made with 'western' building materials. The technical university of Bandung, designed in 1919 by H. Maclaine Pont, meets the requirements for an Indies building style: no artificial appliances, but architectural and construction methods to control the climate with the use of local building materials and indigenous manpower.

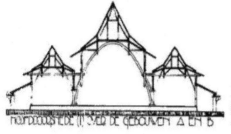

Indische Technische Hoogeschool, Bandung. Architect H. Maclaine Pont. Boogspanten, geconstrueerd uit op elkaar gestapelde planken, die in de dikterichting gebogen en door bouten en beugels verbonden zijn, maken overspanningen van 8 en 15 m mogelijk. Tekening gedateerd 6 maart 1919.

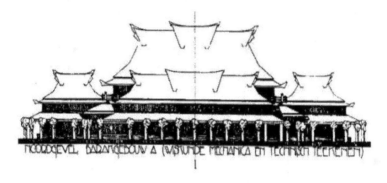

Roof construction of the Technical University of Bandung.
Source: Akihary, Huib

The older Batavia is a trading town, which is built in a traditional Dutch way with main and secondary canals, which are perpendicular to each other. On the sides of the canals are Dutch canal houses, built from Dutch brick, which has been transported to the Dutch East Indies as ballast on a ship. The city slowly spreads to the countryside, to higher, healthier places, where large country houses such as *Weltevreden* are built. Bandung, however, is a city of civil servants and military personnel and the town is carefully planned. The layout is largely determined by the Cikapundung river, which runs from north to south and the railway line that runs from east to west. In the valley of the Cikapundung river a park is created, a green area that lies near the city center. Old country roads are improved and important traffic routes are constructed. They connect the northerly expansions with the city center. In the northern area, buildings for the Department of Internal Affairs, the Technical University, and the Pasteur Institute are erected.

Ineke van der Wal

The volcano Tangkuban Prahu ('inverted boat') near Bandung

The location of Bandung is beautiful. The mountain *Tangkuban Prahu* ('inverted boat') is always in the background with green rice fields along the slopes, the Maribaya waterfall, the fumaroles of the semi-extinct volcanoes and an abundance of beautiful flowers. The organization *Bandung Vooruit* '(Bandung Ahead') urges people to visit Bandung and its volcanoes and manages to attract an ever-increasing stream of tourists (200,000 in 1937), who arrive on a cruise ship in Batavia, and then travel by train or by car to Bandung. Two modern hotels are built to accommodate tourists: the Hotel *Savoy Homann* (with a bouncy dance floor and its own orchestra) and the Hotel *Preanger,* both in the then popular Art Deco style.

The *Braga* shopping street has every imaginable type of store: a fashion store called *Bon Marché*, a tailor shop *Van Hal*, a tobacco store *Toko Tabaksplant* and *Maison Bogerijen* with a shop, a tearoom and large terrace, where you can sit under umbrellas in a tropical setting with an exotic atmosphere. *Maison Bogerijen* employ 130 staff members in their

The Mirabaya waterfall

own bakery where, among others, Queen Emma and Queen Wilhelmina cakes are made. Then there are the *Snoephuis* and the *Firma Huber* with Swiss chocolate and the *Fuchs and Reus* garage with cars such as *Studebaker, Packard, Chrysler, De Soto, Plymouth* and *Renault*. In other streets you can find shops for groceries and beverages, the *DENIS Bank, Toko Buku* for books, the *Majestic Theater* and the *Bordeelsteeg* or brothel alley for Preanger planters. The swimming pool Cihampelas is opened, and it is fed by crystal clear spring water from the *Tjitaroem* river.

Beb, Wim and their young family have found a place where they can grow and flourish.

Ineke van der Wal

CHAPTER IV

Life in the Dutch East Indies

B eb and Wim have an idyllic time in Bandung. They live and work among many Europeans, all of whom have left their family and friends behind and want to have a good time in their temporary station in the Dutch East Indies. Beb settles into her role as 'wife of': she runs a household with children Loukie and Kate, a staff and a husband who is often away. Meeting other families is easy and the servants take care of the domestic work and the children, so that enough time remains to

spend on Beb's own interests like clubs, outings, overnight visitors and correspondence with family and friends.

Beb works hard to write letters regularly to her mother, her mother-in-law and other family members such as Wim's sisters, her own sister and then friends. This takes a lot of time. Koos, Wim's youngest sister, who came to Bandung in 1930 to start a practice as a doctor for women, complains about the burden of the correspondence. She writes one letter a day to keep up. Koos and Beb live so close to each other that sometimes they write a letter together to mother Einthoven. That saves them time. Beb writes neat, but Koos writes with many crossed out words and phrases inserted here and there. Wim sometimes adds a note at the bottom of the letter. Koos' practice is getting off to a slow start: "My practice is now on patient number 18, and 3 pregnancies. Not yet full-time work." That is why she has already received 3,000 guilders from her mother as support. She feels uncomfortable with that. "Mother, I do not want you to have to worry about me," but she does ask her mother to pay all sorts of bills, order books and transfer money to *VVSL* ('Association of Female Students in Leiden') to pay for a wedding gift for her Royal Highness Princess Juliana. The exchange rate of the guilder is a source of frequent complaints.

One of the clubs, of which Beb is a member, is the 'Association of Former Female Students'. This club meets once every month in the evening and the members take turns to give presentations. Twenty four women come to the meeting at Beb's house and all the chairs from the whole house are dragged into Wim's office. Topics include *Education* and *The Excuse of the Papuans*. Wim is a member of the Rotary, a club for men only and they have their own presentations. He gives a lecture on the progress in wireless telephony.

The Kingma family lives next to the Einthoven family and has children of the same age. Father Fokko Kingma is a French teacher at the *Christelijk Lyceum,* the Christian high school. He knows that Beb is an architectural engineer and asks her to be an examination auditor of the final exams at the school. The task is interesting to Beb and she is handed all kinds of papers. "Do I have to read all those papers?" she a asks. "No," is the answer. "You just have to sign them." A simple task that is quickly finished, and three months later a letter arrives from the government, indicating that Beb has been appointed as an official examination auditor for French and English subjects. She is appalled and asks for an explanation. "What have you done? I am skilled in practical subjects and I was thinking about mathematics, why now French and English?" Fokko Kingma is a wise man and he explains: "We did not need any more mathematicians, but we do need people for French and English." "But couldn't you have told me?" "Look at it this way" he says. "You speak French and you speak English. You read and know both languages. The task of an examination auditor is not to ask questions or to take the exam. The task is to be present and ensure that all children are treated equally and fairly. It's a check on the examiners, so you only need to speak the languages which you do, so I would do it anyway." Beb takes on this task reluctantly for the first year, but then continues to fulfill this role for years to come with great pleasure. The school organizes an outing at the end of the school year and that is how Beb goes camping several times with the teachers of the high school.

Beb also starts to sing again. She did enjoy this in The Netherlands and was quite good at it. She becomes a member of a choir that not only performs on the radio, but that also stages operettas. The biggest production is *Goudsprookje's Tooverlied (*"A golden fairytale's magic song*)* by the Dutch composer Machiel M. Koster, with 125 singers/actors: "*24 small orientals, 36 fire devils, court ladies, extras to fill the stage and a show of oriental wealth*". There are 2600 people in the audience for the three performances which took four months of practice, sewing of the costumes and construction of the scenery. The children are allowed to watch and they go twice.

Often one tries to combine the useful tasks with a pleasant task. The many sewing and adjustment work that has to be done is of course more enjoyable when one has company. Beb gets together every Thursday with a circle of friends, who bring the children which are not old enough to go to school yet, and they take turns meeting at each other's homes.

Beb likes to occasionally make a trip to other parts of Java. Wim encourages her to do this, just as he did during his first stay by riding on his motorcycle. She often goes together with Lies Andriessen, an unmarried girlfriend. Over the years she visits the Dieng plateau with fumaroles, the pass between the Sumbing and Sindoro, Magelang, Borobudur, Mendoet and Djokja. The children can stay with Beb's sister-in-law, Koos, or with one of the many families that have children of the same age, such as the families Lels, Bake, Kingma, Fernandes, Süverkropp, Schepers or Eschbach. They also make trips to the various transmitting stations: a car ride to Tjililin in the hills, along and across the rapids of the Tjitaroen River, or to Malabar; these trips are fascinating and romantic at the same time. A visit to the Malabar broadcasting station is a tourist attraction, but also dignitaries such as Mr. Clemenceau (French prime minister), Mr. Treub (Secretary of the Treasury) and the king of Siam pay visits.

In Beb's correspondence there is a constant concern about the health of the family. Child diseases are widely reported and every member of the family stays in bed for a long time if they have a fever or some illness. Beb has rheumatism and receives formic acid injections. Loukie gets treated for worms, has urine tests, a festering knee and then there is also fear of dysentery. Wim has problems with his foot that is being irradiated with a mercury lamp borrowed from friends. When that is resolved, he suffers from abdominal disorders and goes on a diet. Then the children have a fever and they get a red glowing head: "I am so burned," they say. Grandma Zeeman even has to go to the hospital during her visit. Loukie has an eye infection and two birthdays are celebrated in bed; her hands are constantly disinfected with Lysol. Also the diseases of their friends are often the subject of conversation. Jakarta is left behind as the capital city because Bandung is cooler, but it is nicknamed 'the child's grave' because the nights are often so cold that children get sick. And don't forget the insects and animals that can be dangerous: mosquitoes that spread malaria, rabid dogs or a poisonous snake. They find one in the house. Oerig and Kardi - the helpers and gardeners - smash it on its head and throw it away in a ditch in the back of the garden.

Drawing of the house at Kromhoutweg 2, Bandung by Beb Einthoven – Zeeman.

Soon Beb and Wim decide to buy a piece of land at the Kromhoutweg in order to build a house there. Number two is at the top of the Dagoweg, not far from the Christian High School. The Dagoweg is long and runs up the slope of the Tangkuban Prahu vulcano. Beb is obviously involved in the design and construction of the house.

All rooms are on the ground floor, the outside is plastered white, the floor is covered with tiles, a high roof stimulates air circulation and the overhanging gutter provides shade. The tinted glass in lead windows give respite from the sunlight and stark blue skies. The garden is big enough to build a house for the staff members. This means that they can hire an extra helper or *djongos*.

Two cypresses are planted next to front of the house to frame it. Loukie and Albert have also seen the drawings. "They are delighted", and "it is very pleasant and challenging work to design it ourselves," Beb writes. They have to make some cutbacks and negotiations with the builder follow. When Beb's mother later sees the house, she is amazed at the open corridors and the way you enter the house without a front door or a bell or a hall. In this larger house there is also room for a piano. They buy a nicely maintained teak, *Naessens* tropical piano for 425 guilders. Gus sends a booklet from which the children can play.

The year 1930 is off to a great start with the birth of a son Willem Gerard, nicknamed Wink, on January 20th, 1930. Sister-in-law Wies comes to help during the maternity period and during her stay she teaches Kate some nursery rhymes like *It rains, it rains* and *Frère Jacques*. The baby is soon called *Brother* by his sisters and Beb writes: "The cute little receding chin that he inherited from Wim is more pronounced than that of the two girls." The two girls are also called the blonde and the brown, because of their light and dark hair.

On January 22, 1930, however, the sad news reaches them that Loukie, Beb's sister, has died. Loukie was pregnant with her second child and the congenital ailment of her kidneys became fatal. Her son Tip is only 6 years old. Albert, Loukie's husband, decides that Loukie will be  buried in the Dutch East Indies. Her body, therefore, is not embalmed and is not transferred to The Netherlands. Beb's mother has a hard time with that decision. Beb is unhappy that she can do so little for her mother because they are so far apart and she is appreciative that Wim's mother visits Beb's mother to express her sympathy.

Beb does not know what else to do but to continue to write letters with good news about her family accompanied by nice pictures. This,

Ineke van der Wal

however, makes the correspondence somewhat artificially joyful. There is little room for feelings or doubts. Beb, a highly educated woman, will not write about the political situation, the unrest on Java among the native population, or wonder if it is proper that a small group of whites rules over the *Gordel van Smaragd (the emerald belt)*.

Kate, Wim and Loukie.

In August 1930 a trial was filed against Sukarno at the *Landraad* in Bandung. Sukarno is already seen as the undisputed leader of the nationalist movement, which strives for independence for Indonesia. The highlight of this process is Sukarno's own plea entitled "Indonesia accuses". Beb must have known about this. The letters from sister-in-law Koos to her mother are filled with indignation about all kinds of abuses Koos experiences.

One of the abuses, for example, is the fact that Western educated East Indies people are excluded from domestic government and that there is a lack of education for natives. Education is unattainable for the mass of the indigenous population. Around 1930 only 84,609 children of native descent enjoy Western education; in other words: only 0.14 percent of the population of 60 million. An even smaller group goes

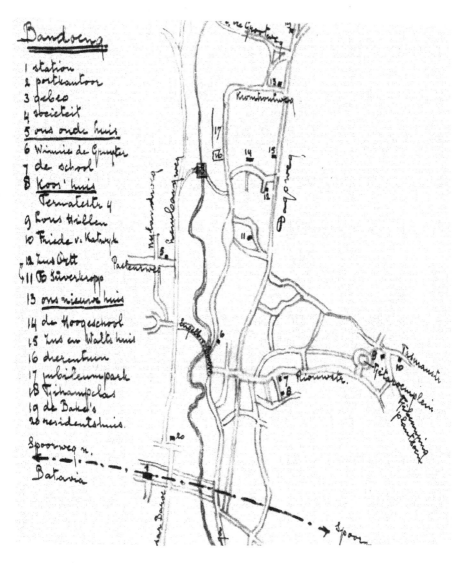

A plan of Bandung drawn by Beb for her mother with among others the old house, the new house and the house of Koos all in Beb's characteristic handwriting.

to a high school (and only in large cities) and on to a university in The Netherlands. After 1920, it is possible to go to the Technical University in Bandung. Sukarno, the independence fighter, was the sixth native student at this Technical University in 1921.

On January 27, 1930, the monument for radio pioneer De Groot is unveiled at the Oranjeplein. It is designed by Prof. Wolff Shoemaker and the *Hollandse Beton Maatschappij* built the monument free of charge. Wim gives an overview of De Groot's career and merits in which he emphasizes his perseverance and how he often performed  under very difficult circumstances that in the end yielded important results. De Groot was an activist who performed unforgettable pioneering work in the radio area:

> *"Only those who know the Malabar, only those who have contributed to this great work, know what is going on in the gorge of that mountain, in these tropical jungles in this inhospitable place and what has been constructed. Only for the indestructible optimism of Dr. De Groot and his deep trust in the plans he designed himself, is one to be thankful for everything that has now been created there. Already when the big transmitter sent its first signals to Holland, De Groot thought about a telephone connection and with that he would have considered his job to be complete. It is clear that Dr. De Groot has formed a staff of helpers, trained by him, who gradually became his great support, but everyone at the radio service will miss this leader who died too soon." There are also words for his dear wife, "who with the greatest devotion surrounded him with her love and support, so that his energy benefited his work."*

Beb, Kate and Loukie on board of the SS *Sibajak* on its way to
The Netherlands.

Wim has to travel to the United States in 1930 to approve a 'standard
clock' the laboratory has ordered. He decides to take advantage of this
trip with a stop in The Netherlands and to take Beb and the children
along. They want to use this early leave (normally only after five years
of work) to introduce their only son to The Netherlands and to share
the grief over the loss of Loukie, Beb's sister. Beb immediately gets
very busy with the preparations, such as making warm clothes. Juffie,
the nanny, is coming along on leave. Kate is four, Loukie is two-and-
a-half and Wink is half a year old, so help is very welcome. Beb plans
a visit to Albert and Tip and to Loukie's grave before the departure.
Wim can take care of the children for a weekend with some help from
Juffie. So Beb goes to Ungaran alone, a sad journey, and she later tells
her mother about it.

Ineke van der Wal

The work goes on for Wim during the ocean voyage. The Aneta Press Office publishes the following press release:

"The Head of the Research Laboratory and the Laboratory of the Radio Technology department of PTT, the engineer 2nd class, W.F. Einthoven, has invented a method, which makes it possible to receive multiple telephony transmissions simultaneously while using only one radio receiver. He will apply for a patent on this invention. Mr. Einthoven leaves for The Netherlands on July, 30 on the SS Sibajak from the Rotterdam Lloyd and will then go to the United States for a study assignment. A two-person cabin will be made available on board the SS Sibajak by the Rotterdam Lloyd, in which the invention of Mr. Einthoven will be tested. For the broadcasts in connection with these tests, the PLE station will be used here."

The radio lab had already been experimenting for a year with this invention, which is intended to make secret telephony possible in the future and to be able to telegraph and make telephone calls simultaneously with one transmitter. The trip is a great opportunity to test this "multiple transmitter".

Wim disembarks in Marseilles and travels with the *Rapide* (express train) to The Netherlands. Beb's mother who has traveled to Marseilles, takes Wim's spot on the ship for this last part of the journey, so that she can enjoy her grandchildren as long as possible.

The family first lives in Baarn with Beb's mother (*Big Grandma*) in the house of Beb's grandfather, who thoroughly enjoys his grandchildren. Then they move to Jeroen Boschlaan 6 in Haarlem, the home of Oma Einthoven (*Little Grandma*). Little Grandma has decided to live with one of her sisters at Van Merlenlaan 4 in Heemstede and to give her whole house to Beb and the children. Beb really appreciates this: "It is so wonderful that you have central heating, then I have no fear that the children will touch the charcoal stove." During the leave a picture is taken of Beb with her three children. Wink is still in the pram and Kate and Loukie are standing behind him with their dolls in their doll

Mother and two daughters each with their own pram.

carriages. Many prints are made of the photo so that several family members receive a copy. Beb's cousin Loukie van der Chijs is engaged to the sculptor Gerrit Jan van der Veen and they decide to ask him to make a sculpture of the two daughters and the new baby. Plaster copies

Ineke van der Wal

are made for the family members. The whole leave is dedicated to family visits: a wonderful day on the water in cousin Han de Voogt and his wife Laine's motorboat and they celebrate *Sinterklaas* and Christmas with the complete family.

When it snows, they make snowmen, which they line up in a row in the front yard. They go back inside to get warm and see someone stealing their biggest snowman by putting him on a sled and running away. Father Wim immediately comes into action. He runs after the sled and is able to stop the thief, a young boy. He quickly makes up an 'appropriate' punishment. Since he still has a snowball in his hand, he forces the boy to take it in his mouth and swallow it. The snowman is placed back in the front yard again and Wim comes back into the house as a hero.

Snowmen in the front yard together with their creators.

Wrapped tightly for the Dutch winter. From left to right: Maria Julius, Mariza Julius, Loukie Einthoven, Grandmother Einthoven, Kate Einthoven, the nanny, Wink Einthoven and Beb Einthoven.

For the return journey in 1931, they again travel on the SS *Sibajak*. Rik packs a toy chest, which everyone learns about because it 'rattles eerily' when they turn it upside down; fortunately only one foot of a doll's bath breaks. On their return trip, they take *Little Grandma* (grandmother Einthoven) to the Dutch East Indies. She will stay with her children for a year. Three of her four children now live in the Dutch East Indies and she herself was born in the Dutch East Indies. She will travel back and forth between her three children: from Wies, stationed at Surabaya where Arnold is a minister, to Koos with her own practice as a doctor for women in Bandung and then again to Beb, Wim and the grandchildren. Beb writes to her mother that the children are being spoiled by *Little Grandma*. When they eat their meals, they want to be fed again by Grandma even though they can already do that by themselves. *Little Grandma* later writes to her daughter Gus:

"I have to tell you about little Wink. Beb always says to the children: "Quiet, children." Wim always says: "Fie!, children" and I always seem to say: "Dear

children." Wink sings himself to sleep every night with: "Quiet mommy, Fie! daddy and dear grandmother."

For children, life in Bandung is wonderful. It is always nice weather and when it rains it is intense, but short. Life does not take place behind closed doors like in The Netherlands and you can wear clothing that is lightweight. The staff is nice to them and does not dare to refuse them too much. They pay many visits to the swimming pool (*Dago* is expensive and beautiful, *Cihampelas* is closer and less expensive), or walk along the *Djalan Pleizieran* (The Fun road), from the Lembangweg, the ravine of the Tjikapoendoeng, past the kampong houses and overlooking the 'sawahs' (rice fields). They have pets: a dog, a dachshund called Holly and also three little kittens: Wimpie belongs to Wink, Miffy belongs to Loukie and Roelletje belongs to Kate. It does not always go well. Beb writes about sick animals and animals that are buried in the garden with a headstone.

The children attend the Montessori primary school and their father takes them there in the car. In the morning it is always a rush to get all the children ready on time. For vacation they go to Pangandaran, which is located by the sea, where they meet the Buning family. There are piano lessons (the girls play four hands with Beb) and violin lessons for Wink. Then there is a constant stream of visitors, which keeps them busy.

The family from The Netherlands regularly sends packages for the children, together with beautifully homemade clothing (blue silk smock dresses). If something is not available in the Dutch East Indies, it can be ordered through the Sears catalog in the United States. These orders are delivered months later and the content of the shipment is often a surprise.

There are many young families in Bandung and the children have lots of friends to endlessly play with. The children's birthdays are celebrated

Kate and Loukie with the staff in Bandung:
Oerig, Baboe, Kokki and Kardi.

with enthusiasm: gifts from the Dutch East Indies, gifts from The Netherlands, visits from family and friends, treats shared at school (100 cookies, each child gets two) and parties are organized. Beb writes to her mother about what it takes to make such a party successful: hats are made from a roll of colored paper with a bow made of a different color paper attached to it and then decorated with silver stars. They leave school at 11 o'clock and play until half past 12. Then they eat at the house, 17 children in all. Tables and benches are borrowed from the school. All the hats must be put on the plates. The menu is noodle soup, croquettes on sticks with colored pieces attached to the sticks, ground beef with carrots, beans and mashed potatoes, cake and ice cream. Each child receives a small gift that was bought at the Japanese shop. Everything has to be finished by 2 o'clock so that all the children can have a nap in the afternoon, because there is a children's

Ineke van der Wal

performance of the housewives' association, which they go to afterwards.

The Einthovens lead a proper life. Bandung has its wild sides, because of the planters from Java who come to enjoy themselves, but Wim and Beb take no part in it. The boisterous parties of D.W. Beretty, the founder of news agency *Aneta* and owner of the beautiful *Villa Isola* do not seem to have been visited either. The wildest activity is a visit to the comedy on Saturday evening together with the *Süverkroppen*. Friede van Katwijk performs as a sour landlady. Then they eat at *Shanghai Dream*; it is 2 a.m. before they are home again.

Summer 1931 with from left to right Louk, Wink and Kate Einthoven.

Koos Einthoven with the three children of her brother Wim.

Beb's grandfather *Opi* dies on October 20, 1934, at almost 90 years old. Because of this, Beb's mother decides to move back to Oegstgeest. Now that the care for her father is over, she is free to go to the Dutch East Indies. She books a trip from March 1935 until March 1936. Beb is immediately busy with preparations; the house is painted, everything gets a big cleaning and extra mosquito nets have to be made. The new electric sewing machine fortunately works much faster. Beb's mother will make a monthly contribution to Kokkie and Juffie for the additional work. To pay for this, the mother opens a credit account with *De Nederlandsche Indische Handelsbank* with 3,000 guilders.

Ineke van der Wal

Beb, Wim, Koos and Lies Andriessen pick up Mother Zeeman in Batavia on March 28, 1935 just in time to celebrate her 64th birthday on March 31st. The three grandchildren wake up Grandma in the morning and take her from the bedroom while sprinkling flowers on their way to the living room. In April, they celebrate Beb's birthday. Grandma Zeeman makes presents with the children: a bookmark, a frame, and a basket. The family has sent presents for the family with Grandma Zeeman, such as stationery, a card, a nightingale whistle, ink patches, a race car, handkerchiefs, a book for children to learn how to tell time, and dog brooches.

In May, Beb and her mother go to Semarang, where Albert and son Tip pick them up from the station and then bring them to hotel Tjandi, where mother and daughter stay. They meet Albert's second wife, Pia. The next day and the following days they visit the grave of Loukie in Ungaran and spend as much time as possible with Tip. Then they drive to Djokja, where they meet Grandma Einthoven (still in the Dutch East Indies for the presentation of the Bosscha medal). That offers them some distraction because mother and daughter have a difficult time after the visit to the grave. On July 17, 1935 Wim turns 42 years old and that can be celebrated in the presence of the two grandmothers, a unique event. They celebrate the birthday with a "wonderful trip to the Wijnkoop Baai and drive back over Soekaboemi, just as Loukie did at the time."

In early December, the shops are decorated with Christmas snow and fake Christmas trees. Grandma treats the family to ice and cake at the *Bogerijen* bakery and between Christmas and New Year they make trips to the Tangkuban Prahu and the Papandayan Crater. They travel via Pangalengan past the tea companies Malabar, Sedep and Sambosa to the primeval forest and on to the newly excavated road to the crater, which they see smoking at a distance. While one is not allowed to enter the crater of the Prahu, for fear of the danger of choking, one can easily descend in the Papandayan Crater. From all sides it bubbles and boils

and steam evaporates. The children do not go too far and the three of them head back. The sulfur vapor scares them. Beb and her mother sometimes feel really stuffed up and then cough a lot, but if there is some wind, they are able to carry on. The clouds that creep into the crater periodically separate and then they see the plains of Garoet in the distance. On the top they eat a sandwich and drink tea from a thermos flask. Later they all drink a cup of coffee at hotel *Beau Sejour.*

Beb's mother returns to The Netherlands on the 4th of March 1936 on board the SS *Marnix van Sint Aldegonde,* which arrives in Amsterdam on March 31st, her 65th birthday. It is a difficult farewell; she no longer sees Tip and it is unknown when Beb and Wim will come to The Netherlands on their leave. Maybe this is not going to happen anymore because mother has seen warships, submarines, planes and an aircraft carrier while on her voyage. Is this a sign of war? Mother is sad when she leaves for Holland. "I dare not expect anything more from the future."

Oma Einthoven, *Little Grandma,* dies on January 31, 1937 when she is 75 years old. She was living at Graaf Willem de Oudelaan 33 in Naarden, and was a widow for ten years. She is buried in the cemetery at the *Groene Kerkje* in Oegstgeest. The furniture is left with the family and the so-called memory boxes and Kate's cradle (taken with the leave) are stored with Beb's mother. She is now the only grandparent for the children.

Ineke van der Wal

On April 13, 1937, Beb celebrates her 42nd birthday: "It was an utterly delightful day," writes Beb. "The children had all bought a gift of 15 cents in *Toko de Zon* using their own money." Beb has great news for the children on that day: she is pregnant. The children are happy about it and hope that the baby will be fed with a bottle, since that is much more fun, and then they can help too. However, they do ask if "Daddy knows about this". Beb no longer expected this pregnancy and this is a change for her, but overall a very happy one, especially because Wim is so happy. Tine Marlene - Tineke - is born on October 31st. This third girl in the family ensures that the make-up of Beb and Wim's family is exactly the same as the composition of Wim's parents' family: three sisters and one brother.

Loukie, Tineke, Kate and Wim, early 1938

The children start their school education at the Montessori school and then go to the Christian High School in Bandung. There are more than 500 students and the school starts at 7 o'clock in the morning, a typical tropical schedule. The school is located on the Dagoweg in a new building (the school was founded in 1928) in a park-like schoolyard, and the children can walk to it. At the 5-year high school, 14 subjects are taught and after school there are many after-school clubs such as embroidery for the girls and carpentry for the boys, plus a lot of sports. The principal is Mr. K. Posthumus. In the school magazine *Announcements* he encourages parents and caretakers (many boarding school children) to get involved in the school. He also advises "that the most important thing parents can give their children is regularity and peace in daily life." Various complaints from parents are discussed, such as unauthorized absence, prolonging holidays, visiting doctors during school hours, vandalism at school, ignoring the dress code, disappointment at not passing exams, and too little time for gym and music. Posthumus is worried about the amount of students that actually completes their education. It is not even half the number of students that start in the first grade. Placement of pupils in the right school is important and parents are often too ambitious, says Posthumus.

In 1938 Maria Hofker-Rueter, Beb's grand-niece, and her husband Willem Hofker come to the Dutch East Indies. Willem Hofker received an order to paint Queen Wilhelmina for the Dutch East Indies headquarters of KPM *(Koninklijke Pakketvaart Maatschappij)*, at that time the main shipping company in the Dutch East Indies. Willem and Maria want to visit the Dutch East Indies and stipulate that they themselves may bring the portrait and that Willem will be paid for making a series of fifty drawings and paintings of Dutch East Indies subjects of his choice. The latter is to provide for their livelihood during their stay in the East Indies.

After they have delivered the portrait in Batavia they come to stay with Wim and Beb in Bandung. They stay longer than planned because Willem Hofker gets sick. The children give Willem the nickname "beard man" because he does not shave during his illness and grows a long beard.

Ineke van der Wal

One of the drawings of Willem Hofker for a KPM poster

Maria gets to know the biologist Van der Pijl in Bandung. He makes her aware of the rich flora of Java, which she chooses as the subject for her first drawings. Willem and Maria later travel on to Bali, the mystical island with its refined beauty and its own culture. They live in Ubud, a small artists' village, where they lead a rather isolated existence and where both can dedicate themselves to their work as artists. They become completely fascinated by Bali, but Ubud offers little practical help. For this reason, Maria regularly visits Bandung for long periods of time, for example to go to the dentist, to enjoy company, to attend a beautiful piano concert and to borrow books from a well-stocked bookcase. That brightens her up. She also has an opportunity to visit with the cook in the kitchen to gather some new recipes and to spoil baby Tineke. Maria keeps a diary and with that she gives an inside look into the preparations for *Sinterklaas,* a Dutch feast with the exchange of gifts celebrated on December 5:

November 30, 1938 *A few Sinterklaas preparations are being made. The children are very nice and enjoyable, and I sew a bit on Beb's electric sewing machine, which works smoothly and efficiently.*

December 1. *Life-size gnomes are drawn and colored and set up in front of the sleeping bags the children will receive as a gift. Beb and I enlarge one each. Now we are all really in the spirit of the holiday especially when 'do not enter' signs appear on various doors.*

December 2. *We find it almost pleasant to see rains in the afternoons for several days before Sinterklaas day. That makes it even cozier, something you sometimes miss in the Dutch East Indies.*

December 3. *In the afternoon after tea we do some shopping. Wim, Beb and I in the car via the Postweg. Bright yellow sunbeams shine through the gloom between the heavy wet air. On the Bragaweg the shops are lit up and it is almost real Sinterklaas. The only non-Dutch items are our summer dresses and socks with white shoes.*

December 4. *In the morning we go swimming and sunbathing in Cihampelas, a wonderful lazy Sunday morning. The next day we work on surprises, poems and packages. Beb is now surrounded by an impossible number of packages, for each of which she needs to write poems. Wim Einthoven is working at his desk, and was in desperation that all his pencils and rubber bands have been 'stolen' for Sinterklaas. I have just come out of my own room, which is full of paper, boxes, shreds, a sewing kit and a box of paints. I am making a Balinese sacrificial tower from a whole stack of boxes and lots of gold paper. A present will be put in each level.*

December 5. *Sinterklaas day. First at half past eight to the dentist ... later at home adding the last touch on the tower and the presents, and then we are a little tired. Beb is so kind and thoughtful for all the packages. The children are free from school and are busy. At half past seven the gift giving starts: Wim always distributes a pile of packages and it is great fun when the children have to search for them back and forth throughout the house. When they are gone for a short while, I quickly place the well-decorated sacrificial tower, a great success. Every year it is more fun.*

December 6. *The children are free from school and play with their friends with their new gifts. We enjoy the peace after all the fuss over the packages, and everyone enjoys fudge and 'speculaas'.*

Wim has seen major changes in his work in a short time. On his return to the Dutch East Indies at the end of 1927, he finds a different Malabar than the one he left behind in 1920 when he departed for Delft to finish his studies. The wireless telegraphy with Morse code signals has been replaced by wireless telephony with the sounds of voices and music. This progress is based on the transition from long-wave to short-wave radio, which takes place at lightning speed and is constantly improved by the development of better and faster transmitters and receivers.

The turnaround from Morse to sound begins on March 2, 1927 when a radio amateur in Bandung hears the radiotelephony from a trial shortwave transmitter at the Philips Physics Laboratory in Eindhoven. The spoken word is amazingly clear and the music that is played later, is impeccable. Three months later, on May 31, Her Majesty the Queen gives a speech to the Dutch East Indies. It is the first time that Her Majesty's voice is heard *live* in the Dutch East Indies and the event causes a huge interest among the public. Loudspeakers are set up, subscribers are given the opportunity to listen to the speech by telephone and the 'Bandung Radio Vereniging' broadcasts the speech in its entirety.

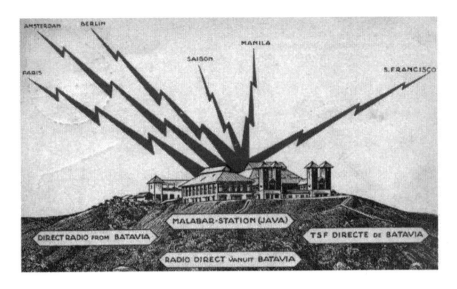

Source: The Early Shortwave Stations: A Broadcasting History Through 1945 (2013), by Jerome S. Berg, page 62.

On June 3rd, 1927, the first cross-phone conversation takes place between the laboratory at Bandung and the Philips Physics Laboratory. This goes so well that the PTT installs a shortwave telephone transmitter in July 1927 and from February 28, 1928 onwards, the public can start making telephone calls from specially built telephone booths. These calls are free until the end of 1928 because the wireless telephony is still experimental. Emotional scenes take place in the telephone booths when parents for the first time hear the voice of their son or daughter after many years. More and more telephone booths are built, but in January 1931 the telephony has already reached the stage, where one can call internationally on the telephone from home to home.

During 1930, telephone calls between the Dutch East Indies and other European countries become available, which is followed by calls with North and South America. Initially, one can only make calls from Java, but in 1933 Bali, Medan, Sumatra and Makassar are also connected. By deploying stronger and more modern transmitting and receiving installations, the period during which traffic can be completed

Ineke van der Wal

becomes ever longer and from May 1934 the continuously available time period is from 9:20 AM to 3:50 PM.

Calls have to be requested one day in advance at the telephone service. In June 1930, 425 conversations are completed that way. A call of 3 minutes costs 15 guilders, a rate which is too high for many a household. Therefore, periods of reduced charges are introduced, usually around public holidays. In 1938, 5,000 of these reduced-rate family calls are set up. The number of business calls is increasing rapidly after the introduction of telephony and the discounted price for longer calls. The total number of telephone minutes with The Netherlands in 1938 is 68,500. There are then 3,300 telephone connections in Dutch East Indies and 70,000 people listening to the radio broadcasts. Together with the Post Office the Dutch East Indies PTT (Post, Telegraph, and Telephone) makes a profit of over two million guilders, which is handed over to the Dutch East Indies treasury.

Especially, the direct radio broadcasts from The Netherlands to the Dutch East Indies are most appreciated by the public such as the solemn funerals of Prince Hendrik and Queen Emma, the wedding ceremony of Princess Juliana and Prince Bernhard and the baptism of Princess Beatrix. Also the broadcasts of the international soccer matches, where the unforgettable Mr. Han Hollander is the reporter. On the evenings of these broadcasts one hardly sees anyone on the street. Those who do not have a radio themselves, go to a friend who is more fortunate. Thanks to the radio, one is able to catch a glimpse of these great events.

The PTT starts with a small short-wave transmission station in Tjimindi, but this station soon can no longer handle the demand, which is why the PTT in 1931 instructs the radio laboratory to build a large short-wave station at Dayeuhkolot. The choice falls on Dayeuhkolot and not on Malabar because building on the high plateau of Bandung is much easier than building in the mountain gorge of

Malabar. For the construction of this modern installation, a young electrical engineer is employed, Henk Lels. He is happy with this opportunity because the crisis in Europe makes it difficult to find a job. Henk comes together with his wife Annie. Wim invites Henk to his home to get acquainted. Henk is a bit nervous about the visit with his boss, but Wim proposes to play chess and that breaks the ice. Wim brought his own chess table from The Netherlands: an antique one with an inlaid chess board and two drawers for the pieces and they play many games while discussing business and life.

When Wim arrives in Bandung, he first becomes head of the Research Department. Soon after he becomes head of the Radio Laboratory as well, but as a so called "second-class engineer". He has to divide his time between the laboratory, the studio and the radio stations. In practice this means that he has long days which include a lot of travel: "Wim is on Malabar every day. He does not come home until nine, eats and goes straight to bed. The following week he goes to Medan. He goes by plane and stays away for 10 days. A new station has been established there." Annie Lels thinks that too much is required from the employees and she appeals to Wim Einthoven about the fact that Henk is often away from his young family.

Wim sees the combination of the two jobs – "Head Research and Head Lab" - as a good opportunity to start with a different setup, which means that the laboratory becomes more involved in the operation of the stations on the Bandung plateau. The laboratory thus becomes a central point for the entire Radio Service where, apart from the production of equipment and everything related to it, tests with the short-wave transmitter are also carried out. For example, a lot of time is devoted to a request from the government to design and produce a suitable radio system, consisting of a transmitter, receiver, antenna and power source, to eliminate the isolation of many civil servants who are at remote locations.

Ineke van der Wal

The aviation industry also comes to the radio laboratory for assistance. The radio laboratories help is invoked with solving interferences on the aircraft's radio installation. The Fokker F9 is the largest aircraft of carrier KLM with seats for 18 passengers and a crew of two people. The test flights above the Preanger mountain landscape to test the radio installation are a pleasant interlude from laboratory work.

Wim at the airport Andir waiting to board a KLM plane

In 1938, The Netherlands Aviation Authority asks the radio laboratory to develop, commission and maintain the supply of complete beacon systems for the navigation of aircraft. This assignment is generally seen as proof of the good name that the radio laboratory has acquired over the years under the capable leadership of Wim. The completion of these beacons is especially important to the Defense Department. Several airports are located in the immense jungles of Borneo and Celebes, and the pilots cannot find these airports without a proper navigation system on the ground.

The radio laboratory works closely with the physics laboratory at the Technical University of Bandung. This way Wim's work not only contributes to radio technology but also to physics. He is thinking about using the large electromagnet of the Malabar transmitting station for the construction of a cyclotron, a particle accelerator, and he also is looking at the production of liquid hydrogen. At scientific conferences the rapid development of the radio is discussed as for example in 1928 in Semarang. Wim is considered a competent physicist, but it is extremely difficult to persuade him to publish about his research. His father complained that he received very few letters from Wim; the academic world complains that he publishes very few papers.

The existing radio laboratory soon becomes too small for all the extra work and on September 20, 1930 a new state of the art radio laboratory is opened. This new complex has a floor area of 4,000 square meters and 33,000 square meters of undeveloped terrain. There are garages, offices, a packing room, a gate with a porter's lodge, machine and battery room, a production department where glassblowers can work, the inspection room, an assembly hall and the central radio warehouse. The assembly hall is a welcome addition, because of its large well-lit space, but it has one drawback: it gets too hot. Since it is not easy to install a ceiling that can stop the heat rays (the hall has a shed roof), Wim comes up with the eccentric idea of cooling the roof with water,

Ineke van der Wal

which is what happens. This method is possible because the laboratory has its own source of water. The system continues to work for years.

The radio laboratory is built on top of a large basement, which is intended for a 'standard clock' that has an accuracy of one in a million (0.086 seconds/day) and was ordered from the USA. This very high degree of accuracy can only be guaranteed by the factory if the cellar meets certain requirements, such as a constant temperature of 18 degrees Celsius (65 degrees Fahrenheit), low humidity, and a sound barrier. Hence no expense is spared to make something special. The massive walls of reinforced concrete, which are deep under the ground and which are covered inside with heavy sound-absorbing material, ensure that there is no vibration, no matter how strong the sound. On the ground floor there is a separate room in which cooling devices are installed to run continuously day and night.

Wim's work does not go unnoticed and he receives several awards for it: One tenth of the 10,000 guilder prize of the *Haagsche Post* in 1929; The *Veder* prize in 1930 and the *Bosscha* medal in 1934. However, it is not just about work. In 1937 he receives a prize together with Henk Lels as a token of appreciation for the joint work for the Relaxation Fund of *Radio Kootwijk* in The Netherlands.

The ceremonial presentation of the golden *Bosscha* medal on Friday August 3, 1934 is combined with other festivities. Wim's mother (Little Grandma) travels to the Dutch East Indies to attend the ceremony. The presentation takes place during the fourteenth Founders' day of the Technical University in Bandung. It is the Natural Science Council of the Dutch East Indies that awards the medal and Ir. C. Hillen, a member of the award committee and also the head of PTT Dutch East Indies, explains what the qualifications were for their choice.

The speech gives a good impression of the inventions that Wim has made in his work in the recent years:

Beb Einthoven, Wim Einthoven and mother Einthoven-De Vogel at the Bosscha-medal award ceremony in 1934.

He succeeded in replacing the large 40 and 80 kilowatt shortwave telegraph and telephony transmitters that were supplied with direct current, with transmitters using an alternating current supply. The expensive and not fully reliable high-voltage machines and accumulator batteries are no longer required now. The result is an important improvement in quality and efficiency, which means that both the number of light bulbs and the electrical energy needed can be reduced.

The second important engineering work is the multiple transmitter that, in addition to having a direct telephony modulation band, has a second high-frequency modulated telephony channel combined with a telegraph channel on the same carrier wave. The great advantage of this is that with a single multiple transmitter, during the hours of good radio contact, three mutually independent connections can be maintained simultaneously, while in the difficult radio transmission periods all energy can be concentrated in a single channel.

Ineke van der Wal

The third work is the construction of a single sideband receiver with an extra carrier wave. Overpopulation of the ether (especially in the area of short waves) has been a problem for years and a solution is being sought. The receiver designed by Einthoven brings the solution a step closer because only one half of the previously broadcast bandwidth of a transmitter is needed. This receiver has another great advantage, namely the influence of the improvement concerning selective fading, one of the biggest enemies of short wave. It was decided to convert all large shortwave transmitters to this new system. The test connection between The Netherlands and the Dutch East Indies with these single sideband transmitters and receivers for short wave, is then still unique in the world.

The Governor General appoints Wim to Head Engineer on April 5, 1936. Wim becomes head of the Radio Laboratory in Bandung, set up and organized by him, where he also brings the training of radio-technical personnel up to par. Beb writes to her mother:

"About five days ago Wim started working in the Head Office. I had hoped that he would be at home properly on time, because five minutes after two you cannot find anyone around, but Wim usually goes to the lab at one o'clock and does not come home until three. At four o'clock, the driver takes him to Dayeuhkolot. So it is very busy and if Wim does not sleep in the afternoon, things are more difficult for him at the end of the day. Even though this is a great promotion (here in Bandung it is said that Wim bypassed ten PTT people, which Wim thinks is a bit exaggerated), he does not feel rosy. "I will now sit at a desk behind a large inkpot", he sighs all the time, and these are precisely the instruments that he is not very fond of."

In 1937, a few American engineers from the group of scientists who are associated with Professor Albert Einstein visit Bandung. Einstein, a friend of Wim's father, is aware of Wim's work in Java. As a token of his appreciation, Einstein sends a book of his own hand with a personal note for Wim. It is a nice gift. The delegation comes with a request to set up a laboratory for experiments with liquid air (compression), but they specify that it must remain strictly confidential.

The visitors also warn that there probably are spies in the PTT organization, who can be Japanese, Indonesian as well as Dutch. The Americans ask, at the end of their visit, whether Wim and Henk Lels might want to come to work in America, but Wim and Henk find their work in Dutch East Indies far too interesting and they want to bring it to a good end.

In 1938, Wim is invited to take part in the tenth International Telecommunications Conference in Cairo. Wim is the head of the delegation for the Dutch East Indies and he first travels to The Netherlands to confer with the Dutch delegation. He flies to Amsterdam with "De Reiger" *("The Heron")* and his departure is even mentioned in the local newspaper. Beb sees him off and eleven others are mentioned in the newspaper article as present. The other delegates, Messrs. W. Domissen and H.J. Schippers, will travel directly to Cairo by ship.

The conference starts on February 1, 1938 at 11 am in the Royal Opera building and will last more than two months with a recess of a few weeks in the middle of that period. The members of the delegation (300 from 70 countries) have the status of diplomats and enjoy privileges such as free travel. They are all received at the palace of King Farouk, the 18-year-old king of Egypt, where they eat from golden plates. One of the dishes is a soup with newborn mice, their eyes still closed and without hair. You grab the mice by the tail and dip into the hot soup, then you eat them. The story gives the children goosebumps when Wim tells them about it later on. During the recess they visit Palestine, the Egyptian museums and the pyramids.

The main theme of the conference is to determine international telegram and telephone rates, general regulations, and to collaborate on the distribution of non-interfering radio frequencies. This conference is a follow-up to the conference in 1932 in Madrid and a next conference is planned for 1942 in Rome. During the conference

During the conference, there is time for trips. Wim Einthoven stands at the far right.

there is a strange incident: Wim will go on an excursion and realizes that he has forgotten something. He goes back to his hotel room and to his surprise finds a Japanese delegation member sitting at his desk and going through his papers. He sees it as another sign that Japan is preparing for an occupation of surrounding countries.

Several countries have their own pavilion on the conference grounds and The Netherlands has a pavilion sponsored by *Amstel Pilsener Export Beer*. For the Dutch there is an extra reason to celebrate; on January 31, a Crown Princess named Beatrix was born. On Friday February 4, the ambassador of The Netherlands receives the conference members to celebrate this joyous event. All members of the conference wear a jacket and a top hat. You have to take a lot of luggage with you for such an event.

At the conference terrain, the Dutch have their own pavilion sponsored by Amstel Beer. At the left, with his top hat in hand, sits Wim Einthoven.

The new large transmission station at Dayeuhkolot was planned to be fully operational in 1935, but this deadline has to be postponed. The rapid developments always require adjustments to the plans and it takes until March 6, 1936 before the station is commissioned with a small three KW transmitter. The small Tjimindi station, which has

Ineke van der Wal

functioned much longer than planned, is dismantled days after the commissioning of Dayeuhkolot. For Wim, this means one station less, which saves him a lot of travel time.

The official opening of the new station will take place as soon as the first 80 KW single-sideband transmitter is finally ready for use and this happens on October 16, 1936. The festivities are kept to a minimum with the exception of a traditional 'Slamatan'. This first 80 KW single-sideband transmitter is given the call sign PMC, and has a wavelength of 16.54 meters. A second transmitter follows soon (in 1937), followed by another and yet another, until a total of 17 large and 12 small transmitters have been set up. The station is not big enough to store all the transmitters so in 1938 (i.e two years after the opening) an expansion of the building is started, to be completed in 1940. Dayeuhkolot is leading in the world at that time. The British are not yet that far along and they ask whether a special connection can be established between Singapore and Dayeuhkolot, so that wireless contact between Singapore and England can be set up. Of course, no publicity can be given to this development.

The romantic Malabar, so high in the mountains, based on long wave transmissions, was the work of De Groot. Dayeuhkolot, a state of the art shortwave radio station made for telecommunications with Europe, with all countries around the Pacific Ocean, and of course with the motherland, is Wim's work.

At last there is now time to think about taking leave. Dayeuhkolot is completed, and the last leave was in 1930. Of course there are doubts whether this is a good time. Grandma Zeeman wrote about warships, submarines and planes, which she saw during her return journey, the government has several times requested Wim to take war measures and the Lels family had to cut short their winter sports vacation in Austria in March 1938 after Germany's invasion. Will there be war in Europe? Is it not wiser to stay in the Dutch East Indies? But their last leave was already so long ago and they really are looking forward to a visit to The

Dajeuh Kolot, the state of the art shortwave radio-station close to Bandung.

Netherlands. Wim is optimistic and thinks there will be no war and if something should happen, he is convinced that The Netherlands will remain neutral, just like during the First World War. They decide to book for June 1939 and their return journey is reserved on the SS *Johan van Oldenbarneveldt* , which will sail back on June 1, 1945.

Ineke van der Wal

CHAPTER V

On Leave

The pleasant outlook of spending some months on leave in Europe brings the travelers in a lively mood. At around ten in the morning the first passengers already arrive on the ship, which does not leave until 1 o'clock. Family members and friends go along on board to say farewell to the passengers. There is a jolly atmosphere with all movement and joy. Those who will see the passengers off are treated to a cold drink. The personnel, in their neat white uniforms and a tied batiked scarf around their head, is busy and walks up and down to serve their customers as soon as possible, because the remaining time is relatively short. The hour of departure approaches. The steam-whistle already sounded twice: first one blast, then two. The majority of friends and family have already left the ship and are waiting on the quay for the departure; The last ones are in a hurry to leave. The quay staff is ready to pull away the gangplank and to release the moorings as soon as the last signal sounds.

Exactly at the determined time the three dull blasts sound on the steam-whistle. The large colossus starts moving immediately. The band on board plays a couple of stanzas of the Dutch national anthem and all stand at attention. After this solemn moment the passengers wave and they throw streamers onto the quay. Photos are being made on both sides and you can hear film cameras buzz. The one streamer after the other breaks, until finally the very last connection between passengers and farewell wishers is broken. The space between ship and

The SS *Sibajak* bound for The Netherlands is ready to leave. The last contact with friends and family is formed by streamers. Source: Vries, Dirk de, *Gordel van Smaragd*.

quay becomes larger quickly. Some devotees try to keep up with the ship by walking along with large steps. In the beginning this still works but gradually they have to change to a trot, to finally give up the race. After ten minutes the friends in the crowd cannot be distinguished any longer and the groups slowly blur into one line. It is hot on the quay because the sun stands at its highest point and after some minutes everyone has left. (Dijkstra, p. 210)

The passengers turn away from the railing and the on board life can start. Beb and Wim have chosen the SS *Sibajak* again, because that is a delightful ship and the journey turns into a very pleasant one. The captain of the SS *Sibajak* still knows them of their previous leave and they are regularly invited to the captain's table. Kate, who just turned 13, is allowed to eat with the adults, but she is not invited to the captain's table, which she of course does not like. Wink and Loukie eat at the children's table and see the great luxury there: the dining room of which a part of the ceiling has been taken away and has been replaced by banisters, so that you can walk around and look down at the dinner guests. There are games for the children again, film showings, the swimming pool is installed, regular trips ashore and lots of meals. Due to their long stay in the Dutch East Indies they know many people, also on the ship, so that the journey is almost like a vacation.

The swimming pool on the SS *Sibajak* made of oil cloth and filled with sea water. In the middle at the last row stands Wim Einthoven and in the middle at the front stands Beb Einthoven

On this leave they will not stay with family in The Netherlands, but they rent a house at the Gevers Deijnootweg in Scheveningen, situated in between the beach and the city of The Hague. Many people who are in some way connected to the Dutch East Indies live in The Hague and the schools are geared to children who visit for a couple of semesters. Kate for instance can join the *VCL* (a liberal Christian school) in The Hague.

It becomes a festive year with many sailing trips, many sleepover parties and reunions with family, friends and classmates. The Einthoven children receive an abundance of attention from Wim's sisters. The marriages of Gus and Wies have remained childless and Koos is single. Small Tineke tugs at the heartstrings because her arms are still too short to let the glasses on the other side of the table touch when a toast is proposed. They go on a road trip through The Netherlands and visit the bell and clock museum and the mausoleum of Admiral De Ruyter. Jan Willem Bake, a friend of Wink, comes to stay for a long time to have more men in the house.

The turtle that Gerrit-Jan van der Veen makes for Kate.

Kate does not want to go on leave. She is thirteen years old and lives well in Bandung, why leave for a year? Aunt Maria helps her pack and gives her a chunk of sandalwood to lay in-between her clothes. This way, Kate can smell the Dutch East Indies every time she opens her trunk. Gerrit-Jan van der Veen sculpts a turtle out of the piece of sandalwood. They visit him regularly because he sculpts Tineke to complete the set of plaques of the children.

Wim goes to work at PTT The Netherlands and he visits the Philips' Physics Laboratory to inspect ultra-short wave telephone systems for the Dutch East Indies. He spoils himself with a Lincoln, a spacious, luxurious automobile, which he hopes to sell after a year for a good price to the son of the landlady. This purchase was recommended by Rik, Gus's husband. They derive much pleasure from their own Lincoln. People are impressed by this automobile, a feeling Gus and Rik sometimes abuse. They, for example, visit a large estate along a river which is for sale. After viewing it they declare that the garden is a bit too small for their taste, they step into their beautiful car and burst out laughing as soon as they drive out of the gate.

Gus and Rik with their Lincoln which they so much enjoy.

Beb reminisces in her letters: The Saint Nicholas celebration (the greatest Sint Nicholas party ever at the Gevers Deijnootweg), Gus and Wies cook a delicious Christmas dinner (what a delicious spread the two of you made) and they fill New Year's eve by playing 'murder mystery' at Gus and Rik. Wink writes years later: 'Aunt Gus and uncle Rik, I remember your house well. I have been there so often. Do all machines still stand in the attic?' Uncle Rik is professor in mathematics and physics and has many machines, with which he lets physical phenomena come alive for his students. Arnold and Wies will receive a new assignment in Hilvarenbeek in the southern part of The Netherlands with a large parsonage and a beautiful garden. The plan is to spend Whitsun at their new house. As long as Hitler stays calm.

Friday May 10, the beginning of the Whitsun long weekend, is a superb morning with a cold and pure air, which is deep blue. At 4:30 a.m. the family is awakened by bombs which are dropped onto the new Alexander barracks and they cause a miserable havoc.

The large German planes fly low and slow which looks very threatening. When they come close, ground fire is opened and that sound crackles and echoes in a frightening manner. Beb and Wim want to pick up Kate and Loukie, who are staying in Oegstgeest at grandma Zeeman's house, but they are unsuccessful. Both on the south side of the city, and between Wassenaar and the Haagsche Schouw, paratroopers have landed, who are hiding inside adjoining farmhouses or barns and there are skirmishes going on to flush out the German soldiers.

Nobody can pass through this area. In the meantime more bombs are dropped onto the center of The Hague and shots are being fired in the streets. Some Germans penetrated to that area thanks to the support from *NSB*-members (the Dutch party that collaborates with the Germans), many of whom live in Scheveningen.

Ineke van der Wal

The family listens to the speech of Queen Wilhelmina on the radio and they hear that there is one possibility left to return to the Dutch East Indies with a ship that will leave from Amsterdam on Sunday.

The first war night turns out better than expected, there is no air raid but the black-out both in house and on the street is ominous. Nobody is allowed outside after 9 p.m., but the landlord nevertheless is able to bring several pots of tea to the guards surveilling the dunes.

Beb and Wim try again to reach Kate and Loukie the next day – Saturday. They reach Leiden, they see artillery, food trucks, ammunition carriages and burned out buses on the way. They do reach Oegstgeest, but are unable to reach Grandma's house, because exactly in that block, four Germans have hidden themselves. Shots are being fired and the area is blocked. Wim and Beb agree: 'If we do not reach the girls, then we will remain in The Netherlands.' At long last they are successful and they gather as much luggage as possible in the short amount of time. By force of circumstance, they have to leave all kind of items behind in Oegstgeest, such as Loukie's little doll together with all clothing of Kate's doll 'Roosje'. 'Unfortunately, Roosje broke in the last minute of that difficult afternoon in May in your house in Oegstgeest. I dropped her, not knowing where she was, and I am still in admiration of the way the child carried this loss' writes Beb years later to her mother, or *Granny*.

Wim embraces his mother-in-law and then bursts into tears. 'Dear good fellow' writes grandma Zeeman in her war diary a couple of years later 'I love you so much and never doubt your will to take care of Beb and your set of four.' Grandma has to cry terribly during the gathering of luggage and when the car, with her only daughter in it, drives away. She waves goodbye for as long as possible and the children are upset by this emotional event. That night they pack all their belongings in such a way that they can travel to the Dutch East Indies with hand luggage only.

Beb writes in 'Wij varen' (We sail) the book which is later published about the voyage of the SS *Johan de Witt* :

> *On Sunday morning we pack the car to the brim, but leave enough space for seven persons: Wim and Beb, the four children and the person that will drive the car back. A lot of kind hands help us. Via some well-known detours, we are able to reach Leiden, but just before the large bridge at the Princessekade we have to stand still. When the waiting time turns too long, we ask the guard about other possible routes. Thus we continue via the Haarlemmerstraat and we observe at the Zijlpoort how the old city fortification has regained its value in this treason-war: The venerable gateway with its great stone mass and a heap of sandbags in its comparatively small opening is a not to be underestimated roadblock against speeding hostile cars.*

Ineke van der Wal

Outside the city, The Netherlands still look peaceful. The green Dutch meadows with a single mill, full blue air, lapping water, everything breathes peace and quiet. We say farewell to our country and love it like we never did before while we travel along the ringcanal to Rijpwetering and Roelofarendsveen, where nobody stops us, not even once. Close to Schiphol Airport the misery of the war becomes visible again. All houses are empty, all windows are broken and the number of houses turned into ruins, is large. Several hangars still stand, but most of them are destroyed. 'You drive through the evacuated area' says the soldier standing on guard. But our stamp of the Ministry of Defense, our purebred Dutch (pronounce Scheveningen or schaap scheerder), our sleeping toddler, the frightened children and the message that we have to catch the ship to the Dutch East Indies, brings him to let us through.'

--- ZEGT U EENS : „SCHAAPSCHEERDER" ---

The Dutch soldiers check whether car passengers are Dutch (and not German) by having them pronounce "Schaap Scheerder', the Dutch word for sheep shearer. Source: Wij varen!

Just short of five o'clock, they arrive at the quay of the 'Nederland Company' in Amsterdam, where the embarkation onto the SS *Johan de Witt* has already started. The staff cannot believe, that they come from Scheveningen. Wim curses because they are not admitted whereas they meet the requirements: they are passengers of the SS *Johan van*

Oldebarnevelt, scheduled to leave on June 1st, and they work in the Dutch East Indies. Another air alarm sounds, the 26th, and then someone taps Wim on the shoulder and says: 'Wim, why are you cursing, I have never heard you do that.' An old class-mate appears to be the captain of the SS *Johan de Witt* and allows the family to board the ship.

The gangplank is pulled away, the journey can begin. The captain orders all passengers to come to the first class dining room and he explains the situation There is danger, of course. There are planes dropping bombs, there are magnetic mines and submarines; therefore,

Stoomvaart My. „Nederland"   S.S. „Johan de Witt"

all measures for a possible rescue must be taken. Sleeping in the cabins is not allowed; Everybody has to stay fully dressed and has to continually wear a life vest. At the first alarm everybody has to go to the rescue boats via the indicated route in a calm and quiet fashion. However, when the alarm for air danger sounds, you have to descend into the ship as deeply as possible. The ship is blacked-out and people try to find a spot where they can sit and get some sleep. Everybody wants to depart, but on Sunday May 12, nothing happens. There is a malfunction in the machine room and the repair takes several hours. The departure will be delayed by a day even though this loss of time is considered dangerous. To prevent the news about the departure to become public, it is decided that no one will be informed about the upcoming hour of departure and that all passengers have to remain on board. Beb still manages to write a note to Wies to explain their absence:

'Dear Wies and Arnold,
Instead of travelling to you, we are on our way to the Dutch East Indies. Without goodbye, without anything, in one fantastic run. Therefore we are unable to see your house in Brabant, but we wish that you will have a good time there, in spite of everything. Much love from all six of us. We were so much looking forward to Whitsun. Wim, Beb Einthoven-Zeeman.'

At last, they depart on Monday, May 13 at 4 p.m. This time has been chosen because the German aviators are especially active in the early morning hours. Now the ship will be able to leave IJmuiden directly after the onset of darkness and it will try to be as far away as possible from the Dutch coast the next morning. Before their departure, the many vessels that block the entrance to the North Sea Canal are moved aside and then the ship sails in to the well-known gateway to the North Sea.

There is nobody to send them off. No streamers, no music, no cars on the quay. They stand on the deck in their life vests and see The Netherlands glide by. The bridge of the ship is protected with sand bags. The ship sails into the lock and they hear that magnetic mines were scattered there by a German plane. The convoy that left before them on Sunday afternoon, has been hit with full force: one ship ran on a magnetic mine, another one was hit by machine-gun-fire and a third one was hit by a bomb coming from a plane and barely made it to the United Kingdom. This convoy functions, in fact, as minesweepers, so the SS *Johan de Witt* manages to cross the canal intact.

The ship that ran onto a magnetic mine is called the *Rensselaer*. The SS *Johan de Witt* takes its passengers on board after the lock in their second attempt to reach the United Kingdom. The SS *Johan de Witt* is now really packed. The North sea is empty. The ship is blacked-out entirely, but the clear moon makes everything visible. At sunrise, they see three planes coming toward the ship, but they fortunately are British. Later they pass British minesweepers and a fast moving squadron of British cruisers.

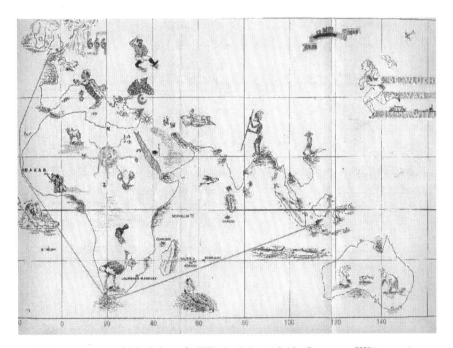

The voyage of SS *Johan de Witt* in May 1940. Source: *Wij varen!*

At the mouth of the river Downs they meet a British investigation boat, which summons them to anchor at Deal, so that the *Rensselaer*-passengers can leave and the ship can be inspected. Here they see the remains of the convoy which left The Netherlands on Sunday, May 12: the SS *Sembilan* and the SS *Bussum*. The SS *Johan de Witt* proves to be the last ship, which got away from Amsterdam. They can continue to sail into the Channel, along the South coast of the United Kingdom and by means of Portsmouth on to Southampton.

Ineke van der Wal

Before they reach the harbor of Southampton, the captain convenes the passengers again in the pitch-dark first class lounge. On the completely blacked-out and invisible ship, he reads the proclamations of Her Majesty the Queen and the Superior Commander of the armed forces: 'Her Majesty the Queen and the government have left the country. To avoid further bloodshed, it has been decided to bow for the supremacy and to hand over our country to the German military governing board.' 'We saw nothing, we only heard sobbing' writes Kate.

They arrive in Southampton on May 15. Willem has some money in a bank account at Lloyds Bank in London which can be transferred telegraphically to Southampton. Willem even added to this bank account before they left Bandung and this extra amount is very useful now. Here they must decide which destination they will choose: Will they stay in the United Kingdom or do they want to travel on to the Dutch East Indies? They decide to go home, to Bandung. A decision which comes frequently to mind in the later war years.

The crew uses the quiet days in Southampton to return the ship to good working order. The SS *Johan de Witt* was out of service for five months and there is quite some due maintenance. Warm and cold, fresh and salt water flows again, the dining room is furnished again and can function. The ship takes in provisions and water and the passengers can do some shopping with tradesmen, who come on board. The family can finally open their luggage and it appears that their hasty departure and the many helping hands have caused some confusion: A hat box containing Wim's twenty years old top hat is on board, but Beb's hat box with all the administration of the year of leave has stayed behind. Also Wim's pajamas are still in The Netherlands.

The plan is to sail to Batavia by rounding the Cape of Good Hope in South-Africa. The first part of the journey will take place in a convoy, forty ships in total, with protection of a couple of English war-ships and planes. This means slow sailing, about seven to eight miles per hour with a change of direction every fifteen minutes to achieve a zig-zag pattern. The other convoy ships are merchant ships of several citizens, some of which have been fitted with anti-aircraft guns.

The SS *Johan de Witt* has a floor plate in the middle as a protection against submarines. There is fear of sea mines, but especially of submarines. The captain has received a radio report which states that an English ship, approximately 150 miles away, was attacked by a German submarine. As a precaution, the music and smoke lounges are transformed to communal dormitories; sleeping in the cabins is not allowed. All passengers must wear their life vests continuously; even at night one has to sleep fully dressed with the life vest on. There is some discussion whether you can take off your shoes when you go to sleep, something that the children ultimately decide to do in spite of prohibition. Each time when the alarm sounds, they have to rush to the deck and remain close to the assigned rescue ship. The alarms are this frequent, that there is never time to finish something quietly, such as wash yourself entirely or eat a full meal. The question arises what you do in such a case and it is discussed extensively. When you know, that an alarm will come soon, do you start with the nicest part of the meal, the dessert, or do you have faith and do you keep it to the end and do you eat your main course first? The life vest is annoyingly thick. You cannot sit close to the dining table and that is reason for much fun because in the course of the journey scraps of food stick to the life vest.

During the night you can't see anything, also because of the total black out and it is unclear what happens, but in the morning when they wake up, they can count the number of ships in the convoy and realize that a ship is lost. On May 24, the convoy is dissolved. The planes do a low fly by and the passengers cheer to them. After a couple of hours you lose sight of the other ships because they sail away in different directions.

The SS *Johan de Witt* is now by itself and it raises its speed to fifteen miles per hour. The passengers can sleep in their cabins and the life vests can be stowed away. The ship remains blacked out though. Gradually the passengers start to feel more safe, stories are told, garments are exchanged, games are played and Beb realizes that her cousin from Batavia, Annie Grevenstuk-Zeeman, is also on board.

Six days after the dissolving of the convoy they reach Dakar, the most western city of Africa. The inner harbor is blocked by floating barrels, to which nets are attached to repel submarines. Cannons have also been placed and two planes circle above the ship, while they moor in the outer harbor. They see other Dutch ships and a Belgian one on its way to the Congo. Everyone hopes to be able to disembark to do some shopping and to take a look in a French colony. The authorization to land is not given however, and it is also uncertain whether they can load oil. Furthermore, no rate of exchange is published, not for the Dutch guilder nor for the Dutch East Indies guilder. The fact, that all lights on the ship can be illuminated again is not enough to cheer them up. They are perhaps out of the danger zone, but they are still a long way from home in safe Java.

The SS *Johan de Witt* eventually does receive, oil, water and provisions and on June 2 they continue their journey. The ship is still blacked out and they apply a strong summer time so that they can enjoy the light in the evening for as long as possible. As soon as they enter the tropical area, the swimming pool, made of oilcloth is set up, and everyone can drink coffee on deck in pajama and kimono. Passengers, all together 420, do their best to entertain each other, with games, a choir and lectures. The on board medical doctor gives one about the human body, someone else about the Malayan language and the habits of the domestic population. 'Thanks to the cooperation of some members of the crew with our passenger engineer Einthoven it was possible to install a loudspeaker, which proves an enormous improvement for the speakers.' (Wij varen, p. 148)

One Thursday June 6 they pass the equator where they see large schools of flying fish and porpoises. At 4 p.m. they celebrate with a 'thé-dansant' and the day is concluded with a showing of several films by Wim about Pangandaran and an excursion to Cairo and Jerusalem. 'It is hot and stuffy in the dining room because the ship is still blacked out. After several films and a break, Mr. Einthoven thinks it will be enough, but a vote carried out by sitting or standing, shows clearly how much this diversion is appreciated, and Mr. Einthoven, defying heat and humidity, shows yet another long film.' (Wij varen, p. 149)

On Monday, June 17 Cape of Good Hope is in sight and everybody is fully dressed and on deck at 8 am because they hope to be able to visit Cape Town to do some shopping, but they do not receive authorization to disembark. The on-board hairdresser is the only one who can go shopping and he leaves with numerous shopping lists from various passengers. Purchases can only be made in English pounds; the Dutch guilder has no value anymore. The hairdresser manages to buy a variety of items. Wim receives pajamas and there is chocolate in abundance. Also telegrams can be dispatched here and Wim sends one to Henk Lels, to tell him that they are on board and well.

The engines start again on June 20th and they sail into the wide sea. They will not visit any ports and will sail straight to their final destination and the expectation is that the ship will arrive in Batavia on July 9. In other words, twenty days at sea without any break. Everyone actively tries to beat the boredom with any thinkable kind of entertainment: Presentations, singing lessons, a play, sports and games for the children. The boys are put to work with plywood and they make several models of submarines and destroyers, the girls braid baskets. Birthdays and anniversaries are celebrated and in the evening it is bridge, chess and card games.

On July 6 and 7 farewell dinners are organized; they toast to the Queen and the national anthem is sung. Monday July 8, everyone is busy

Ineke van der Wal

packing when at two o'clock they see the first vague contours of land and then finally Sunda Strait and the Princess Channel. At Anak Krakatau two Dutch destroyers, the *Evertsen* and the *Witte de With* approach them, with their flags on top. Signals are exchanged and if the latter is close to starboard, the Commander speaks to the passengers with his megaphone and wishes them a warm welcome in the Dutch East Indies. The crew of the man-of-war greets them with three cheers, which is received with enthusiasm. On July 9 they reach Tandjong-Priok, the port of Batavia, which is entirely guarded. Nobody is allowed onto the quay. That is a war regulation, but behind the fences a lot of friends are waiting: Koos, Lies Andriessen, the Schippers family and Henk Lels. Koos joins them when they go the Van Lenneps' home, where they have lunch and she also comes with them to Bandung, where Oerip has taken good care of the house. After 8 weeks at sea, they are back home again in their comfortable 'Kromhoutweg-house' where Itji waits for them with macaroni à la maison, with cheese and tomatoes.

They send a telegram to uncle Ies, who lives in Switzerland, to announce that they arrived safely. Beb writes 'I was so grateful to him, that he had forwarded our first telegram concerning the safe arrival so promptly, but as he never sent back any message himself, I assumed that the did not want to be the go-between anymore. Only much later did I receive a message from him via somebody else. So I decided to ask the cousin of Too, Juul van Regteren Altena, who lived in New York.' The answer from mother Zeeman never arrives in Bandung. The letter is stopped by the Germans and only returned to the original sender in September 1945.

The letter that Mother Zeeman tries to send to Beb via Juul van Regteren Altena, who lives in New York. Mail from 'neutral' countries is sometimes still forwarded, but the German occupier returns the letter marking it 'Postverkehr eingestellt'. The letter returns to New York in September 1945, of course opened by the censor.

CHAPTER VI

War in the Dutch East Indies

The Einthoven family tries to resume normal life in Bandung as soon as possible. Wim goes to work, the children go to school and Beb tries to provide clothes for everyone. Each of them arrived with only one suitcase and nothing more, but fortunately there is still clothing in storage and new items can be made. Due to the long journey, the children arrive after the starting date of their schools. The director of the high-school makes the nice gesture to let Kate choose which class she wants to join. She sees the name of her friend Meta de Vries on a large list of 11 classes and opts for that one. 'I worked very hard to eliminate my backlog. I wanted to become a normal member of the group again. But that was a big mistake. I suddenly seemed to be turned into a celebrity. People pointed at me saying 'She is the child who experienced the war in Holland.' Even while playing tag in the *Tjihampelas* swimming pool, I was stopped and asked 'How was the war?'

German language classes are no longer available at school. After the German invasion in The Netherlands, all German citizens have been arrested and interned, but this is generally not perceived as

Swimming pool Tjihampelas

problematic. The girls go to dance class and complain about their dance partners. Wink starts his music lessons again, but he doesn't like them and Aunt Maria Hofker comes to stay to listen to all their stories. She makes a booklet with watercolors named 'Bandung en Pangandaran' that she dedicates to Wim as a special thank you for all hospitality rendered to her.

Wim's sister Koos also comes to stay. Koos transferred her practice to a colleague, who wanted to settle in the Dutch East Indies, because Koos wants to go on home leave. She is staying with friends when The Netherlands are invaded and she needs to change her plans. A former student of Father Einthoven – Dr. Mansoer – offers her a place in Medan. His practice is very busy and they decide to divide the work: he will concentrate on surgery, Koos will do the deliveries of babies. Willy, Koos' loyal assistant, goes with her.

Sinterklaas and Christmas 1940 are celebrated at home, even though gifts from The Netherlands are missing. Contact with The Netherlands is already terminated. This means for example, that no more dividends are received from The Netherlands, which results in a decline in income. Beb struggles to make ends meet. The remuneration at that time is nine hundred and fifty guilders a month.

Princess Juliana - in exile in North America - delivers a speech in New York during Easter 1941, using the motif of resurrection to call on the United States to join the allied front. The speech is also broadcast in the Dutch East Indies.

A drawing from the notebook *Bandung en Pangandaran* dedicated to Wim Einthoven in august 1942. Source: *Maria Hofker's Indische impressies.*

The United States chooses to stay far away from the European war although sabres do rattle.: in July all Japanese assets in the United States are frozen. In August President Roosevelt warns Japan that further expansion in the region will force the United States to take all necessary steps to protect American interests in Asia. After finding Japanese uniforms and weapons in a barn of a Japanese farmer in California, many Japanese residents are imprisoned.

In August Beb decides to go on a trip with Elisabeth Andriessen again, this time from Djocja. They travel via Solo along the south coast and the mountain lake Ngebel to a hotel above Malang and from there via Modjokerto and the antiques museum designed by architect Maclaine Pont to a hotel called 'Eagle's Nest', which really is nestled against the mountainside.

Wim telephones her there on the evening of August 31st and asks Beb whether she has read the newspaper. As newspapers only come in the course of the next day, Beb knows nothing and Wim mentions that he has become an Officer in the Order of Orange Nassau. The official papers arrive from the Dutch government in London. Wim tells that it was a special ceremony at the laboratory. He noticed early in the morning that something is going on, but everyone gives evasive answers. He is kept in his office and one by one they come by to chat. They have to keep him busy, because they want to make a nice setup and he is of course not allowed to see it beforehand. He wants them to leave, because he wants to work. When the last person rises and says, 'Come and look', Wim doesn't want to go and invents various excuses. Eventually they persuade him to come anyway, and then he sees all the staff gathered together with the military, stationed there since May 10, 1940. Mr. Hillen, the director, gives a beautiful speech and presents Wim with a medal of honor and Wim is very happy.

Beb later writes to her mother:

'I so much regret not having attended the ceremony. There were many flowers, many of which I found when I came home together with several acquaintances' congratulations received by Maria Hofker, who took care of the household and the children. It's a real shame that I was not at home that week, otherwise I would have seen it all.'

Willem delivers a speech on January 31, 1941 for the Bandung branch of the *KNV* (Royal Physical Society) about the development of radio towers in the Dutch East Indies. Especially now that the mother country sees war with Germany and the Dutch East Indies reckon with an invasion by Japan, it is a relief that the key functions run properly and that sufficient staff are trained to operate and maintain the equipment. Maintenance is an especially daunting task because the import of materials from Europe has ended. Once the radio towers are finished, the laboratory can start working on other projects to prepare the East Indies for a possible war. Two projects stand out: the balloon plan and the bomb shelter.

At the radio laboratory it is a well-known secret that Wim is actually the spiritual father of the balloon plan over Bandung. On his return trip to the Dutch East Indies he heard about the defense system over London with tethered balloons and thought it was an excellent idea. These captive balloons are designed to protect the city from air attacks and he advises the city council to apply the same system over Bandung. After much effort, he finds a couple of high-pressure containers to collect hydrogen to fill the balloons. A pair of old boilers are reinforced from the inside and buried a few meters under the ground, and connected to the hydrogen plant. Then it ends, because there is not enough hydrogen. The only factory producing hydrogen is the radio laboratory itself and the total supply is just enough to cover their own needs and the needs of the aviation industry.

Dijkstra writes in 'Malabar': 'We all knew of the attraction of eccentric technical ideas to Mr. Einthoven, an exceptionally gifted technician. The enthusiasm he displays while carrying out these plans should be directed to worthier causes. Sometimes we had to hold him back when his ideas went a bit too far. '

For the next project though, his enthusiasm is much needed. Bandung has a bomb shelter for members of the government. The Governor General calls on members of the government to take shelter there, when the threat from the Japanese increases. Wim wants a shelter to place all radio systems underground, thus ensuring telephone and radio contact after a Japanese attack. His idea consists of digging under a hill and to build an underground warehouse. This plan will have to be implemented, however, by the radio staff themselves, because there is no extra capacity available from the Ministry of Mining. Wim takes the lead. 'When it comes to matters like these, just like the late Mr. De Groot, he stops at nothing,' writes Dijkstra in 'Malabar'.

Somewhere above Dago, past the large water reservoir of the hydroelectric power station, there is a narrow tunnel. This tunnel goes straight through a hill, and served in the past as a passage for water for the power plant.

It is this 150 meter long tunnel that is converted into a bombproof cellar for storing the radio equipment. Side-passages are created and the tunnel is widened. The walls of the mountain consist of a kind of limestone, which makes changes conveniently easy, which is good because the radio staff have neither the experience nor the tools for this work. A road to transport all the material is also built. After the completion of the work, the traditional offering (called slamatan) is observed but this time instead of a buffalo, a black goat is sacrificed.

Much valuable material is brought to safety such as transmitters and large water-cooled lamps. A month or two later, however, they discover that the area is very humid and additional measures need to be taken to protect the transmitters from mold. After the war the operations can be re-started immediately with the materials out of the shelter, because the tunnel system outlives the Japanese bombardments.

Just when it looks as though the decision to return to the Dutch East Indies was the right one, the American naval base at Pearl Harbor is attacked on December 7, 1941 by Japanese planes, and a large part of the US fleet is destroyed. The Japanese empire wants to end Western domination and wants to set matters straight in East-Asia. Caucasian people have to be expelled and Japan must become self-sufficient with the rich raw materials from the Dutch East Indies and Korea.

Ineke van der Wal

The tunnel above Dago which became a warehouse.

The next morning the Governor General of the Dutch East Indies, Mr. Van Starkenborgh, addresses the population in a radio broadcast and he denounces the cowardly attack by the Japanese on Pearl Harbor. According to the Governor General Japan's intention is clear and is also aimed at the Dutch East Indies. He concludes his speech with the words: 'The Dutch government accepts the challenge and takes up arms against the Empire of Japan.' As of December 8, 1941, the Kingdom of The Netherlands, the Dutch East Indies included, is at war with Japan. Japan responds by attacking the US base in the Philippines and destroys half of the American bomber planes and two thirds of their fighter planes in two days.

The ultimate goal is a Japanese empire, which includes all the countries surrounding Japan that will be governed on the basis of Japanese philosophies. The Japanese feel that the yellow and the white men are eternal enemies and as long as the white man stays in Asia, there will be no peace.

Immediately after the declaration of war, many men are enlisted for military service. This creates a teacher shortage in several high schools. The director of the children's school asks whether parents with a university degree can act as replacements. Several mothers respond to the appeal and Beb and her friend Friede van Katwijk offer to help out with mathematics and Latin respectively. Together they can support each other, which proves necessary. Director Posthumus advises them: 'You are not well experienced and children of this age can be quite difficult. If you don't know how to handle a student, send him out of the classroom. I will come along and I will make it very clear that this behavior cannot continue and I will give the student a proper punishment.'

But both Friede and Beb feel that if something goes wrong, their lack of experience will probably be the cause and Mr. Posthumus can be incredibly strict. They decide that no child will be sent out of the classroom under any circumstances and so this advice proves counterproductive. The children think it annoying to get lessons from their mothers, but there are several children in the same situation and this is the only option to open up schools again in a limited way.

Christmas 1941 is celebrated at home with visitors. Willy, the assistant to Koos, likes to spend time with her family at Christmas and

150   Ineke van der Wal

therefore departs from Medan in early December. Because of the declaration of war it turns into a difficult journey, but she makes time to visit the family at the Kromhoutweg. She talks about Koos, tells them that she's fine, that she moved to a nicer house and is adjusting. Willy decides not to go back to Medan because everything is so up in the air. Later it turns out that this news from Willy represents the last news about Koos for a long time.

Cousin Tip also celebrates Christmas with his uncle and aunt. Tip was immediately called to enlist together with many buddies who are 18, but still in school. From December 15 to January 1, Tip is stationed in Bandung along with his friend Max Geerlings. The boys try to visit as much as possible, even though it is very difficult with transport and blackouts. The family gives Tip what chocolate they have, he takes a bath and reads magazines. He has volunteered for the Navy and is soon to be stationed at Surabaya, where he remains until early March. Tip then writes a letter to his father Albert, in which he announces a trip to Australia. After that they lose contact.

During the New Year's celebrations the family speculates about the year 1942, that is now ahead of them. Wim is very optimistic: he does not believe in the possibility of a Japanese landing on the coasts of Java and even less in attacks from the air. He thinks that the Japanese will not be able to find a base from which they can reach Surabaya and Bandung with their planes. Moreover, the Japanese are thought to be poor pilots with inferior machines that can be easily found and destroyed. He agrees with the prevailing view that Europe is superior to Japan:

'A white man's disastrous miscalculation about the Japanese, a world scale mistake. The sorry truth was that for years, white men - including soldiers and politicians who should have known better - had been looking at the Japanese without ever registering what was before their eyes. They only saw what they wanted to see: sub-human specimens in dirty gray uniforms, who were not able to form an intelligent fighting force, or have a fighter plane like

the type O, or zero, made by Mitsubishi. White people thought Japanese
planes were made out of bamboo and rice paper with mouse powered engines
with near sighted pilots in them.' (Daws, p. 60)

At the traditional meeting of the PTT-staff on New Year's morning, PTT-director Hillen points out the seriousness of the situation and they talk about the Japanese aviators who carry out attacks on radio stations in the outer regions of the archipelago. Like other countries, Japan organizes their attacks with intense radio traffic and propaganda in Dutch and Malay. To hinder these types of transmissions, the radio laboratory quickly produces some jamming transmitters. Also, a large-scale radio listening post is created for the Lembangseweg in Bandung to receive everything that can be of importance to their defense.

It's not just air strikes: in January 1942 Japanese troops land in East Borneo and North Sulawesi. The Allies react on January 15 by creating the American-British-Dutch-Australian Command, 'ABDA', led by the British General Sir Archibald Wavell and headquartered in Singapore. After destroying the great English battleships *Repulse* and *Prince of Wales*, in mid-February Japan conquers Singapore, which prompts the general to move to the *KNIL* (Royal Dutch East Indies Army) headquarters in Bandung. The English staff are surprised by the neat rice fields they see in Java: 'It looked as though even the weeds were planted where they were supposed to be. It is the most manicured country on earth.' (Daws, p. 56)

The Japanese turn out to be stronger than expected, but in Java, everybody still feels safe. They simply cannot believe that the Japanese can reach Java.

This optimism is in vain: Japan moves further and further to the center of power in Dutch East Indies. On February 27 the allied fleet squadron, that was supposed to protect Java against enemy landings, goes down during the Battle of the Java Sea. General Wavell flees to

Ineke van der Wal

RICE FIELDS ON AND ON, PREANGER   Copyright. Town Studio No. P-46

The rice-fields on Java, which are laid out systematically with dikes, so that the water level can be adapted to the size of the rice plant. The English army is taken aback by the systematic planning of it all. The method is still in use today.

Australia and the *KNIL* stands alone. Two Allied cruisers and a submarine of the Royal Navy, while fleeing, manage to cause serious losses to the Japanese in the Bay of Bantam. Because of these losses, the Japanese General Imamura - commander of the 16th Japanese army and responsible for the conquest of the Dutch East Indies - has to wade to dry land while carrying a life jacket. The Dutch get a chuckle out of that but there is no more time to laugh when in the night of February 28 to March 1, 35,000 Japanese land on the northern and western coasts of Java and conquer the main military airbase at Kalidjati on their first day.

On March 2 as many Dutch troops as possible are gathered together - about 3,500 men - to advance to Kalidjati from the west. After a hike of about twenty kilometers, they approach the target in the morning of March 3rd. Heavy Japanese bombing stops this initiative. The Japanese

Navy Zeros are much faster than the lumbering Brewsters of the Allies. On their journey back, Japanese aircraft drop fuel tanks, to store fuel so that they can operate from their distant base.

That Wednesday, Bandung is bombed for the first time and many more bombardments follow. Bandung is still unable to believe that a victory for the Japanese is imminent. When the airport Andir is bombarded, the inhabitants of Bandung do not seek cover but run out in curiosity to observe the devastation.

Schools are closed and Kate and Loukie now help out at the girl scouts day-nursery or at Covim (the big women's association for war work). The girls soon discover that the hall of their school is being used as a hospital and that nearly fifty wounded Australians and some Frenchmen are hospitalized there. They can visit every day, they help the nurses and practice their English and French. Beb decides to bury her silverware in the backyard and Willem hides his officer's medal, his photographic equipment and his watch at the Observatory in Lembang.

Wim also secures the transmitters and destroys parts of the laboratory. Wim and Henk Lels do this work during the night. The families at home feel the tension even though they do not really understand what is going on. The next morning, the relief is great when both men return home. The two men personally disabled the 'American' lab that night.

The Japanese derive part of their effectiveness from the fear they instill: after a successful attack, the military often behead several prisoners of war to keep the rest in check. All ranks of the KNIL know about this practice. In some cases, the Japanese even decide to take no prisoners of war at all and just kill everybody. This happens to a group of soldiers in the mountains.

Ineke van der Wal

The Bosscha-observatory where Wim hides several personal belongings hoping to retrieve them after the occupation. Source: *Daar werd wat groots verricht, Nederlandsch-Indië in de 20ᵉ eeuw.*

A week after the raid in Java the complete *KNIL* is beaten. At the Kalidjati airport General Ter Poorten surrenders. Governor General Van Starkenborgh initially argues that complete surrender will only be possible after consultation with Queen Wilhelmina, but Imamura is adamant. 'In the Indies, it took no more than the killing of 1,000 Dutch soldiers to convince tens of thousands to about face and go sit in the corner'. (Daws, p. 94) Beb writes:

'And then, despite all the contradictions in the newspapers, surrender came on Sunday, March 8, 1942. The resistance lasted three months. Sunday the troops moved into Bandung, a battered, filthy row of soldiers who seemed incapable of doing anything and we are deeply ashamed that we surrendered to them. They come from the north of the city, along the Lembang- and Dagoweg looking for shelter. Many people are put out of their homes, but we find a truck brigade in our street, which only comes in to wash themselves,

ask for cigarettes and bananas or simply grab them, constantly looks for weapons, frisk people, steal 200 guilders from one of our houseguests and steal a watch. They disappear early in the morning, but have wreaked havoc in some homes. And those who cannot return to their homes, find it further destroyed by the local population, as encouraged by the Japanese propaganda. Many members from the navy and the air force left at the last minute to go to Australia, but the air force sadly lost many of its wonderful men during their sorties.'

Resistance against the Japanese persists on the Philippine island Luzon, where Manila is located, but the remaining Americans are driven to the Bataan peninsula, where they persevere until April 9 in spite of disease and food shortages. On May 6, 1942 Corregidor, the last Philippine island under the American flag, is conquered. This means that it took Japan only five months – from December 7, 1941 till May 6, 1942 – to either kill or capture all the US ground troops stationed in Asia under the command of General Douglas MacArthur.

The occupiers immediately start setting up camps. All soldiers must report to them and are imprisoned behind barbed wire. After that all other men are interned. The remaining families are left with no income, and all kinds of activities are organized to help the women and children. Some women sew via the Roemer Visscher Association, other women bake cakes, which are then sold for a large sum. Some men are forced to continue their work because several functions are vital, such as running utilities and the radio laboratory. These men are allowed to remain outside the camps.

The occupier has a simple way to show that protest against the forced labor does not work. They choose an employee and threaten him with a gun. On the radio laboratory they choose Mr. Schippers. The Kempe Tai - the Japanese military police - let him choose between a bullet in the head or the heart. Why did the Japanese choose Mr. Schippers? He was one of the participants at the radio conference in Cairo. His room was also searched. Wim is wondering how much the Japanese know.

Ineke van der Wal

Will he and Henk Lels be arrested for the destruction of the 'American' lab? The Japanese behead not only soldiers, but also civilians. At Nirom, a radio broadcasting group, the Dutch National anthem kept playing after the capitulation. The broadcast leader and two of his aides were immediately executed.

The Japanese ban the use of the Dutch language in public, Dutch signs in shops, hotels and restaurants have to go and everybody has to fly a Japanese flag and bow to Japanese military. Bowing correctly is strictly enforced: you have to hold your arms and hands tightly against your body and your nose should be about level with your knees. The Japanese system of counting years and the Tokyo time zone are introduced, a time zone difference of two and a half hours. The street scene changes drastically. The *KNIL*-soldiers were neatly dressed in uniforms and shoes with laces, the Japanese soldiers wear rubbery shoes with the big toe separated, caps with flaps at the back for sun protection, puttees on the legs and heavy weaponry. In the first few months of 1942 the locals consider the Japanese army as their liberators, but on March 14 the occupier makes it clear that no Javanese will be appointed to high government posts and six days later they are banned from all political activity in Java.

It is in this period that Beb begins reading aloud to her family. There are no more cinemas, the streets are dark and you cannot go out in public. The children borrow the book Adriaan and Olivier written by Leonard Huizinga and they enjoy it so much, that she decides to read it to Wim. 'In these awful, nerve-racking days when Wim and I both lost five kilos (about 11 pounds) in weight in two weeks, such a precious, humorous book is a very good distraction and is beneficial to both of us.'

At the end of April 1942 the laboratory is assigned an 'economist' in uniform, with a Samurai sword. Nearly every senior employee at the executive office is assigned such an 'economist'. The 'economist' takes his place behind a desk and the employee gets a separate, small table somewhere in a corner. The radio laboratory is treated mildly again, because the whole radio laboratory has just one 'economist' assigned to them. He knows next to nothing about radio technology and he does not interfere with it. The administration department gets his full attention though and they are very busy making statements and copies of all kind of things. All these documents are sent to some office, where they are further examined. The Japanese have taken over the largest radio station in the Pacific, which is greater than the Japanese facility in Nagasaki and better than the English station in Singapore.

The men who work at the radio laboratory do not have to live in a camp, but that does not mean that they escape the high-handedness of the invaders. In May all the radio people are suddenly arrested. Five rough Japanese with an Indonesian interpreter arrive early one morning and knock and ring at the door until it is opened. The man is given five minutes to dress and pack a small suitcase. No time is given to eat or drink. Beb runs after Wim and is allowed to hand him a sandwich. Then she starts to call around and is reassured by the news of other employees taken prisoner and also by the direct action of superiors, even the Japanese superiors. At 9 o'clock that same day there is a joyous reunion and a 'see you next time' for participants. Such a lucky chain of events is rare, so thereafter everyone keeps a packed suitcase by his bedside.

The internment camps for men and the military are soon followed by camps for the women and children. These camps need to be much larger than the camps just for men so buildings like a school or a factory – the buildings of choice till then - are not big enough. The Japanese decide that entire neighborhoods have to be evacuated, these areas are surrounded by a fence and then 'new residents' can move in. The evacuation of these neighborhoods takes more time than initially planned and as the transfer of families into Bandung has already started, the result is that Bandung becomes overcrowded. The Japanese force everybody still living in their own house to accept guests or 'paying guests'. The Van Welsum family, a man, his wife, an adopted nine year old daughter and a dog come to live with the Einthoven's. He worked at the provincial roads control in Poerwakarta. Also the De Hollander family – mother Riekje with her little son Arie and number two on the way - come to live with them. In order to find room for them all, Wink and Tineke sleep in Wim and Beb's room.

In July, Wim and Mr. Van Welsum are sent to a men's camp, but both are sent home. The following month, Van Welsum is summoned again and then has to remain in a very large internment camp for men located in an asylum in the South of Bandung. Mrs. Van Welsum decides to move in with a friend whose husband is also captured and from then on all kinds of visitors come and go through the Einthoven's family house. A woman comes with two children, a boy just two years old and a girl not quite one year old, and a third child on the way. She stays until her delivery, a month later. Meanwhile, Riekje Hollander gives birth to a baby girl, but it dies after five days. 'It was such a sad funeral in a deleman', writes Beb later. A 'deleman' is a two-wheeled carriage that can be pulled.

At first, the women's camps don't look too bad. Every family gets a small house, where they can have some furniture but no help from staff and everybody soon receives orders to work in the big soup kitchens. However, the conditions worsen quickly, people in three houses are 'merged' into two houses in order to find room for newcomers. The food is not too bad in the beginning, much better than in the men's camps, where it is far from sufficient. The Red Cross pays 9 cents a day to all men and women, to buy some sugar for example. The women's camps are not closed initially, so women and children can freely walk in and out. The Buning family – with whom the Einthoven family used to vacation at Pangandaran beach - seizes this opportunity to enjoy the garden at the Einthoven house. Daughter Ank writes: 'Uncle Wim was still free and shaved himself with an electric razor to the surprise of the village youth from Lingadjati. My eyes almost fell out. Aunt Beb created a relaxed atmosphere and we were served 'stimp stamp' (a kind of stew with fresh vegetables) which I was never able to match. Maybe we also looked at the moons of Saturn or were the telescopes already hidden away? Anyway, the night cactus bloomed and I can still remember the smell.'

The women's camps are closed unexpectedly. To show the Japanese and the native people that the Einthoven family occupy a special position and are allowed to walk the streets freely, they each receive a white cotton band with a large red sphere and some Japanese characters on it. They are instructed to wear the band on their arm when they go out onto the streets. With this band Kate and Loukie can visit their friends and they can participate in education. The European schools are closed and education is taken over by mothers in the camps. Officially, classes cannot contain more than three children but the mothers usually allow up to 6. One of the classes is in the *Tjimahi* camp where Kate sees a performance by the comedian Corry Vonk. She waves a saucepan in her hand and says, 'Ja pan, Ja pan de zon is bijna ondergegaan.' (Yes pan, Yes pan, the sun has almost set), referring to the rising sun of the Japanese flag and hoping for the demise of the Japanese. That phrase is often repeated. Of course, the girls also use their visits to smuggle medication and messages into the camps. The white band comes in handy in those cases. If a Japanese person stops you because you forgot to bow to him, you arrogantly point to your white band and then, to your great surprise, both the Japanese and the native people back off.

Shortly after their arrival, the Japanese issue an order that no one is allowed to listen to shortwave radio anymore. Europeans may not even possess a radio receiver. This orders also applies to the radio laboratory. All devices present at the department, which are not required for testing, must be turned in. Listening to messages in public is no longer possible and one will have to change to listening clandestinely, which is not so difficult because there are plenty of occasions to do so. Klaas Dijkstra writes in 'Malabar':

'Mr. Einthoven however (who finds it very hard to adjust to the new situation) was so imprudent to have a listening device installed in his office, apparently under the opinion that the order did not apply to him. It was typical that our 'economist', who had noticed this of course, did not object. But the Kempe Tai (the dreaded military police) are of a different opinion, because that very night he was taken from his home and brought to their headquarters. They beat him with belts on his legs before interrogating him, but he is nevertheless released after one and a half hours and is allowed to walk back home. This time they show mercy, although the traces of the 'interrogation' remain visible for a long time. Later it turns out that one of the indigenous spies – it is apparent that there are lots of them - has betrayed him.'

According to an ancient prophecy from the 10th century from *Djaja Baja*, the Japanese rule will only be temporary and last no longer than 100 days, a period corresponding to the ripening of corn. Many Europeans cling to this prediction. And behold, on the hundredth day after the capitulation (a Sunday) Bandung is startled by machine gun fire. Located high in the sky are several aircraft, too high to be identified. They turn out to be Japanese planes, flying over the city with the intention to trick the European population.

As the liberation did not take place, people start to look for a different explanation of the 'prophecy'. Perhaps it really refers to the time needed for gestation of a baby in a womb, about nine months. In September 1942 various people seem to know that Japan has surrendered. This is proclaimed with such certainty that even the most inveterate pessimist would doubt it for a moment.

Wim, who quickly warms up to rumors, can even say exactly how the capitulation took place. The American fleet steamed to the Philippines, the Japanese home fleet shows up and is destroyed. After this, the Americans have a free hand and they put their troops ashore. Shortly after this battle, the capitulation took place. How did the rumor come about in the world? Nobody knows. It seems fairly certain that the

Japanese have a hand in it, otherwise it is not understandable why they do not clamp down on the boisterous behavior of the European population. However, the joy does not last. Already on the next day, those who can listen to foreign stations know that a capitulation did not occur. At Christmas 1942, Beb and her family members are lucky to be without overnight guests in their Kromhoutweg house. Beb writes:

'We just had had evacuees out of Buitenzorg for a couple of days. All the Dutch out of that region were transported to Bandung in a lame fashion and everyone in Bandung still living in a decent house, offered to help for a couple of days, before the transport to a women's camp. We received the Van Vliet family and something like this, we had never experienced before. It was a mother with her three children, a girl of 14, a boy of 10 and a little one. During transport the little boy had fallen with his face on the edge of a pail and there was a wide black and blue stripe from halfway across his forehead to below his nose. He looked like a skull with large eye sockets. When I plucked him from the deleman, I thought he was about 11 months old, but the sister said he could walk well, and he indeed did. When I asked how old he was, she said two and a half years. That seemed impossible to me and I was even more convinced when the mother's first task was to breastfeed him. But she confirmed upon questioning, that the child was two-and-a-half years old. The Japanese had told her that she would receive everything she needed in Bandung, which was the reason why they had brought nothing, no clothes, not even toothbrushes. '

The Japanese staff is steadily expanding at the radio laboratory. Each department receives an 'expert' who, after settling into his new job, takes over the work to the extent possible. The idle European staff are basically supposed to decide for themselves how they want to spend their time.

Ineke van der Wal

Members of the European and Indonesian staff of the Radio-Laboratory at the end of 1941. Second from left at the front row is Alexander Hasenstab; third from left is Wim Einthoven. At the far right is Henk Lels. Source: *Radio Malabar*.

Wim, who sees his position, as head of the radio laboratory, taken by someone else, works exclusively with the vacuum pump device for glassworks, his favorite work activity. He thinks ahead to the moment when the Dutch East Indies will be free again and he constructs a large thermos for storing liquid air. Another person keeps himself busy by making an electric furnace for melting glass. A third person goes for metal rectifiers, a fourth makes thermal headphones, a fifth tries his hand at paper capacitors and a sixth one produces bakelite objects. In other words, they are doing nothing important but trying to pass the time. Only one man receives a special order: the creation of a very modern commercial receiver for the groundstation *Rantja Eke*. This is obviously not a rush job.

Although no one has dared to ask the radio laboratory staff to construct a radar installation, there is increasing pressure to do so. The sense is that the army and the navy have a very great need for this new means of detecting enemy objects and the army leadership would greatly appreciate it if one of the laboratory staff would volunteer to make tests in this area. (The acronym Radar means Radio Detection and Ranging.) Every one wonders why the European staff remain at the laboratory, and why they are not sent home. The reason why is revealed to them much later.

In August 1943 all working men of the radio laboratory together with their families are sent to the so-called 'paradise camp', camp Oosteinde or the *Tjiboenitkamp*. This means that the servants of the Einthoven family, who lived in the outbuildings for 16 years, are now out of work. Beb worries that they will become poverty stricken and looks for a job for them. She finds a place with the Indonesian Governor, but when she tells the staff that they can work at the governor's mansion, the 'djongos' (male servants) stand up proudly and announce solemnly: 'I gladly work for the Dutch, but not for the natives.' Beb does not know how this worked out for them.

Drawing of the house in the *Tjiboenoet* camp by Beb Einthoven-Zeeman.

The *Tjiboenit* camp consists of a small neighborhood with five streets, lined by a bamboo fence that you cannot see through. The Einthoven family only gets a small house and they can take very little furniture with them. Many things are given away and they also leave many things behind in their former house. One of the items they take with them is a painting which they hang at the end of the hallway opposite the entrance door. It depicts a forest path, and they call it 'the path to

164 Ineke van der Wal

freedom'. The men continue to work and go outside every day, the women and children are not allowed to go out after the first month, but they can get food from outside and the *baboe* (maid) can get the laundry. The rest of the chores they have to do themselves.

Tineke's stuffed animal, a bunny, did not come with her and she needs it to go to sleep. Tineke says she is sad because she thinks the bunny is sad, alone in their old house. Beb says: 'In your imagination you can always go outside, you can always go to your bunny.' Tineke is not convinced because she feels the bunny cannot come to her. Beb then makes a bunny from a girl's slip and Tineke carries it with her for years. This is the beginning of a long period in which the families make clothes and toys from old clothing that no longer fits or from materials that they can find.

Altogether, 72 families are moved to this family camp. Many know each other and despite the hardships, this gives them fellowship. The children are now back amongst peers and organize themselves. Wink is asked to be head of a group of children who distribute food and he does it with enthusiasm. Beb is asked to give lessons and does so with Annie Lels. Annie has already begun teaching English to her daughter Paulien and offers to teach other children. Wink has never had English lessons before so he gets his first lessons from Aunt Annie.

Fortunately, they are able to bring many books with them so Beb continues to read to them, because there is not much else to do. Many books are shared also. They read *Poeske* by A.M. de Jong, author of the series *Merijntje Gijzen*, that Wim loves very much. Other books are: *Hollands Glorie, De geschiedenis van San Michele, De Citadel, Dr. Vlimmen, Het laatste Huis van de Wereld* (from Bep Vuyk), Frank van Wezel's roemruchte jaren (also by De Jong), *Jody en het hertejong, Petroleum, Het lied van de vuurrode bloem, Het eiland der demonen, Grand Hotel and Love and Death in Bali*. The last two are by Vicky Baum and they are both excellent.

The food at the family camp comes from outside, from a guesthouse and is not good; the bread they eat is simply bad. It is made with tapioca flour and shows large spots of slimy, translucent jellyfish, but nothing else is available. Wim decides to start buying rice for lunch from a not too expensive local store close to the laboratory. At night they fantasize about meals that their cook, 'Itji' used to make: macaroni with cheese and tomato and delicious bread with toppings.

Sinterklaas 1943 is celebrated in the Tjiboenit camp. Wink makes a wooden Christmas tree for his father out of two pieces of wood, which slide into one another. He even writes a poem:

There is a pine tree hidden
in our small backyard
it is only there since this morning
it carries two treasures in its crown.

The treasures are notes with instructions to find other presents. At Christmas time Beb places the little tree on the sideboard, decorates it with five candles and wraps a silver garland around it. The family is happy to have it.

CHAPTER VII

To Japan

The radio laboratory staff wonders why the European staff of the laboratory are not sent home, relieved from their duties, and why are the Japanese so lenient with them? In the last half of 1942, they receive an answer to that question. Three Japanese men come to the laboratory, who do not wear a uniform. They are better mannered than the military and speak fairly good English. It seems that they have a higher education.

Quite quickly the staff learns that they work for Sumitomo, one of the three largest companies in Japan, and have come to prepare for a takeover of the radio laboratory. Sumitomo is a large company working in the field of electrical engineering and everything associated with it. One of the three men, it appears later, has studied at Harvard University in the US; he is the boss and he is the designated new managing director of the radio laboratory. The two others are an accountant and a manager. The European staff of the laboratory has observed that there is an ongoing controversy among various Japanese institutions and they see it here as well. Any cooperation is out of the question, since everyone works on their own. The accountant from Sumitomo demands multiple copies of the engineers' work in English. Even the thick list of warehouse supplies, with the most peculiar, fictitious names, needs to be translated.

A few months after the arrival of the three Japanese gentlemen, the radio laboratory is handed over to Sumitomo. The transition takes place with great formalities and several senior Japanese authorities give speeches. In these speeches they stress the importance of the radio business for Asian countries. The remarkable thing about the transition is that it does not include the big Radio Central Warehouse which remains under the management of the PTT-service. This means in practice that the laboratory cannot obtain any parts and therefore cannot produce anything. No wonder that the new acquisition of Sumitomo operates with a huge loss. With remarkable candor the Japanese accountant reports every month that the numbers are getting worse.

Sumitomo also asserts itself in the *Tjiboenit* camp. All PTT families are summoned to move to a separate part of the camp; a fence is built around them, guards are stationed at various points and contact with other internees is prohibited. For many families, this means again dragging furniture to another home. But that is not the worst part, which is the uncertainty about the reason for this camp within a camp. Of course, the Japanese do not reveal the reason for the longest of time.

It takes until November 1943, when all sorts of important Japanese people barge into the house of the Einthoven family and demand that the entire family be present. The Japanese tell them that Wim and four of his colleagues will be transferred to Japan to work there on behalf of the Japanese army. Wim angrily refuses and says he will never let this happen voluntarily. In response the Japanese force him to cooperate. One of the Japanese pushes a revolver between Kate's ribs and says that women and children are to be taken along as hostages. Kate stays cool and thinks 'Oh, what a pity, I will never be able to tell anyone, because there is no one who will believe me.'

Wim resists tooth and nail against this plan. He is convinced that the Japanese surrender, cannot be far away and he wants to be present when the radio service needs him after the surrender. So far, he has not asserted himself, but after the notification of their departure, things change and Wim refuses any cooperation to prepare for the trip. 'Never have I seen him as recalcitrant as this' writes Klaas Dijkstra. Until the last moment, Wim hopes that something will intervene, so that the departure will be suspended or postponed. After another success of the Americans he is sure that the trip cannot go on. The war in the Pacific does not go well for the Japanese. The Japanese futile attempts to conquer the island of Midway mean that already in June 1942, six months after Pearl Harbor, the Japanese end their advance and change their strategy to preserving the conquered territory. The Americans penetrate ever further towards the Philippines so that a step to Japan can be made.

The Dutch try to delay the departure in many ways. A Dutch petition to leave the women and children in Java is rejected. The order comes from the army and nothing can be done about it. The prisoners consider sending a request to the queen to gain time. Each day of delay counts and it cannot be long before the seaway to Japan will be closed. Meanwhile, the danger that they will be torpedoed on the way increases every day.

Beb, meanwhile, reluctantly tries to prepare for the trip. What should they pack? How much luggage can they carry? How will they get suitcases? What happens to the belongings that are left behind? Where are they going? Will they be able to give the children an education? It is now clear that 4 other families will be going as well, namely, the families Lels, Leunis, Levenbach and Hasenstab. Beb consults with Annie Lels what they will take and when they actually need to be ready, because the date of departure is still kept secret.

Then, to sow further unrest it seems, it is suddenly decided that the camp has to be vaccinated against cholera (3x), smallpox (2x) and typhoid. This is done in the Japanese manner: an injection every other day by a native doctor who does it skillfully and is able to keep everyone calm. To be vaccinated every other day seems too often but the doctor assures them that the doses are very small. Nobody has a bad reaction to the shots, but it is difficult for the children. Tineke cries loudly once, and after that the staff is more sympathetic. Loukie does not receive any vaccinations because she has jaundice, but this gives you the unsettling feeling that Loukie is not well prepared for what is coming. For months the children play a game called 'You have to get an injection.' Tineke has a toy bear and uses a pin to poke the bear for his vaccination. The children play what they have experienced.

In order to complete the group of prisoners, Riek Levenbach with her three children is summoned from the great Bandung women's camp, Tjihabit, where conditions are very crowded. In the women's camp, the food situation is still pretty decent. Messrs. Leunis and Levenbach, who were in a men's camp for a year already, already experienced real hunger, before they are brought to the PTT encampment. Corrie Leunis is the last person to be added to the group, straight out of jail. She hid an Englishman and was betrayed and sentenced with nine others to three years imprisonment. Her treatment was very bad; she's terribly skinny; a little taller than Beb but weighs only 95 pounds.

Starting from the Japanese announcement, the five men are summoned regularly to the Japanese office near the camp to receive instructions. These instructions are given by one officer, who always brings an interpreter. At the last meeting, and after he has sent the interpreter away, he closes the door carefully and says in perfect English to the stunned men, 'Gentlemen, I'm sorry, I cannot do anything for you and I cannot prevent you from being sent to Japan, but I'll give you one piece of advice: when you are forced to go to work, work as slowly as possible and keep asking for more literature about your topics. The resources will be exhausted soon. I wish you all the best.'

On the night of January 24, 1944 the dreaded day has come. The Japanese choose to carry out these kind of transportations at night so that there is as little publicity as possible, but the whole camp knows that the group is leaving. Almost everyone has woken up to say goodbye. It is a heart touching farewell because nobody knows if they will ever see each other again. Henk's sister secretly comes from her camp to say goodbye to her brother. Henk recognizes her in the crowd and waves to her from behind the window of the bus.

The night is beautiful, the moon is shining, and the Preanger plateau seems large and empty. They pass Soekaboemi with the corner store where everybody has eaten pastries, past the entrance to the Botanical Gardens in Buitenzorg and the beautiful alley invites once more. They arrive in Batavia where they stop at the building of the Trade Association Ruysch, completely filled with Kempe Tai, the dreaded military police. Breakfast is handed out with very thick sandwiches that are difficult to bite into with slices of ham and such poor margarine as they have never before tasted or smelled. They eat amidst Japanese who all chew loudly. And they receive water, delicious fresh water. They are again loaded into the bus and driven to Priok, which seems completely untouched by the war. In Port Priok there are some shipwrecks, but the pier where the group's ship is docked is completely intact.

Two Kempe Tai guards, the youngest of the two speaks Malay and acts as interpreter for the oldest, tell in their well-known screaming voices that they are the guards and that the Dutch group is required to comply with all orders. They see another group, all Dutch men, being led onboard, so sad. Wim recognizes one of the men, but they cannot exchange a word. The group of men is stowed in the bow and it looks as though the ship, a small Japanese cargo ship, lacks space for this group. The Dutch families have cabins that are entirely furnished in Japanese style: there is almost nothing in the room but six blankets, with six tiny hard, high pillows containing seagrass, six lifejackets, six clothes hangers and a net. When you enter, the first square meter lies low, you have to take off your shoes there, then you go up one step, under which you can place your shoes and then you're in the sleeping area, where you can only walk with slippers. So for most of the day you walk around with slippers, hence the Japanese slow gait.

Outside they can only walk in the small corridor past their cabin, but they are not allowed to go on deck. The food is all Japanese, not bad and sufficient. The meals are served on six small square black lacquered trays with several black lacquered boxes each with a lid that can be used as a saucer. There are also some porcelain dishes with side dishes for the rice, which is served in tall lacquered bowls. They eat in a circle on the floor, with all the boxes and trays around them. Luckily, it was recommended to bring a spoon and fork for everyone, because they only receive chopsticks to eat with. The only drink on board is very weak Japanese tea served in an ugly aluminum kettle with six blue bowls.

On the first evening the Japanese are not yet organized enough to provide the prisoners with Japanese food and then they receive big bags with sandwiches. The group from the laboratory try to send some to the other Dutchmen below deck, but this is prohibited. They are told that they absolutely must not seek any contact and the guards watch carefully to make sure that this indeed does not take place.

The prisoners of war have to clean the toilets while a Japanese guard watches, such a miserable sight. From 8 to 9 in the morning only, water is available to wash themselves. It is crowded in the two small rooms, where four wash basins hang side by side and these are to be used by the Japanese men, the Japanese girls and the Dutch families. The toilets are tight and small and you have to squat. The doors don't close and they are raised about three steps up so if the ship rocks, you're afraid of rolling off. Tineke especially has a difficult time.

Ineke van der Wal

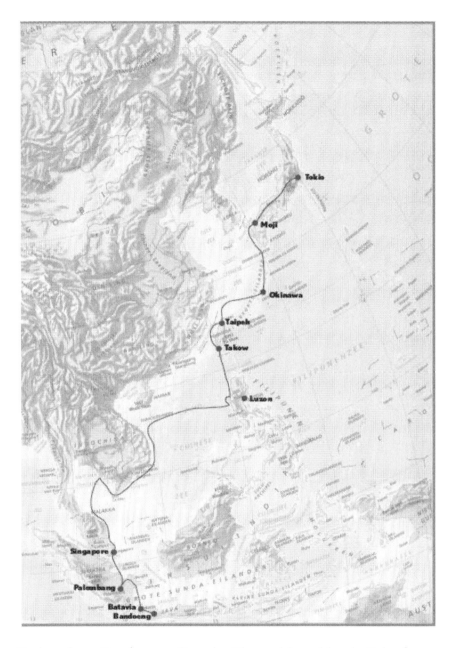

By bus from Bandung to Batavia. Then with a ship via Palembang, Singapore, Malacca, Indo-China, Philippines, Takow and Taipeh (Taiwan) to Okinawa and Moji (Shimonoseki) and over land with a train to final destination Tokyo.

The Temple with the Chrysanthemums 173

The ship sails north, but on the second day the ship changes course and sails up the Musi river towards South Sumatra. They sail close to Palembang, where water and oil is loaded at a large jetty. Then back along Pladjoe, which is in full swing. Pladjoe is the port of Palembang with the oil refinery of the Batavian Petroleum Company, all now in Japanese hands. The Japanese on the dock are staring at the Dutch and when the ship sails away they wave to the Dutch on the ship while making circles with their hands, their symbolic greeting, the sign of the rising sun. The last day on board many are seasick and Tineke and Beb both stay in the cabin, in spite of the heat and having to lie on the hard floor. Wink celebrates his birthday on the little Japanese ship. They have a few treats for him, which they were able to grab at the last minute during the chaos of preparing to leave. Unfortunately planning for his birthday was a low priority.

The 'guides' - there are three of them, Tsutsia, Takahashi and Kishida - tell the families that the ship will sail to Singapore where they will wait for a bigger ship, which will then sail to Japan as part of a convoy. The wait can last two, ten or twenty days. The next day the ship moors in Singapore at the same dock where one previously used to come ashore on the voyage from The Netherlands to the Dutch East Indies. It seems that not much is destroyed, although there are a few wrecks.

The group is transferred to a small ship. First the Japanese board, then the Dutch PTT group, and finally the other male prisoners of war who were stowed below deck. The guards and Kempe Tai make sure that it is impossible to make contact with the other Dutch people. After waiting a long time a bus takes them to the Adelphi Hotel. The hotel is located next to a nice park which is across from an English Church - St. Andrews Cathedral - along a busy road on the corner of Coleman street and North Bridge road.

The group is divided over two giant rooms, each about 25 x 25 feet with a veranda of 8 feet wide that has a view of the sea. The Lels and Einthoven families, all ten of them, are put in one room. There are two

beds on the veranda with two easy chairs and eight beds in the room together with a long table and ten chairs in the middle. The two men, Wim and Henk, decide to sleep on the veranda, Annie with her two children and Beb with her four children are inside. The beds are clean, with good mosquito nets, but the chairs are full of lice. There is a sink in the room and at the end of the hallway there is a bathroom and a toilet which they share with the two other families. On the first day, they clean themselves thoroughly and go to bed very early. Everyone is very tired from the first leg of the trip due to seasickness and the inability to sleep comfortably on the hard wooden floor of the cabin. While they are enjoying lying in the European beds, there is a knock on the door. A Kempe Tai guard comes in to see if the group is complete and returns early in the morning to count them again. He places a big pack of cigarettes on the table for the men. Generally, the Kempe Tai knock before entering, but they don't wait until you say 'come in', so you always have to be prepared for their arrival.

Once everyone has somewhat recovered, there is plenty of time to take a look at the members of the group. There are indeed five families of which the men were working at the radio laboratory: Einthoven, Lels, Levenbach, Leunis and Hasenstab, a total of 22 people, divided evenly into 11 adults, 11 children, 11 men and 11 women. The eleventh adult is Mrs. Hasenstab's sister. There are four children in the Einthoven family: Kate (17), Loukie (15), Wink (14) and Tineke (6); Two Lels children: Paulien (10) and Murk (4); Three Levenbach children:

Frits(6), Hans (4) and Marijke (2 1/2) and two Hasenstab children: Reinier (19) and Hans (7). George (Geo) Levenbach, who is an electrical engineer and his wife Riek, came to the Dutch East Indies in 1939. Geo is of Jewish descent and wanted to leave Europe. Jack Leunis and his wife Corry already lived a long time in the Dutch East Indies.

The family Hasenstab, father Alexander, mother Irene, her sister Frieda and two children are originally German, but have Dutch passports. They are not pro-Nazi, but are not loyal to The Netherlands. The four other families do not trust the members of the Hasenstab family (frequently referred to by the letter H), and they become outsiders. The Hasenstab family occupies a special position in the group because since the beginning of the deportation they try to endear themselves to the Japanese by making the other Dutch members of the party look bad and betray them when they break a rule. Mr. Hasenstab was already not well liked in the *Tjiboenit* camp. The family managed to claim the biggest house; a house that was on a small hill and therefore had grass that remained fairly dry in the rainy season. The lower paths become muddy puddles and because the paths are separated by barbed wire that surrounds the special PTT-camp, one had to walk across the grass to keep one's feet dry. However, Mr. Hasenstab did not want others to walk through 'his' garden. He would hide in the bushes with a stick and scare people when they tried to take a shortcut through his property. Everyone knows, however, that Mr. Hasenstab has strange habits, so they don't care; it is peculiar.

During the first three days, they are not allowed to leave their hotel room. The walk down the hallway to the bathroom and toilet is the only distraction, so they take this trip many times. From the bathroom one can look into a side street and see a real Oriental shopping street full of activity with many little street vendors, portable food stalls and children playing. After three days of house arrest, they are allowed to go into the park opposite the hotel. The three guards go along and additional guards are posted by the gates of the park to make sure that

Ineke van der Wal

there is no chance for them to talk with or make contact with other people. If they do so anyway, they will not be allowed to go outside anymore. They can walk around, play ball games, or just sit, while the children can dig in the bomb shelters. However, when the holes in the shelters become too big, this activity is terminated.

From the park one can see the end of the bay and a row of graves with English names on them. The Dutch people are an attraction; local people come and watch, and wonder who the Europeans are. The Dutch, in turn, look at the Singapore people. Singapore is very busy. There are cars – most of them are running on charcoal - electric trams crowded with people, and lots of pedestrians, all Asian. On the corner stands a police officer directing traffic, usually a large, well-built Sikh. The shops are Chinese, the soldiers and sailors, as well as the entire population of the hotel, are Japanese, but the majority of the people are natives of the peninsula. A kind of curiosity are the pariah-women who are dressed in blue with big hats doing manual labor, like digging shelters. There are many rickshaws pulled by lean, lithe pariahs. On February 15, the anniversary of the capture of Singapore, it is very busy and crowded on the street. A large procession goes by singing the same song, probably an Indian anthem.

Quickly the families start teaching the children again as there was no opportunity to do so on the ship. Beb continues with algebra, Annie teaches English, while Geo Levenbach begins with physics and chemistry. Wim believes that his son Wink is ready to learn trigonometry and they start with Kate's book. Wink discovers that his father is not such a good teacher; he can explain clearly, but Wim believes it is important that children learn to understand the material by doing many exercises. So, Wim explains two chapters in a short time and then says 'now go and do the problems but if you cannot figure it out, you come to me, but first you should try it yourself.' The group stays in the hotel for six weeks and in those six weeks Wim goes through the whole book of trigonometry with Wink. This is quite intense but there are no other activities. Wink works on a problem, then on the next one but gets so bored that he starts to watch the traffic. After watching that for half an hour he gets bored again and he returns to solving his trigonometry problem.

The three guards also have rooms in the hotel and they sit in the hall to monitor the group. Two of them are Kempe Tai and one of them is a guard from the Sumitomo company. They are not unpleasant and try to help whenever they can. They allow a British-Indian barber to cut hair and do some errands when they request so. Kishida buys Riek Levenbach a pair of hiking boots, they try their best to buy biscuits (expensive but inedible), and they are able to find eggs at 70 cents each! When they run out of paper for the children, they buy a slate and chalk, so that the children can do homework again. Wim Einthoven asks the guards to phone the laboratory in Bandung to tell them that they have arrived safely, but it remains unclear whether this actually happens. Tsutsia, the youngest of the guards, even comes into their room once and talks about politics for a while, but also tells them about his duty to bring the group safely to Japan. The guards have orders to transport the entire group to Japan and when in danger, they must sacrifice themselves for the group and tie everyone on rafts. The chance to be torpedoed appears to be the worst near Formosa (now Taiwan). Tsutsia sees this as a difficult assignment and is not looking forward to the next part of the journey.

Sometimes the differences between the Japanese and European cultures are very apparent. Once, while they are outside in the park, Wim, Riek and Annie walk around the lawn, Wim in the middle with a woman on each arm. Oh my, this is something: the youngest of the Kempe Tai is appalled and asks why Mr. Einthoven does not walk with his own wife. This behavior is really frowned upon in Japan.

Everything is being done to avoid boredom and to maintain a comfortable atmosphere. The three books they have with them are shared by everyone. One reads in the afternoon, another in the evening, and a third in the hours in between. Even Wim reads the two books that were in his suitcase, in case he was arrested: *Hunger Fighters* and *Microbe Hunters* by Paul de Kruyf, an American writer who explains scientific research in simple terms. The third book is from Wink's backpack: *Extraordinary Voyages* of Jules Verne. The little ones have fun all day with games, which were loaded into the backpacks at the last minute. After a few days the big kids secretly seek adventure and start looking around the hotel. They know that there are times when they can hide themselves. There is a small corridor behind the room that winds around to a hallway used by the service staff. Wink and Paulien Lels often go there to play. The staff condones this. The families are in close quarters and it is sometimes difficult to keep up their spirits. In the room where the Leunis, Levenbach and Hasenstab families reside, the atmosphere is sometimes tense. Annie Lels writes that she is so happy that she is in the other room with the Einthoven family.

Unexpected things sometimes happen and you talk about it for days. For example, on February 20, the adults are playing cards in the bay window, when suddenly five Japanese men enter. They just came from Bandung, are working for Sumitomo, and have come to greet their 'colleagues'. Annie writes: 'On such occasion, Wim is almost rude, he does not shake hands, he does not offer a seat and is very terse with them'. Wim is the oldest and most senior in rank and feels responsible for the group; he is angry, upset and does not hesitate to show this. Also unexpected is the sudden arrival of a newspaper after Wim has persistently asked for it. It is the *shonan shimbun (shonan* is the Japanese name for Singapore, *Shimbun* means newspaper), an English newspaper. Wim is very happy about it, others find it depressing and scary, all those stories about Japanese victories, the killing of English troops and the progress of their victorious imperial armies into Burma. On top of that, names of cities are mentioned which they cannot look up, because they don't have an atlas as they are not allowed to access their luggage. The carry-on luggage from the ship is all they have and there is of course no atlas included.

The food is Japanese, always rice, as much as they want, with some side dishes in Japanese cups with lids. It doesn't always taste good. One sajoertje (a vegetable dish which resembles soup), which is served almost daily is nicknamed 'dead mice' within 48 hours. If one person opens his cup and announces in a grave voice the contents, all others keep their cup closed because just the smell is already nauseating. Once a day they receive fruit, usually papaya and pineapple, plentiful and delicious. This abundance is mainly due to the fact that Geo Levenbach and the younger Hasenstab boy have severe jaundice. Sometimes a dish is being served that is considered a rare specialty by the Japanese and it is called *sashimi,* raw fish. It's a slice of fish, looking like smoked salmon, but white, in a blue porcelain dish with a little ball of crushed red radish spiced with red pepper. It looks very nice and doesn't taste bad, but Beb gets real sick after eating it for the first time – a fish poisoning probably – so they do not dare to eat it anymore.

Breakfast is once described by Kate as some squeezed tea leaves, raw *kankoeng* (sea cucumbers) and a little mud. The ugly piles on the plate indeed look that way. Fortunately, they have some supplies that they brought with them so they can feed the children rice with butter and sugar. The Chinese, who run the hotel, slowly realize that this group is not a fan of Japanese cuisine and prepare more and more European meals. The group encourages and praises them for their efforts and even the children eat their food on those days. On Princess Beatrix's birthday the Lels and Einthoven families celebrate by ordering ice cream. It comes in cute little chocolate-colored portions and appears to be ... brown bean puree, made from Indian kidney beans which are a bit sweet. Sugar is rationed and comes in very small portions. As a solace, they can order coffee, a luxury that costs the group more than 200 guilders during these six weeks.

Corrie Leunis is of course very happy to be released from prison. She finds the whole trip a big improvement compared with her previous life in jail and even gains weight. She does not understand why Wim is so bitter or why he has lost weight. She talks for hours and the group

Ineke van der Wal

listens, after all they have lots of time. Corrie has been through a lot and suffered. She shows them a handkerchief which all the women, with whom she was imprisoned in the women's section of the Semarang jail, have signed. Corrie is now busy embroidering all the names to kill time.

They stay in the hotel for six weeks, hoping for signals from outside, but they never discover anything and can only wait for the events that lay ahead of them. It is obvious that this is their life from now on: other people decide what they can and cannot do. The crossing to Japan becomes more dangerous every day and they ponder therefore, 'the sooner the better.' At last, they are told the day before, that they will leave at 1 pm on March the 8th. This time they take the announcement seriously, because everyone receives an envelope in which they must defecate. This is how the Japanese check if the group has any diseases. There is not enough time for each person to fill their allotted bag though, so some of them 'borrow' bowel movements. They all have a good laugh about it, which releases some of the tension.

There is not much to pack, they only have hand luggage. They eat a little earlier that day and are given some food for their first meal on board. Everyone receives a neat square bamboo box with a piece of paper on top with Japanese writing. Inside are a ball of rice, some side dishes and a pair of chopsticks. A bus takes them to the port which is busy. They see their baggage on the wharf with many, many other suitcases. The Japanese give a few speeches; the luggage of the other passengers is thoroughly searched, but when they come to the Dutch group, Tsutsia jumps forward with his wide red Kempe Tai band on his arm and they are allowed to close up their baggage without being searched. After a long wait, they walk in a large line towards the ship.

The walk would normally take about seven minutes, but this time it takes more than half an hour, because they have to wait over and over again and that proves difficult when you are carrying heavy bags. The second class is their destination and after yet another long wait in the gangway they get to their fairly tidy cabins. There are only 18 beds, so Murk has to sleep on the floor and Tineke and two Levenbach children share a bed. All their luggage is in the cabins, but it is completely mixed up, so it takes a while before everyone has their belongings. At 6 pm a signal sounds: the beginning of the blackout. All portholes have to be closed, they are all painted black and covered with a thick black curtain. It is rather stifling inside. The next stop is the dining room where a corner is set aside for them. The guards make sure that they stay separated from the other passengers. Again, a lot of shouting and orders from the guards; they are never satisfied.

It appears to be a large ship called *Teia Maru,* but Wim soon recognizes it as the SS *Aramis* owned by the *Messageries Maritimes,* a French mailboat company. It is the same ship he sailed on when he made the crossing from Marseille to Port Said to go to the Convention in Cairo. Later they find a life jacket with the old name, indicating that Wim's suspicion is correct. This ship is not marked, just like the ship that brought them from Java to Singapore. Under international law, ships used to transport prisoners of war must be marked with the letters POW in white.

The ship sails away from the wharf and remains lying off the pier for a few days. Nobody is allowed on deck. One evening the guard takes the group upstairs for an hour, but he is severely reprimanded. Only when the ship is moving, they are allowed to go up on a portion of the deck. There are also Japanese on board, mothers with children and sailors. The Dutch women are busy working on their embroidery or other needlework as soon as they sit, but the Japanese women remain idle. As a result the crew go directly to the Dutch women when they have something that needs mending. A tear in their pants, a broken suspender, a hole in their socks, everything always neatly washed, is brought to them. The crew is grateful and give the children treats to express their gratitude. It is a mixed, curious group of passengers. They see some Siamese boys, who also lived in the hotel and to whom the children occasionally spoke on the stairs, disobeying every command.

Ineke van der Wal

Also on board are some Japanese officers going on leave accompanied by women and children. Down in the hold of the ship are products from the Dutch Indies and perhaps booty or prisoners, but they don't notice it.

It's only March and it is still cold. Sumitomo has given them three chests with warm clothes and blankets which they sort out and distribute. It turns into a cheerful morning. Annie writes: 'We laughed out loud, the men are all jumping around in their identical outfits that are either too large or too tight with a hat that is too big or too small. They even find some leather kid gloves.' Much of the clothing is too small for the Dutch men though, which means in practice that some of them have no warm clothes, no thick sweater or warm underwear, which is very uncomfortable when you have to sleep on deck at night. Women are not allowed to wear skirts on board, only padded pants, called *mompés,* which are warmer and easier.

Every day there are rescue exercises in order to save the crew and 860 passengers in case of an attack. A ship can sink quickly, so it is important to come on deck as soon as possible and eventually into the lifeboats. Most attacks are expected to occur at night, while it is pitch dark; that is why you have to feel your way along to reach the appropriate deck. The siren sounds, you tumble out of bed, put on your shoes and a life jacket and then grab your bag. You go into the hallway and then you count the doors with your hands along the wall, turn left, count your steps to the stairs, and then count the number of steps up on the stairway. You turn left again to the next stairway. Go up more stairs and go through a double light barrier of two thick black cloth curtains and finally you're on deck. Adults have to carry the children who are too small to walk.

The Leunis family takes care of Frits Levenbach, the Levenbach parents take Marijke and Hans, the Einthoven parents carry Tineke, and the Lels parents carry Murk. The older children take care of themselves. For Wink, this means that he is stuck put between other people. He tells: 'The hallway and the stairs are so narrow, that I get lifted up off the floor and cannot feel the stairs with my feet but it doesn't matter. I am swept up by the mass of people and as long as I keep myself vertical I know that sooner or later I will get my feet back on the ground'. On deck there are places where you assemble and the children have to make sure that they stay with their parents. The adults have a rope, which is rolled up in a special way so that they can tie the children to their bodies. Adults then have to tie themselves to rafts. The temperature of the sea water is so low, that it is unlikely they will survive, but they all do their best.

Some crazy incidents that occur, amuse them. For instance, they have to practice lowering the small children in a basket into the lifeboats. Tineke and the Levenbach children enjoy this adventure. Each ship has a rope ladder and a few ropes and both the adults and older children have to learn how to climb down the rope ladder, which is good for hours of amusement. Later they are told that the baskets cannot be used after all and that the men have to carry the small children on their backs. This is practiced over and over and of course the small children find it very exciting.

It is recommended that they sleep with their clothes on, just like in 1940 when they left The Netherlands. Actually the guards feel that you should also sleep with your life jacket on but that proves to be a very uncomfortable way to catch sleep. Even the shoes come off. When you go to sleep, you put your belongings near you so that you can quickly dress yourself in the dark in a few seconds. On the 11th of March, they are told they can't bathe anymore, because it is too dangerous: it takes too long to get dressed again. On the 12th of March the water in the cabins is shut off. Whether they like it or not, they will remain dirty until the end of this strange journey.

The SS *Aramis* is the ship in the middle of a convoy called Hi-48. It is made up of a total of sixteen ships with several tankers with crude oil and destroyers. The journey eventually takes sixteen days instead of the expected eight days. Along the way they are attacked four times by submarines and lose five ships from the convoy. The ships are hit, catch fire and sink quite quickly. If you happen to be on deck in the middle of the night and you're not looking in the direction of a burning ship, then you will miss it. They only know for sure that five ships are lost when it is confirmed by one of the guards. The SS *Aramis* is actually hit once by a torpedo but it does not explode.

The group knows that they are travelling to Japan, but the route is unknown and is not shared with the passengers. Wim makes a sextant using simple components and with a map in his pocket diary he is able to figure out that the route is not direct. The ship sails as close to the shore as possible; first along the Malacca straits then northwards, across to Indochina and continuing further north past Cambodia. Most of what they see is a deserted shore line. One day they see a big white monastery built on the rocks, with a lighthouse and a radio station, but no people, no cabin, no ship. One evening when they emerge after dinner, there is shore on both sides and with SS *Aramis* in the lead, they sail into a bay with all the other ships of the convoy.

In this natural harbor somewhere in Indochina that you can only enter via a very narrow rocky entryway, they come across a large fleet. They anchor here and suddenly a seaplane lands on the water next to the ship. It taxis closer and begins to exchange messages with the bridge and after fifteen minutes it lifts off again and disappears. They never hear why they stopped in this port and what the visit from the sea plane was all about. Maybe they detected enemy aircraft.

The next morning, there appears to be some life in the area, because different little boats with white sails come close and try to sell them food such as chicken, eggs, bananas, and pineapples, but they are not allowed to buy anything, and it is strictly enforced. That's a shame because the food on the ship is awful. The second class dining room is located downstairs in the ship and it smells stale and sour. You get nothing but rice and even that is not enough. In the morning you get some water that is left over from cooked beans, then in the afternoon you sometimes get a small portion of the beans, but most of the time only a small pile of unknown vegetables with a little meat tendon to add some taste.

From Indochina the convoy crosses to Luzon, the Philippine island on which Manilla is located and here they are attacked for the first time. At half past one at night the siren goes off and they all make sure they quickly go upstairs. As soon as they arrive on deck the whole ship starts to tremble, it is hit and it trembles for several minutes. They all stand at the railing and wait in silence, they are not allowed to talk, lights flash around them and there is thundering noise everywhere. Their ship fires a shot - it has a small auxiliary gun on the back - followed shortly by a second shot. This produces so much noise that Wink drops on his knees. In the distance they hear more shots, and see something burning. It becomes clear to them that this is serious, because the men looking at the stars realize that their ship is now sailing due south at full speed heading back to where they came from. It all comes unexpectedly, it's quick and then it's over and pitch-dark.

After an hour and a half the men are allowed to quickly fetch some blankets and they try to sleep a little, but it does not work. The problem is that the life jacket pinches you on all sides. Just imagine, you're wearing cotton pajamas, a pair of wool pants on top, a wool jacket with long sleeves, a pair of woolen socks, an evacuation bag stuffed with all kinds of things - eyeglasses, jewelry, photographs, important papers – around your neck, a belt with a coiled rope to tie to your children in case something happens, and a towel in case somebody gets hurt and is bleeding. On top of all that you have to wear this rough life jacket.

The children are very sleepy. The mothers start sitting on the joists along the side of the deck so that the children can sleep on top of them. But as soon as they are settled a screaming Japanese guard comes and tells them that they have to sit in the middle of the ship. After ten

Ineke van der Wal

minutes, when the children are just dozing off, a second screaming Japanese guard comes and chases them away from the well-deck. If the ship is hit, all the iron lids that cover the pits will fly up and this can be dangerous for the prisoners. So the mothers move to a place somewhere halfway when a third loudmouth guard comes and says they need to watch out for a potential explosion that might cause any of the cranes to land on their heads. They look up and realize that a crane can land on them, but it can also fall the other way and try to doze on.

Only the next morning they can freshen up real quick and eat some food. In the middle of the day the alarm sounds again, but this one turns out to be false. The next night they can sleep in their beds to wake up at the entrance of a harbor at the southern tip of Formosa, Takow, now called Kaohsiung, Taiwan. The ship remains anchored until the entire convoy, minus some destroyers, is reunited again. Six people come on board to speak with the captain.

Then the convoy crawls north along the coast of Taiwan, the Japanese name for the island. Close to the tip of the land, the group is suddenly directed to their cabin and everything is blacked out. They wait in a dark cabin and it is difficult to keep the children busy. What is there to be seen? To their surprise, they sail into the port of Taipei where the convoy probably is seeking shelter.

After Taiwan it seems that the ship sails west towards China, but a new attack causes a change of course. The children have just been put to bed and to help them fall asleep quickly, the adults stay in the cabin with the Leunis family. They hear a heavy thud. The ship is jolted and immediately the siren sounds. Murk, who sleeps soundly, can barely get his jacket on. During many more loud bangs they hurry to the stairs, where they are frightened by the crowd. 'Kedomo, Kedomo' - children, children - Henk calls and then the military give them some space. Once on deck, they see nothing but ink black darkness. All around there is heavy cannon fire. A flare is fired from the bridge and for a moment it looks like day-time. They keep hearing very severe dull rumbles, explosions of depth-charges. Jan and Wim, who stand on the other side of the deck, see a giant flame of fire, one of the torpedo ships is hit. Everywhere commands are shouted, which the Dutch of course cannot understand. Tsutsia and Takahashi (Kishida they hardly ever see on board) push the children and women to a corner underneath their assigned lifeboat. They can see the boatmen, with phosphorous lights on their hats, running up and down to and from their positions. Doedoek! *(Squat!)* they shout. The women squat down on and over each other, the children cling to them. They are told not to talk and they remain sitting for hours like this until the early morning. Then they can count how many ships are missing: a total of three destroyers.

They pass the island of Okinawa, it is always reassuring to have land in sight, and then the direction remains westward, toward Shantung on the east coast of China. Again they have to sleep on the deck crammed in with the whole crew, with gale-force winds coming straight from Siberia, a dark, sloshing sea that causes the lifeboats to bang against the side of the ship, anxiously hurrying as quickly as possible down to the toilet. The next day, there is an alarm while they are having breakfast. They see immediately that they are sailing back to where they came from, so real danger again. After half an hour of waiting in suspense, they can return to their breakfast, where they find the last cans of sardines, which mix so well with rice, fortunately still untouched. Again, there is discussion about what you should eat first when you know that another attack is probably coming: do you eat the tasty sardines first or do you keep them as the last delicious bites? The Einthoven family opened their food box and enjoy some extras. They always share with the Lels, Leunis and Levenbach families, so it empties quickly. The Hasenstabs have much more than the rest, but they don't share; sometimes the Lels family provides something for them all. The two other families, who were driven out of their homes earlier, have nothing.

Ineke van der Wal

A convoy sailing under the protection of the destroyers is the safest way to cross the ocean, but it is also dangerous. Annie writes on March 21: 'Today we almost sailed into one of the other ships of the convoy. A collision - that is what we were still missing on this trip.' The ship suddenly stops, then steams backwards at full speed, and it takes a while before all the giant ships are back in position. It is pitch-dark at sea, hence the wrong maneuver.

March 22nd. Screams from the guards, even before the siren goes, the families are ready. When they arrive on deck, they see the destroyers running on ahead at full speed. It looks as though they are creating a smokescreen. Later an airplane flies over several times with one bomb missing. It is freezing cold on deck. After an hour, they can go back to the cabin. On March 23 they try to keep a positive mood by opening a few food cans in honor of Loukie's sixteenth birthday. The next day the guards discover that Annie is keeping a diary and it is confiscated. Fortunately, she gets it back again even though the last two pages are torn out.

On March 25, they finally arrive at the port of Moji, on the southern Japanese island of Kyushu, and they remain all day at anchor. It's a good-sized sea passage, which gives access to the Inland Sea. The coast is crowded and crammed, with many factories, small Japanese houses and a temple with a *torii,* a Japanese gate. All the passengers have to put their luggage on deck, but there is no news about moving on, so at seven thirty they put the children to bed and promptly at 8 PM the guards shout 'lekas, lekas' *(quick, quick)* and they have to go ashore. The entire harbor is lit up, no black out, no sign of war. They take a small ship to the customs warehouse, and are told to take out all their important papers, which are then stamped. Then they wait, and wait, and wait, with terribly sleepy toddlers and close to 11 o'clock they are suddenly returned to the SS *Aramis* with the same small boat. After long delays on board they can again go to sleep in their former cabins until six o'clock the next morning. They get an early breakfast, get back onto the small boat, and again go through customs. All the large baggage is put on the dock and must be opened. A courteous English speaking Japanese comes with their Kempe Tai guard, and without looking at the luggage, he declares everything as satisfactory and they can repack again. They are happy to be standing on solid ground.

The next stop is a dirty shed, where a year's worth of dust has collected. There are two benches so that the ladies can sit, but there is no room for the men and the children. They have been given some food from the ship and the Einthoven family has canteens with water. If one of the children has to go to the toilet, they can leave the shed to go to the filthiest toilet they have ever seen. The urinals are clogged and spill over the side so that you have to wade through the urine. They feel miserable. They sit there until 2 o'clock and then again hear the guards cry 'lekas, lekas'. They quickly grab their stuff together and walk through Moji, trudging along with all their cabin baggage, their blankets, knives, forks, spoons, bags, and backpacks.

They can only take what they can carry. Tineke has a bag with something in it, that's already heavy for her. Beb carries a suitcase and a big bag which she wants to switch occasionally to lighten the load, but the guard keeps yelling 'lekas, lekas'. At one point Beb puts her bag down, exchanges her bags from one hand to the other, and then the guard strikes her because he is angry with her. Tineke is furious with the guard and bites the man's hand. The guard's hand is at the right height for her to bite him and she wishes it to be painful because 'he must know that I am very angry and that he cannot beat my mother.' Beb is obviously startled and angry with Tineke, who does not understand this, yet. Fortunately the guard does not act upon it and lets it go.

Their destination is a ferry, a huge jam-packed ship with two floors, on which they cross the harbor to Shimonoseki, a port city on the main island of Honshu. Upon arrival they walk through a long covered bridge over many railways. It takes them at least twenty minutes to arrive at the station from which their train will leave. They are allowed

Ineke van der Wal

to sit in the hallway on the ground and wait for the train to leave at nine o'clock in the evening. The train goes to Tokyo. Is that their final destination? Kishida continues to monitor them constantly but Takahashi and Tsutsia go and get some food. The bamboo boxes they bring back contain a ball of rice, some side dishes and of course two neatly wrapped chopsticks. They get a lot of attention and they see masses of traveling Japanese people. Most wear European clothes but there are also women in kimonos that are rarely colored. Many walk on 'getas', the Japanese clogs, a board with two cross pieces of wood underneath and two bands that go between one's toes. They do not yet know that they too will walk on these getas later on.

On the train they sit at the front and there is place for everyone. All windows and curtains must be completely shut. That's okay because it is constantly cold. They keep their coats on and wrap themselves up in the blankets and try to get some sleep. The train ride will last 22 hours and they will travel along the Inland sea overnight. That is where the largest naval port of Japan is located, so of course they are not allowed to look outside. The curtains are allowed to be opened fifteen minutes after sunrise and then they get their first impressions of the country of Japan. The train runs along the east coast of the Big Island and they see that the morning is bleak and gray with cities that are also bleak and gray. The cities are in fact Kobe and Osaka with connected neighborhoods with densely built housing. This is what they see for hours on end. It looks like a stressed, overpopulated country. Sometimes they see green fields with some crops and a multitude of small farmhouses with thatched roofs. There are many fences and hedges, and it seems that everything is hidden, except their little temples along the road. They are served food out of baskets again, but also a few rolls which are very dry but still appreciated. In the afternoon they see Mount Fuji in the distance, the famous holy mountain with its white top and green slopes. Other mountains are also still full of snow, but in the foreground they see the plum trees that already bloom.

At six o'clock they pass through the fully lit city of Yokohama after which they reach the main station in Tokyo. They have hardly disembarked when all the lights go out due to an air defense exercise. Part of the group can see where the Japanese guide goes and follows him to the exit, but the Hasenstab family, who are the only ones to have been in Tokyo before, have not seen him and get terribly lost. The Japanese guard is close to a fit. He fears they will escape to their old friends. It is an anxious quarter of an hour for the guide, but then the family is found. Nobody seems to be available to pick up the group, so they are again made to sit in a corner on the ground. The children are terribly sleepy because they did not get enough sleep on the train or on board the ship.

The Japanese have to make a phone call and look for contact-persons in the big dark station with only a single tiny emergency light. They wait and wait until 11 o'clock when finally a representative from the Sumitomo company arrives to take them to a station on a beltline. They are told that the train stops only briefly and therefore they need to get on quickly. The three guards go first followed by Henk, Murk, Beb and Tineke, while the Hasenstab family, all five of them, slip inside another door. The door slams shut and the train leaves. The rest of the group remains on the platform with the Sumitomo-man, who speaks only Japanese. Again, the Japanese guards are close to a fit and at the next stop, two of them quickly get off and go back. The first part of the group is instructed to get off at Megoro station and wait for the others. They arrive half an hour later. By then it is March 28.

The group is back together again and the trip can continue. They all have to pick up their hand luggage and walk for half an hour to their destination through the pitch-black city. You don't see anything, the blackout is strictly enforced, and you only sense that there are tram tracks in the street. Murk Lels sleeps; Henk carries him. Marijke Levenbach is also carried and is asleep but little Tineke must walk just like the Levenbach boys.

Ineke van der Wal

To make matters worse it starts to rain. Finally they turn into a side road and see an illuminated entry but are not allowed to go in. One cannot enter a Japanese house with your shoes on, so all the shoes must be left on the sidewalk before they are allowed to enter the 'hallowed halls'. The group enters a fairly large, clean but unheated room with a few chairs and many benches on which they can sit and wait. Japanese girls walk to and fro and they ask for tea, which they get; finally something warm. The group is divided. The Levenbach and Einthoven families remain in the first house, the other families go to a second house in the same yard. The Einthoven family are assigned two rooms on the first floor: one for Wim and Beb and one for the four children. The luggage is not there yet, so they decide to lie down with their clothes on under the silk comforters in European style beds, and they all fall asleep. They sleep late, which is just as well because there is no breakfast. The staff was unable to arrange that this quickly. They get some lunch, which is typical Japanese served from black lacquered pots.

Drawing of the house in Tokyo where the families are kept as prisoners of war made by Beb Einthove –Zeeman.

Everyone is exhausted and sick. They have lost weight and have hollow, thin faces. The bad food aboard the SS *Aramis* and the nights on deck have taken their toll and Sumitomo is shocked by their condition. The following days they are served oatmeal with sugar for breakfast, and both lunch and dinner come from the Imperial Hotel.

It is too little, but delicious after the filth on board the ship and it keeps them warm for a while. It is cold in the house, although there is a neat central heating, but running it is only allowed in December, January and February. There clearly is a shortage of fuel in Japan.

The entire household staff - they all live on the property - Takesan, the housekeeper, the three cooks, Yamposan, Burukawasan and Hyokisan and the two maids Soemidja and Mitsuko, make an appearance. Takesan is a kind of secondary supervisor. She is over 60 and does not have to be as submissive as the young Japanese women. Then they meet Mr. Hirata, their liaison with Sumitomo. He has been in America for four years, 'he had studied English,' so they call him Mr. Hirata and not in the Japanese way with *san* after his name. Later the whole group is also presented to the representatives of the local authority. Even the children have to show up. 'We must all bow down and listen to a long speech,' writes Annie.

The next day the men are given instructions by a high-ranking officer of Sumitomo. The men will have to work hard (13 consecutive days, the 14th day is free), or otherwise will be severely punished. The men must swear to an oath, which among other things states that they will not try to escape. According to the Geneva Convention, such an oath is not allowed. The men make some money, but that money is not paid out to them. Hirata controls the money and if something needs to be paid, he provides for it.

Wim protests on behalf of everyone against the employment and requests contact with the Red Cross or a representative, but there is no response. The best thing to happen that day is the arrival of their luggage. Finally they can take off the dirty clothes which they have worn and slept in for so many days. Three days later they can take a bath. There is a neat clean bathroom and they all bathe themselves and they begin to feel human again. The bath is only fired up once a week, other days they get a bucket of warm water to wash themselves.

Ineke van der Wal

<u>O A T H</u>

1. Regarding your personal conduct, you will be under the surveillance of the SUMITOMO COMMUNICATIONS INDUSTRY COMPANY, Ltd. - the said surveillance to be carried out at the request of the Japanese authorities - and more particularly, you will be under the charge of the General Affairs Department of that Company."

Whatever you are directed to do by the said General Affairs Department, you shall attend to immediately, always considering it as an order coming from the Japanese Government, and shall not disobey or evade it through any misconduct.

2. As for your work and behaviour at the laboratory, you will be governed according to the rules and regulations issued by the laboratory.

3. Regarding your clothing, food and dwelling, you are to take whatever is provided by the said Company and shall bear a portion of the cost and expenses thereof charged and arrived at by the said Company.

4. On your way back and forth between your home and laboratory, you are strictly prohibited from getting off the automobile in conveyance, and from riding together with any person other than those permitted by the Company.

5. You are strictly forbidden to go outside the designated area.

6. You are strictly prohibited from communicating with any person other than those in charge either over telephone or by telegram; and shall not communicate by letter with any people on the outside, nor listen to radio, nor take any photograph.

As to any reading matter, such as newspapers, magazines, and books, you may read only those that are permitted.

<u>O A T H</u>

The oath to which the five men 'employed' by Sumitomo must adhere. Non-adherence will be punished severely.

Japanese companies need prisoners of war, in order to meet the increased output demanded by wartime production quotas. The Army is responsible for control and supply, but the prisoner of war camp facilities are the responsibility of the companies, which use the prisoners of war. In 1907, the leading nations of the world, including Japan, had agreed in writing that enemy prisoners could be made to do hard labor such as road or farm work, but they were not to be used in any industry involved in war production. Moreover, the The Hague Conventions stipulated that prisoners of war should be paid for their work. The Geneva Convention on prisoners of war was signed by the Japanese representative in 1929, but at home the Japanese government never did ratify the Geneva Convention on POW's. The Japanese feel therefore that they are not obliged to comply with the terms of the Geneva Convention. About 25,000 prisoner of war are put to work under pressure in private industrial companies to maintain the momentum of the war industry and make weapons that are to be used against their own comrades. (Daws, page 97, Goetz, page 23)

The place where the group is staying, was assigned to the Chilean representation before the war, but they have long gone, of course. It is located in a neighborhood where all houses are built in a European style. The site is fenced in and there are several houses whose beautifully landscaped gardens overlap. There is a road with a driveway for cars, several garages and housing for the staff. The house in which the Einthoven and Levenbach families live, is the largest on the terrain. Downstairs is a large dining room, a big sunroom and a large reception hall. On the first floor are four bedrooms, two for each family and a bathroom. The house is large and does not feel pleasant; the house where the other families live, is smaller. The Hasenstab and Leunis families live upstairs and the Lels family lives downstairs in two bedrooms and a sitting room. The houses are beautiful, but quite bare, as if Sumitomo made the arrangements quickly. The big house is connected to a big kitchen, which Sumitomo uses to provide food for receptions and dinners. Sometimes they see a delivery van that picks up food for Sumitomo. It smells good, but completely Japanese.

Ineke van der Wal

At first, there are Japanese people in two other houses on the property, but they leave quickly. Some speak briefly with them, but all are afraid of being discovered because contact is strictly prohibited. They are decent people who are not hostile, but the intention clearly is to isolate the Dutch group and not to have any contact with other people. Tineke later sees an opportunity to visit the abandoned houses. She finds things that are left behind, which they can occasionally use.

The food from the Imperial Hotel stops after two weeks and then the schedule of home cooking by the Japanese cooks begins. Sumitomo arranges food stamps for them and also buys food on the black market. In the morning they get oatmeal together with a cup of tea and a slice of bread. At one o'clock it is a mixture of rice with barley, and other grains with some vegetables in a thick sauce and a cup of tea. In the evening the one o'clock lunch dish is repeated, but they also get a bowl of soup beforehand. Everything is tasty, but it's the same every day, there is no meat, hardly any vegetables, no fat, no sugar, and nothing in between. It's not healthy, especially not for growing children. They have been advised to chew the food properly to release the few vitamins, but it is annoying. You're sitting at the table chewing for a long time. Wim turns very skinny and he dreams of macaroni with cheese and tomato, and tasty pastry.

On April 13, 1944 Beb turns 49 years old. She writes: 'I have absolutely nothing to offer to the others who come to congratulate me and they have nothing to give me.' Loukie made a small *Hardanger* piece and Wim purchased some roses via the housekeeper that arrive in the morning. Only later do they learn how to make small gifts for such special days from leftovers or stuff that they salvage from the kitchen waste. 'This is easy for me, I can make a drawing of the two houses,' Beb writes, 'everyone likes such a drawing as a memento.' They also learn how to save bread and other food to make a dish to serve; just a suggestion of a treat.

Beb does not know that all of their birthdays are also celebrated in The Netherlands. Her mother travels to Gus or Wies, where the birthday is celebrated together. They save coupons, so they can eat something special on the day. This time they have 'poffertjes' (mini pancakes). They sing for the birthday boy or girl and all of them write a letter that they plan to mail once contact is re-established. The Bake family - friends of the Einthoven family in Bandung - sometimes celebrate with them; they are stranded in The Netherlands, unable to leave when the Germans invaded. The Zeeman and Einthoven families keep up these birthday celebrations until the southern part of The Netherlands is liberated and transport between the North and South is no longer possible. Beb's mother writes in her congratulatory letter to Beb that she lives in Baarn with a family, who willingly share their place. Staying alone in Oegstgeest would have been difficult, after the house was requisitioned by the Germans. Beb's mother writes about some relatives: the cousin of Beb, Loukie van der Veen, is put out of her house and the two girls are sent to live with other people for the duration of the war. Gerrit is often gone. Lou Einthoven is a hostage. He was allowed to go home for two weeks, but then had to say goodbye, which was very difficult. Lou's children are in hiding. Beb's mother buys a large bag for Beb's birthday. She decides that she will put everything that she wants to share with Beb after the war into this bag. A friend of Beb's mother has died and Beb's mother writes that 'she longed so much to see her children from the Dutch Indies. I hear such stories over and over again and then I get so fearful that I will not be re-united with my children. That's my reason for staying alive and I will do my best to stay fit in body and mind. May it happen for me.'

Annie Lels writes on April 27: 'Except for Wim, the other men can easily fill the empty hours.' They enjoy the quiet time just like the women do. Jan tinkers and draws. Geo studies Japanese and Henk has been busy for more than a week on a model crane for Murk. What disturbs them most is that they are completely devoid of any news. What is happening while they are locked up in this courtyard? They

Ineke van der Wal

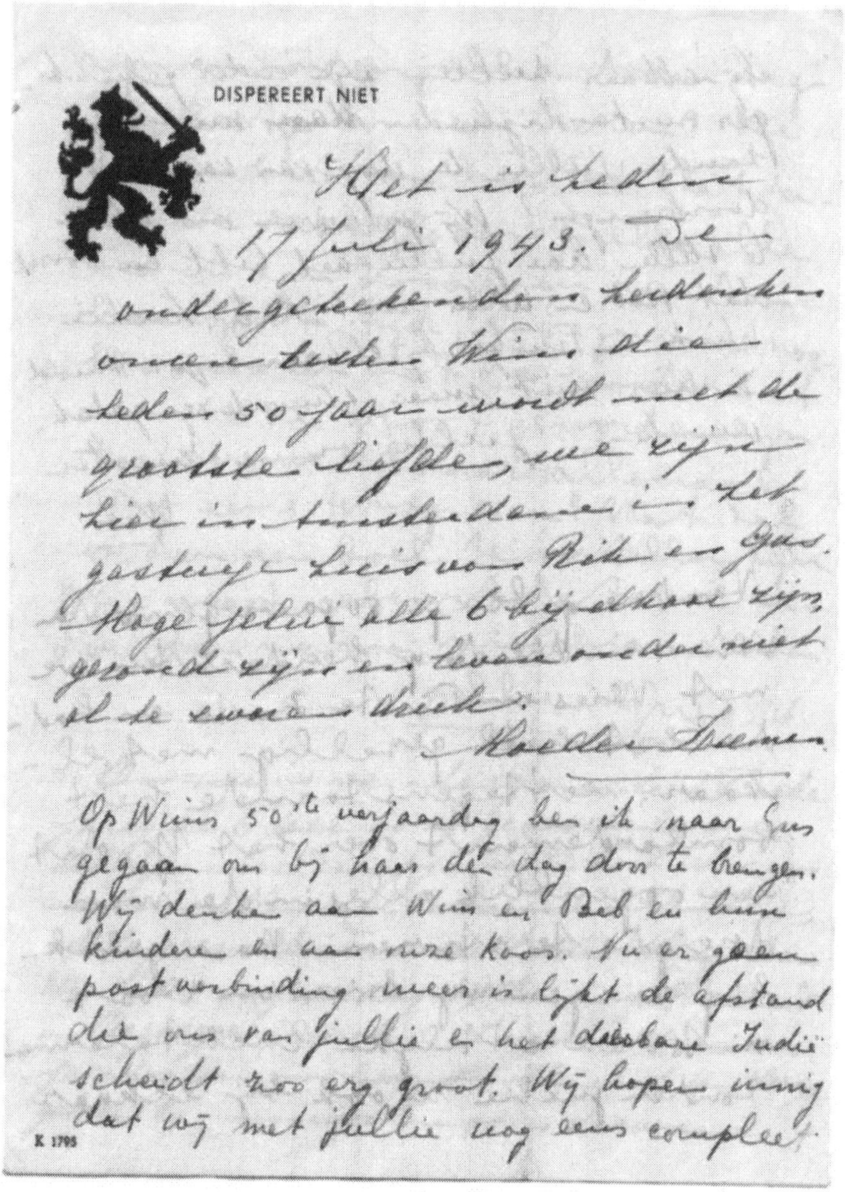

DISPEREERT NIET

Het is heden 17 Juli 1943. De [illegible] herdenken onze beste Wim die heden 50 jaar wordt met de grootste liefde, we zijn hier in [illegible] in het gastvrije huis van Rik en Gus. Moge gelieve alle 6 bij elkaar zijn, gezond zijn en leven [illegible] al de zware druk.

[illegible] Zeeman

Op Wims 50ste verjaardag ben ik naar Gus gegaan om bij haar den dag door te brengen. Wij denken aan Wim en Bab en hun kinderen en aan onze Koos. Nu er geen postverbinding meer is lijkt de afstand die ons van jullie en het dierbare Indië scheidt zoo erg groot. Wij hopen innig dat wij met jullie nog eens compleet.

K 1795

The Einthoven and Zeeman families come together in The Netherlands to celebrate Wim Einthoven's fiftieth birthday. They write a congratulation letter to him on 'resistance' stationery with the Dutch lion.

enjoy the garden and the fact that they have their own rooms. They make some contact with the staff and learn some Japanese words, and the mothers are busy making clothes so that everyone can be warm and have well sized clothing. The children grow out of their clothes and the group gets a chance to buy some fabric to make new clothes. On one of her expeditions Tineke finds some Christmas lights that she takes home. 'I could do a lot since I was small. If you're only five years old, people are more forgiving of your actions, unlike Wim for example, who was too old already. I was fairly adventurous and was able to play everywhere.'

On April 29, they receive tea with milk and cookies to celebrate the birthday of the Emperor of Japan. The Dutch, in turn, celebrate the birthday of Juliana on April 30, by wearing orange and drink tea together, of course, this time without milk and cookies. They don't have any food for themselves, which is not very comforting. You can never give something extra to the children in between meals. The kitchen maintains a rigid regime.

In late April, two cars arrive to fetch the men to be presented to the President of Sumitomo, but after that silence kicks in again. Will this work ever commence? They begin to think that they will serve as exchange material for all those students who were sent to the United States on a scholarship from Sumitomo and who, at the outbreak of the war, were interned by the Americans. If only it were true. These exchanges take place on the island of Lorenzo Marques, an island off the east coast of Africa. But then, at the end of May, a new resident appears at the court, a special Kempe Tai guard Hamaichi Tanaka who will live in the gatehouse with his family. From there he can look out over the group and the gate, which was soon erected after their arrival to prevent them from leaving the site. Tanaka will accompany the men to work; it will happen after all.

On June 4, the men go to a ceremonial introduction, as the Japanese call it, in the laboratory to become acquainted with the 'colleagues' with

Ineke van der Wal

whom they will work. The eighth of June is their first day. At half past seven they leave with a packet of sandwiches for lunch and come home at half past six, tired from hanging on to the handles in crowded trams and trains. The trip to Sumitomo's laboratories at Ikuta Noborito takes an hour and a half. First with a tram to the Dayama station on the beltline, crammed into the tramcar from the beltline to Shinjuku, and then by a suburban train to Noborito. After a ten minutes' walk up a steep hill, they arrive at the laboratory at nine o'clock. Willem and Henk are assigned a room together and the others get a room in another building. Everyone receives a design from the Japanese engineers, but only Wim gets material to actually make something.

Sumitomo engineers know they cannot really trust the Dutch, but they are asked to write long reports for the army, who organized the whole 'show'. In order to type these long reports, it is quickly determined that Corrie Leunis joins them. One day some officers come with a lot of amazement and look at the large pile of paper, which they have produced. 'I don't think anybody has ever read any of it,' writes Geo Levenbach. They mostly make calculations, and don't perform any practical work. It therefore remains mysterious. Were they brought from Java to do this work? 'The work signifies little, a college sophomore could do it', according to Beb.

Wim has to build a measuring device for vacuum tubes. He creates it in such a way that with a small alteration the device is capable of receiving news from San Francisco. In the evening when they walk to the train, the news is shared, in camouflaged Dutch. At one point they get the impression that Tanaka understands Dutch, although his English is very broken. After a few days of sharing their news, an engineer inspects the 'measuring device', but does not see how it can be changed into a receiver. The next day, however, Wim and Henk are moved to another room. The measuring device is supposed to come later, but that of course never happens.

Geo Levenbach reported on the research conducted in Tokyo by Wim Einthoven during the internment in 1944-1945.

1. *Integral curves for the Joule-Kelvin effect were searched for to determine which temperature drop at a certain expansion, could be expected to obtain liquefied air. The only experimental data available at first was a table from Hütte $pv = f$ (RT), from which analytical curves were determined by approximation with a power series $p = f$ (v T). At constant entropy $p = f$ (T) was calculated using several integrations and differentiations. The accuracy could be verified with a few well-known measurements, but left very much to be desired, because the deviations of the relationship PV-RT of the unit, that are important for the effect sought, are very small.*

2. *Better results were obtained by graphical integration of the Joule-Kelvin impact assessments published in 'Physikalisch - Chemical Tables', which later became available.*

3. *The behavior of liquid air and gaseous air at different temperatures and pressures were initially examined.*

4. *According to the method in 2), an extensive set of curves for the particular temperature-pressure range was determined. Point 3) had not yet produced known results.*

All data and results were lost during the journey from Japan.

The women and children have to entertain themselves at home and in the small courtyard and it is not always easy. Always in the same place, always the same daily routine, always the same food, no possibility to leave, and not being able to make your own decisions, slowly drains all energy out of you. Wink says, 'My great enthusiasm and thirst for adventure were dampened by remaining in the same place day in day out and by only being able to look at books. It slowly destroys your mind. I left the courtyard once to go to the dentist, all the other days I spent in the courtyard. It is a luxury prison, but it remains a real prison, from which we cannot and are not allowed to leave.' Earthquakes,

Ineke van der Wal

which occur regularly, provide some distraction, but after a few times, everyone knows that they cause no damage. Sometimes a small group, escorted by guards, goes to the hospital. That too is a distraction. Annie Lels writes about it in her diary:

June 28th: *Yesterday the doctor from Sumitomo came. I let him examine me because I have some problem with my breathing after the journey here. A 'gift' from the woes that we suffered. The doctor is afraid I have pleurisy and tomorrow I have to visit the hospital for further examination. It would be nicer if I could leave our prison for a better reason.*

June 30: *Yesterday I was driven out of the gate that I walked into three months ago while it was pitch dark. The drive to the hospital in a wood-fired car lasted at least forty five minutes, so I have seen a lot of Tokyo, the metropolitan city with eight million inhabitants. The neighborhood where we live has an oriental air because of the rows of shops, closely packed side by side, selling nothing but junk. The center looks very modern, with large concrete buildings, broad canals and streets, wide squares and modern architecture. But ..... the city is dead, completely dead. There is no large department store and all the shops that were ever there, are closed. There is no activity, no signs of trade and very little traffic. Only the trams are crowded. At the hospital we have to wait for a long time in a small, dreary waiting room, where a bunch of nuns are also waiting for their turn. The Levenbach family were first in line. Hirata went with them to take them to the doctor. I was left alone with a European lady, who had just arrived. Moments later, she was called away.*

When she stood up, she (deliberately?) dropped a handkerchief. I picked it up and returned it to her with a few English words. Imagine my surprise when she replied, 'Dank u wel, mevrouw.' (Thank you, madam in Dutch) She immediately left after that. I was just getting over the shock when she came back, sat down beside me and started a conversation. I warned her that I could not talk to other people and she got up twice to make sure Hirata had not returned into the hallway. It was exciting. She was really trying to get information about us, but I did not dare say more than that we were not free and had just arrived and generalities like that. She turned out to be German, married to a Dutchman, a planter from Delhi. Her husband was interned in British India. Later I realized with horror that she therefore had to be a member of the N.S.B. (N.S.B - The National Socialist Movement in The Netherlands that collaborated with the German occupier). She was called away again, and for a little while I was alone when an unusual couple entered the waiting room...Burmese people. They were dressed in very fancy sarongs with lots of beautiful jewelry. They immediately began a conversation in English and suddenly the man was bowing to me and handed me his card: Captain ... attaché. Apparently he expected the same courtesy from me, which I obviously could not render to him. They also continued to ask all sorts of questions, but all I could told them was that I was Dutch. I was examined by the doctor who took two x-rays. I only had bronchitis, for which he gave me liquid medication. Then we visited some stores! It was against the rules, so we had to hurry, hurry. But we came home loaded with packages. We did the best we could, but it was barely anything.'

The hospital they visit is St. Luke's hospital, a former American hospital in Tokyo. Beb goes to the hospital for new glasses, the children go to the dentist there and Wim visits an internist, Dr. Ikeda. In his office hangs a portrait of Professor Einthoven. Dr. Ikeda has met Professor Einthoven and admires him. He asks Wim if he is related to the Professor and when Wim confirms this, Dr. Ikeda asks Wim to put his signature at the bottom of his father's portrait and he offers Wim all help whenever possible.

Around the houses where they live, is a garden, which all families love. Beb writes a lot about it and enjoys the changing flowering seasons. In spring, there is an abundance of flowers, followed by the rainy month of June. July and August are very hot and dry with very few flowers. Then, in the autumn the flowers return. She describes camellias with white, pink and red spots and the chrysanthemum, the imperial symbol with sixteen petals.

Ineke van der Wal

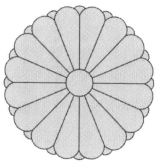

The Chrysanthemum, or Kiku in Japanese, is a symbol that represents longevity and rejuvenation. When first introduced to Japan during the Nara period (710 – 793 AC), the Japanese Royal Family was fascinated with the Chrysanthemum. Eventually, during the passing of the years, the Chrysanthemum became the Imperial Family Emblem.

In spring the cherry trees blossom with a wealth of pinkish-white splendor. Japanese gardens are planted with a great variety and diversity because one has to adhere to the rule that two of the same trees cannot be side by side. They get permission to plant their own private garden. Wim and Wink help with digging, and remove a stubborn tree stump. Loukie and Beb plant the garden and take care of it, and even Tineke gets a small plot. They harvest some delicious tomatoes and they grow beautiful flowers from marigold seeds that they were able to smuggle with them. The marigolds only start blooming in September but the large orange colored area gives them faith. In the garden some round slabs of wood cut from the trunk of a tree are used as decoration. The children play with these discs, and in their imagination they become islands and homes for dwarfs. They make some dwarfs from scraps of fabric and give them names. Beb says: 'This garden has been our great joy. It was the only place for us to go outside.'

The Japanese promised education for the children, but it never comes to anything, so the adults continue their lessons. Beb starts French and German lessons, Annie teaches English, Geo teaches physics and chemistry and Tineke receives some private lessons from Beb. After trigonometry had been so successful in Singapore, Wim starts with logarithms and differential equations, and does it at the same fast pace as before. It is sometimes difficult for the children to keep up but if they manage they progress real quickly. Wink decides to do math problems with Tineke for fun and Beb is delighted with this distraction. Wink experiences this way that you learn things best when you try to teach someone else. Kate and Loukie are further ahead with physics and chemistry than Wink, so Wink gets private lessons from Geo, who manages to make Wink very enthusiastic because of his inspiring lessons. Wink tells, 'These four teachers, my father, my mother, Geo Levenbach and Annie Lels were able to teach us better than 99% of all other children. We always received answers to all our questions.' They learn a lot, also because there is nothing else to do. Work is your only distraction. Wink has the advantage that he can work with the books from his two older sisters, but Kate does not have this advantage. Kate realizes that when she comes to the end of her book material, Loukie and Wink will catch up with her, and that is no fun when you are the oldest.

Wim is working on some thermodynamics problems and is looking for some characteristics. These are multiplications with 7 or 8 digits and he is not getting correct results. Wim is trying to find where the error is and Wink offers to help. Wim actually thinks this is a great idea and Wink works on the problem for two days and finds three mistakes. All three were just two lines of numbers where the digits were moved over by one position. It's a welcome distraction from the regular problems for Wink.

Ineke van der Wal

The only photo made during the imprisonment in Tokyo which survived. Not all members of the group of 22 are present. The middle row is formed by 5 Japanese staff members. People in the photo are identified on the last page of this Chapter.

The summer is very hot and humid and you sleep so poorly that you are still tired the next day. Every night before you go to sleep, you first kill mosquitos, so you don't get bitten. Once they count the mosquitoes and find that they swatted 100 of them. They try to put mesh on the windows, but they cannot find good material. The Japanese have drums full of water everywhere in case of fire, but the drums are great breeding grounds for mosquitoes. Wim asks if he can put some drops of oil on top of the water but they respond: 'oil on water? No, this water is needed to extinguish fires, oil is not allowed on the water.' Wim says: 'It is to prevent the mosquitoes from landing on the water' and then the Japanese ask: 'Mosquitoes, what have they to do with water?' Wim points at the creatures that swarm around in the water, but the Japanese say, 'But these are not mosquitoes, can't you see?' It's not that this guy is ignorant, but he simply does not have the education to know that they are mosquito larvae. Such are the difficulties that you have to contend with.

The people at home suffer from the hot summer and the fact that they have too much time on their hands. Annie Lels writes on September 9, 'The month of August was piping hot and the atmosphere among this group of prisoners was also piping hot, but not in a good way. I'm so glad that the Einthoven family belongs to the group, otherwise it would have been unbearable.' Annie writes less and less in her diary. She used to write daily in the beginning, now it's every two weeks and later it is reduced to once a month and only if something unusual happens.

During the remainder of 1944 the five men are transported regularly to the lab. The transport is becoming more and more annoying because there is a great shortage of railcars and more and more people are forcefully pushed into them. In the car, the five men often cannot stay together and sometimes Japanese try to practice their English. Tanaka immediately squeezes through to the culprit, whispers something in his ear and forces him to get off at the next station. The only news they can get is by memorizing the headlines of newspapers in the train and translating them later. Geo knows best how to do this and he is improving. In July he reads that General Tōjō Hideki, who is both prime minister, minister of war and the Army chief of staff, has been fired. It looks as though not all is going well. At the end of August, Geo reads that a large city in Europe has been liberated. It is a city with a curved river running through it. He writes down the Japanese characters and says the signs represent *Ripa*, but he cannot think of any major European city with this name. After some back and forth discussions someone suggests that perhaps the signs should be read backwards, not *Ripa* but *Pari*. It's Paris that's been liberated by the Allies. He also discovers, that there is something going on in The Netherlands, but he cannot figure out whether The Netherlands have been liberated or not.

Paris in Japanese characters

パリ

The Netherlands in Japanese characters

オランダ

Here you can see how difficult it is to read Japanese characters.

The group celebrates all birthdays, but that usually happens without the Hasenstab family. For example, they celebrate Henk's birthday on October 11, 1944. The highlight is an ABC-rhyme composed by all the members of the group. It describes in a humorous way many aspects of their amazing existence. Beb still has a can of condensed milk, some coffee and the cook donates half a jar of jam. They gather together and enjoy homemade gifts and an almost forgotten treat: coffee and a piece of bread with jam.

In November it starts to get cold and they ask for coal to fire up the furnace, but it never comes. They only get a charcoal pit that's called a 'hibachi'. You use this small pit in your house to warm your hands. It keeps you comfortable for a little while, but there is danger of carbon monoxide poisoning. You can avoid this poisoning only if you are in a well ventilated - so cold - room and can breathe clean air. The hibachi is no help and Wim looks for a solution. He finds that he can use the coal dust – considered waste by the Sumitomo kitchen staff - and turn them into coal dust briquettes with which he can stoke the central heating furnace. They use these briquettes in the afternoon, so they can sit and work quietly. Making the briquettes is a demanding and especially dirty job. First you have to sift the debris from the coal. This is then mixed with salt, paper and water and kneaded to a mixture that is pressed into molds. These molds are made from wooden planks discarded by the kitchen and once they are filled, they are put outside to dry. Therefore you need to make sure that, if it is going to rain or snow, the molds have to be brought inside. Wim and Henk spend hours in one of the barns working to develop the technology and then to teach others. The mixture hurts your hands which become sore and chapped. Everyone hates the job but they do it anyway. They treat their hands with petroleum jelly which is all they have left but the sores never go away. It is Wink's job to fire up the furnace. It is an arduous task which is difficult for him, especially in the beginning. There are not enough briquettes to keep the furnace running all the time so they have to choose their days and hours carefully. Wink has to work with a minimum amount of briquettes for a maximum amount of heat, which sometimes works and sometimes doesn't. In the evening when Wim comes home, he helps Wink to tune the furnace for the best result.

Ineke van der Wal

In late November they see reconnaissance flights over Tokyo and that results in a lot of chaos. The sirens warn them of the approaching planes, the *keikaikeiho* - planes far away - alarm sounds and then everyone has to immediately stop working and go home. The men wonder whether it is not safer to shelter at the Sumitomo laboratory than to board a tram, but discussion is of course impossible. When the planes come closer the *kushukeiho* – air danger close by - alarm sounds and all traffic stops, everyone runs out of the train and tries to take cover in an unfamiliar street. They try to get under a roof, but Tanaka calls to them, and they have to run to the other side of the street, which may be safer. It is actually not clear why, but they do it anyway. The first time they saw an enemy aircraft, was in June and an intense blackout was ordered then. There had already been several practices, but never as intensely as in June. Takesan said that the Americans were coming. The next day, the men did not have to go to the lab, because Tanaka had been on guard duty all night. Later it turned out that this was a lone experimental aircraft that caused the alarm all by itself. Now, after five months, they see American planes again and they are thrilled. It seems that the Americans are now able to reach Tokyo easily. They obviously do not know exactly what is happening. Japanese newspapers give biased reports and they only get part of the story, but the thought that there are people working to free them, and that finally something is happening, gives them hope.

The Lels and Einthoven families have the intention to celebrate Sinterklaas on December 5, 1944 and to make a party out of it. They can barely buy anything so they will have to make gifts themselves which makes the celebration unusually special. Loukie writes later: 'It was so bad that we picked the tools out of other people's garbage. The whole Einthoven family makes a *Mah Yong* game together. They find small pieces of waste which they shape into the same size and Beb draws the marks on it. Wink makes shelves that you can hang up against a wall. He uses boards which are considered scrap by the kitchen. Warm slippers are a very popular gift. Beb makes a pair for

Annie and a pair for Wim and she stuffs them entirely with cotton from duvets. Wim finds two scarves for himself in a small, cluttered shop, that they pass by on their way to the laboratory. When Wim visits the doctor, he finds a set of lenses in a shop from which you can make binoculars and he gives them to Wink. It is a magnificent gift and authentically Japanese. Besides these gifts they create some silly gifts. For Wink, they make a chimney sweep out of a black quilt because he is always stoking the furnace and can look so very dirty. Annie Lels uses some fret-saw blades from the fret-saw the housekeeper bought, to make a miniature stove, cute and unique. Wim has been entrusted to make sure that the refrigerator in Tokyo works. It is a curious contraption and often something is loose, so Annie surprises him with a small fridge made out of a shoebox. It has a likeness of the emblem of General Electric on it, just like the refrigerator they had at home. And they write poems. Beb writes a poem with 18 stanzas, six lines each, repeating the last two lines with the same phrase throughout the poem. Even the children are a big help finding words that rhyme. The cook does his best and makes some biscuits. Actually, the biscuits are more like flour slices, because flour and water are the only ingredients; sugar and fat aren't available anymore. Of course they drink the eternal tea, with nothing added, but they create a joyous evening. With so few resources, you can still create an intense family life and as a child you appreciate this. In that respect, it was a time like you would never actually experience in peacetime and you learned from it while having fun.

Annie Lels writes on December 10: 'We finally decided to move to the living room of the main house. The house with the kitchen is the warmest and we enjoy the heat that we get from the homemade briquettes. Here we have a lovely room overlooking the garden and most of the day the sun shines into the house. When the sun shines, the weather is nice and you can sit outside, but without sun it can be bitterly cold. Another reason to move, is Mr. Hasenstab; the Lels family wants to be away from him. Alexander Hasenstab speaks regularly about *the caste* when he talks about the other men and also uses anti-Jewish or anti-Dutch statements. He invents all kinds of things to thwart and betray the families. Japanese guards are not pleased with Mr. H. and refer him back to the group. At one point Mr. H. states that he cannot work anymore, 'ostensibly for health reasons,' writes Geo. The Japanese don't mind Mr. Hasenstab's complaints, because they too find him difficult. 'So Mr. H. does not work anymore' writes Annie, but that also increases the isolation of the Hasenstab family. Sometimes the Japanese guard gives news to the men on their way to work, but ask that they do not pass on the information to Mr. Hasenstab.

In December it is decided that a second shelter must be dug and that the men have to do it themselves; therefore they do not need to travel to their work anymore. The beautiful garden is dug up considerably. The women are meanwhile busy transforming black woolen coats into thick pants since the women are required to wear these in case of an air raid. They are good protection against the cold, and you can easily run to the shelter in them. It is clear that the Japanese are expecting an upsurge of the bombing.

Christmas 1944: they all wish that this really will be the last Christmas that they experience in wartime. The initial bombings in Japan and the second front in Europe give them hope. The Einthoven and Lels families celebrate Christmas and they have a Christmas tree, a very pretty one that reaches the ceiling with lots of Christmas decorations. They found the tree in the attic of one of the empty houses in the court. The cord with electric lights that Tineke found and that was repaired by Wim and Henk at the Sumitomo lab, hangs on the tree. The cook bakes biscuits again, mixed with some herbs Beb still has, in the form of stars and wreaths, and they wrap them in red paper. Annie and Paulien make a small stall with Mary and Joseph and a cradle in the manger. Annie is teaching Christmas songs to the little ones and Wink performs Christmas songs on his violin.

They come together on Christmas Day and Annie reads the Christmas story from the Bible. Beb writes: 'It is written in such beautiful language, it deeply moves you, but it is finished before you realize it, it is so short and without much elaboration.' At night they read the story of the Three Kings. And while they are all together, suddenly their Kempei Tai guard, Tanaka, comes in without knocking and steps inside with a flute under his arm. The families have received a bottle of beer from Sumitomo. After saying no 10 times, as is the tradition in Japan, where politeness dominates such pleasantries, he drinks two glasses of beer with them and plays on his flute. He starts with a few European tunes, then some Japanese ones. Finally he dances some young Japanese boys' dances and he sings some songs to accompany himself. It turns out that he was a leader and folk dance teacher in a big boys' boarding school and now he likes to perform for us as a farewell.

Tanake has asked for a transfer because he thinks that guarding this group is too boring. He is not allowed to leave though, so he stays with them in Tokyo until the end, but he did not know that yet at the time. Although the Dutch women and children are present, he doesn't bring his wife and sons, as is customary in Japan. He enjoys Wink's violin playing and gives him a music book as a present. The book contains the world's hundred best songs such as *Ave Maria, Santa Lucia and Old Kentucky Home.* They are in utter amazement at this unexpected kind gesture by Tanaka.

The Japanese remain incomprehensible, very sensitive to nature, but without compassion for people. They can be cruel and sentimental, but fortunately are usually friendly to children. On New Year's Eve, they are surprised to find that the entire house gets cleaned. This is apparently common practice in this country - to start out clean in the New Year. The cooks make a real deluge in the kitchen. They stand on top of the warm stove to scrub everything. At about nine in the evening the Dutch families come together after putting the little children to bed. Paulien Lels is the youngest, who is allowed to be

Ineke van der Wal

present, but very soon the siren goes and there is an air raid. All lights must be turned off; only a small burner with a very large, black hood on top can stay on. They sing something together, and even though they carefully wrote down the words, they cannot read them because of the darkness. Everyone takes a turn to sing a song by themselves. Wim sings *Le roi a fait battre tambour* and later he reads to them one of Dickens' Christmas stories *The umbrella* just like he had once done at home. This is his favorite story just as it was for 'Little Grandma'. At the stroke of midnight they sing *Uren, dagen, maanden, jaren* ('Hours, days, months, years') with a cup of tea in their hands. They're a small group of Dutchmen lost among the millions in the capital of the enemy. At 5 minutes after 12 the siren sounds again and then there is violent gunfire so the gathering breaks up quickly in the dark, because they don't dare to keep even the small burner lit. They stumble upstairs to the sleeping children to be ready to carry them downstairs if the planes come closer. At 3 AM and 5 AM they hear the alarm, but are allowed to stay in bed. These bombings gives them faith and hope for the New Year which is what they need right now. The day after Christmas, they had the horrible experience of seeing a large bomber being shot. That makes you so sad.

It is especially the uncertainty that can be very upsetting. There is an English library, where they can sometimes borrow books from and the first English book that Wink borrows is *Listen! The wind* from Anne Lindbergh. Despite all the English lessons Wink has had, it takes him about an hour to read the first page. Then Wink is fed up and wants to do something else, but there is nothing else to do, so he starts on page two. When he finally finishes the book, he cannot borrow another book. No one knows why. Henk Lels tries to get a newspaper. 'We're supposed to be here as scientists, we would also like to live like scientists. Can we subscribe to a newspaper?' For a month they regularly receive a Japanese newspaper, until a Japanese higher up in the hierarchy hears about it and terminates that privilege. Crazy things sometimes just happen and then all of a sudden are not repeated. Wim regularly asks to speak to a Red Cross representative or the Swedish delegation; it is a prison of war's right as stated in the Geneva Convention, but he is always refused. The concept of 'right' *(kenri)* in Japan is a totally different concept from the one in the Western world: A right is not something that is due to you because you exist, but a right is something that is given from the outside and from above and therefore may be withdrawn at any time.

Wink is becoming more and more comfortable with the central heating and the furnace can now stay on night and day. Wim has managed to obtain grit and with this new grit it is much easier to produce the briquettes because it does not have to be pushed into a mold. The salt and paper ingredients have not been available for a while and this sticky coal grit which only needs water, is an improvement. It is Wink who discovers this new process. He realizes that the grit sticks well and is easier to knead. He consults with his father who says 'Yes Wink, that's a good discovery and that is exactly what research is all about.' It is thus easier and less time consuming to make briquettes. Wink also notes that the cook removes the slag from the kitchen oven every day and disposes of it outside. He can use this still warm slag to cover the bottom of the furnace so that the briquettes don't easily fall through the grate and burn longer. Wim thinks this an excellent initiative and he urges Wink to remain friends with the cook. Wim attempts to take the slag directly from the kitchen stove to the furnace, but that concept is not understood. The cook knows that Wink takes his slag and thinks it strange. People who come from such different backgrounds, often distrust each other. The guard, for instance, is always concerned that they will run away or that they are in contact with the Americans and this is yet another strange thing: making fire from dust and slag. The cook gladly shows visitors how Wink comes running, picks up the slag, and places it in the furnace. The winter of 1944 to 1945 is the coldest in forty years. It is no wonder that despite the effort everyone is making, the large house is still not warm. If the sun does not shine, it remains cold all day and then they cannot study or do homework

Ineke van der Wal

because they get too cold by just sitting still. After eating they remain warm for about half an hour and then they slowly become cold again. They are all skinny and want to save calories by not moving too much, but it is hard to pass the time this way. They walk around a bit or lay in their beds wearing all their clothes underneath all their blankets.

On January 26 the men go back to the lab in Noborito. They don't object because they are more likely to get some news this way. Traveling to work is very tiring and the work itself is not interesting. Yet they are mentally better off when they work than when they sit at home all day.

It is beautiful, freezing weather but on February 1 the weather changes into a very rainy storm type and a flu starts floating around, even the Japanese are affected. Loukie starts first, then Tineke does not feel well. Wim comes home on February 3 after work and doesn't feel good. Two days later Beb is in bed; only Kate and Wink stay healthy. A doctor comes because 13 of the 22 are ill, and he prescribes some medication. All of them are violently ill, but that does not last long. After four days you feel better, but if you're not careful, you can get sick again. On the 7th Wim no longer has a fever and on the morning of the 8th he wants to take a bath. Beb advises against it, but he insists. Wink fires up some briquettes to heat up the bathroom. After bathing Wim goes downstairs to help get the food. Nobody knows when it happens, but in the evening Wim starts shivering and Beb takes his temperature. It is 40.1° C (or 104.1 F), more than he ever had when he had the flu. He complains of pain in his left shoulder and they immediately ask for a doctor. The doctor doesn't come until the 10th (of February) in the afternoon. He pats him here and there and says in his limited English: 'Nothing serious.' The fever meanwhile goes down somewhat. In the morning it is 38° C (100.4 F) and in the evening it goes up to 39° C (102.2 F). The doctor is interested in Wim's constipation, which does not mean anything when you stay in bed all day. This reassures Beb even though Wim remains depressed, but the Japanese calm down and no longer listen to Wim's complaint

Wim has himself to blame for this attitude of the Japanese because of an incident in October. When Wink, Paulien Lels and Mrs. Hasenstab all became ill with jaundice and Wim came home that evening with a slight fever, he immediately thought that he also had jaundice. The next morning his fever was gone and he was out of bed, but did not want to go to work. The primitive Japanese did not understand that; either you are sick and stay in bed, or you can get up and go to work. Tanaka vented his rage against the healthy men, so in the evening they convinced Wim that he could not behave this way and made him stay in bed. For a week Wim stayed upstairs with books on a table beside him. This resting period was very beneficial to him. The men had worked for a long time at end and Wim got really tired and thin. For those who stay at home the food is somewhat sufficient, but it is not enough for the men traveling back and forth to work. Fortunately, Tineke doesn't finish her food and Loukie and Kate leave some of their rice and some leave half a piece of bread, so that Wim can take something extra to work. Beb spreads some fat – which they are lucky to still have – on Wim's sandwich. The first tin of fat was shared by the six of them, but this disappeared so quickly, that Beb decides to keep the other two tins just for Wim. Only on the Monday, when the men have their day off, which is every other week, the other family members can use some fat for their bread. The fat is a bit rancid, but it tastes still OK. Wim always claims that the sandwiches made by Beb are the best of all, because they are spread with a bit of fat while the others are spread with jam, or a little bit of dried Japanese salmon (a very inferior type of what should be a delicious fish).

After Wim rested for a week, Hirata surprisingly shows up with a Sumitomo doctor. Wim's urine, which at first was orange, is now much lighter in color; his constipation is gone and his eyes are no longer yellow. The doctor performs some tests and doesn't find anything wrong. Wim, despite his protests, is ordered to go to work again the next day. Fortunately it all ends well, but this incident tells the Japanese that Wim is overly concerned about his health.

Ineke van der Wal

In February Wim asks the doctor for some drugs other than a laxative maybe a sulfa drug. The doctor completely ignores him, maybe he did not know what he was asking for or there are no drugs left. They get no support from Hirata, who always comes along to their doctor visits. Several days later Wim repeatedly asks if Dr. Ikeda, the doctor who has the portrait of Father Einthoven in his office at St. Luke's hospital, can come. They still ignore him. On the fourth day at noon Wim cannot go to the bathroom. He eats very little, only the soup and the milk taste good to him. He gets a cup because he is ill and Beb also gets one, but she gives hers to Wim. Later he eats a tangerine which was given to him as food for the sick. On the fifth day after he had an aspirin, his temperature is 37.6° C (99 F). This is encouraging although Beb decides to try and feed him hoping to get more food in him that way. Beb is also weak because she just went through a flu attack herself, so she spends lots of time dozing next to Wim in their double bed. Wim doesn't sleep well and wants to drink a lot at night, but when there is another air raid, he asks for the curtains to be opened so that he can see all the searchlights.

On the morning of the sixth day, Wim says he is too stiff from lying still all the time and he sits up straight with his legs dangling over the side of the bed. After five minutes he gets tired and lies down again. Beb puts a folded quilt behind his pillow. He already has a pillow under his knees. That afternoon Beb reads to him, but in the evening Beb finds that Wim is not at all well. He has eaten; Kate gave Wim her soup and Wim seemed to enjoy eating both his own plate as well as hers. But half an hour later, he throws up and is confused when he tries to speak. Beb is worried but at night one can never get a doctor. Beb prepares Tineke – who is still ill – for the night and then Wim. He says 'This is the solution, I am comfortable now.' Beb also crawls into bed because she is still very tired. Beb writes:

When I woke up early in the morning, Wim had difficulty breathing; I called softly 'Bibi' but got no answer and thought to myself, 'Thank God, he sleeps' and remained quietly beside him. But at six o'clock I got very concerned, and when I turned on the light, I noticed that he was unconscious. He had not drunk any water, so he probably became that way early in the night, because he usually drank three glasses of water. Immediately I went to Henk Lels who quickly got dressed and went to the Kempei guard, who lived in the gate house at the entrance of the yard. He came at once, and by eight o'clock a doctor came, again with Hirata. They tried very hard to reach Dr. Ikeda, but he was sick. He promised to send one of his young employees. The first doctor gave Wim an injection. Wim winced a little but then became very quiet, even though he had been moving his hands a lot. I sat by Wim's side continuously; Loukie sat beside me; the others thought it was too scary. At a quarter to ten he held his breath for a moment, Loukie went downstairs to see if the doctor was still there and came back with Henk Lels, Katy, Tineke and Wink and while we were all standing around him, and without him opening his eyes and without any discomfort or even a deep sigh, the difficult breathing stopped and our dear, dear Daddy left us. We all gave him a goodbye kiss and could not think about our terrible loss; we only saw his relief from the horrible sufferings he had endured during the last year before he died. It was so quiet and peaceful that we had to be grateful rather than upset or angry. The children felt this very strongly as well.'

Kate writes: 'There was an expression of intense, deep peace and serenity on his face. It was the first time that I saw someone die and it was still beautiful.' Wink tells: 'Mom was very brave, and talked us all through it, talked about the meaning of life, and we children wept.'

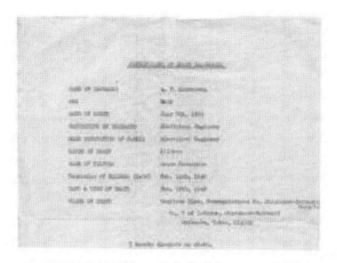

Official declaration of the death of Wim Einthoven made up by a Sumitomo doctor both in Japanese and English on very thin rice paper.

Ineke van der Wal

In the picture on the left page, the middle row is formed by 5 Japanese staff members.

1. Reinier Hasenstab;
2. Alexander Hasenstab;
3. Riek Levenbach;
4. Loukie Einthoven;
5. Wim Einthoven;
6. Beb Einthoven;
7. Jan Leunissen;
8. Annie Lels;
9. Henk Lels;
10. Geo Levenbach;
11. Corry Leunis;
12. Hans Hasenstab;
13. Wink Einthoven;
14. Yamposan;
15. Sumidja;
16. Takesan;
17. Mitsuko;
18. Hyokisan;
19. Paulien Lels;
20. Frits Levenbach;
21. Tineke Einthoven;
22. Marijke Levenbach;
23. Hans Levenbach;
24. Murk Lels.

Missing are Kate Einthoven, Irene Hasenstab and Frieda Kelling.

Ineke van der Wal

CHAPTER VIII

Away from Tokyo

After Wim's passing, Dr. Ikeda's assistant arrives first. He is a pleasant young man who speaks English well, but he cannot do anything anymore. Shortly thereafter a Sumitomo official physician comes to diagnose Wim's death. The Japanese all act in the same formal way: They enter the room, they stop and then stand at attention. They then walk to the bed, make a deep bow, stand upright as if to say a prayer, bow again, and then stiffly take some steps back; only then do they turn to the people in the room and start talking. The entire household staff appears. Hirata comes quickly too, as well as Tanaka. Later in the day several other people from Sumitomo come, some from the lab and some from the department of human affairs. Also an important delegation from the Kempe Tai arrives.

The next day goes by in the same way, albeit not as busy because it is the first day of a major air raid. It starts at a quarter past seven in the morning - a time when they have never had 'keikaikeiho' (planes far away) before - and it lasts until a quarter past five in the afternoon. However, it is not constant 'kushukeiho' (air danger alerts) but they are not allowed to burn coals for heat, they can't cook and there are no trams, so no one comes to visit. Later they hear that a carrier ship has come so close to Tokyo that small aircraft can reach the city. So far they have always been attacked by large planes, but this is a completely different type of aircraft. They always come in waves, all in all there are about 750 aircraft over the city.

Sumitomo asks what Beb wants to do with Wim's body. She knows immediately that Wim should be cremated, so that he does not have to remain in this hostile foreign country. The coffin is supposed to arrive the next day, but because of air raids, it is not delivered until 5 o'clock in the afternoon. It is a simple white wooden coffin made of soft smooth Japanese wood. At first his coffin looks very simple but when they later see other coffins, they realize Wim's one is not so bad. In the coffin they find a mat and pads of rice paper. The Japanese do understand how awkward it will be when Japanese men will place Willem in his coffin, so the Dutch men offer to help. They wrap Wim in a sheet with Beb and Wim's monogram on it and they also put a monogrammed pillow under his head. Then Beb, the four children, and the men from the Lels, Levenbach and Leunis families, place Wim in the coffin. It is placed on trestles in Beb and Wim's bedroom and they cover it with a white silk cloth.

Meanwhile bouquets arrive from all the families in the house, the staff, the lab, and the president of Sumitomo in Tokyo, Dr. Kadju, altogether about ten bouquets. They are all of the same type: a small bamboo table with legs approximately ten centimeters high with two thick bamboo vases attached on top. In the vases are a few newly budding branches of trees, some carnations and a flowering branch without any leaves but beautiful, entirely unfamiliar flowers, that have a dark red square in the center covered with narrow yellow petals.

Mrs. Leunis and the girls make a garland of flowers and add three of Tineke's hair ribbons, one red, one white and one blue, in such a way that they look like the Dutch flag. The coffin stays throughout the night and the next day and all the Japanese from the house come back to pay their respects. Suddenly a photographer arrives and takes three pictures. Afterwards he is allowed to photograph all the families in the garden, but for the Einthoven family it is of course too late; they are not a complete family any more. On February 17, at four o'clock in the afternoon, five cars arrive. The first one will carry the coffin, the other four cars will take the group, who have not been outside the compound for a whole year, to the crematorium. Annie Lels cannot go, she is still too ill; The Hasenstab family is not invited.

The crematorium is a peculiar temple-like building where at least sixty coffins are stacked on top of one another, almost all equally poor and ugly. The coffins are made with planks from crates with the painted signs or addresses of American or foreign factories still on them and they are roughly jammed together with large cracks.

The Dutch group has a Kempe Tai priority and is allowed to place Wim's coffin on a table. All the men and Wink carry the coffin downstairs out of the house and into the crematorium. The Japanese never take flowers with them so all the Japanese bouquets are left at home. However, they do bring the bouquets from the Dutch, and of course the wreath with the red, white and blue ribbons and so their coffin stands out compared to the bare coffins of the Japanese. They ask Beb if she wants a priest, but she refuses. Later on Beb regrets her decision and thinks that 'at least we might have made an acquaintance while we were in captivity'. Henk Lels gives a eulogy in which he speaks very warmly and emotionally; he tells what Wim has meant to him at work, how much he learned from Wim, which could be summarized by the words: 'Good is not good enough.' Beb thanks Henk, and then the four Japanese who had come along (again without their wives) bow formally and that is the end of the ceremony; it lasted less than fifteen minutes. They are given good food and even sakè.

Two days later Beb and Henk Lels, accompanied by Takesan and Tanaka, drive to the crematorium to receive the urn with the ashes. The Japanese made an effort to find a beautiful urn, but it is too fancy, dark blue with a lot of gold, not appropriate for Wim, so Beb asks for a simpler urn and they bring a plain white cylindrical one. Jan Leunis calls it later 'so technical'. The urn comes in a box of beautifully finished oak and is carried in a white silk cloth with a knot on top. Beb stuffs the inside of the box later with padding to make sure that the urn won't break during travel. While they are waiting for the Japanese trying to find another urn, they can observe their surroundings. They see more new caskets, many for small children which are brought to a special counter. They calmly admire the Buddha statue displayed in the center alcove and some bright green vases displayed in two side alcoves. In front of the beautiful antique objects stands a messy table and two kitchen chairs - such an unusual contrast. They are taken to a side building where the 'undertaker' awaits them and in the *tokonoma,* a place of honor, stands the box next to a vase of flowers. The Japanese hand over the box while bowing reverently. Henk carries it to the car, where Beb takes it on her lap. At home, Geo Levenbach and Jan Leunis customize a small table, which came with the funeral, with a neat edge so that the box fits tightly. This way the box has its own place in the bedroom that from now on will be occupied by Tineke and Beb.

A few days later Beb is suddenly called by Hirata and Henk Lels goes with her. Hirata hands her a nicely decorated envelope and tells her in his Japanese way that it comes in the name of Sumitomo and is for 'the honorable spirit of the deceased'. The envelope contains 500 yen, then the equivalent of 500 guilders. Beb asks if she and the children can visit the laboratory where Wim worked; it was at first agreed but then it never happens.

Annie Lels spends a lot of time with Beb these days. The whole group is so crushed. Beb and Annie both feel that Wim died not only from pneumonia, but more because of his inability to adapt to their circumstances. This especially makes a deep impression on them. The idea that he had to relinquish the Radio Laboratory to the Japanese and had to work for them. This was a huge inner struggle: he wanted to sabotage, but he knew he couldn't because he was also responsible for his wife and children. It is the tragedy of men who are unable to maintain control of their lives and ensure the safety of their children. Tineke says later: Beb is a strong woman, also a strong woman next to Wim, she will be able to cope. Perhaps Wim felt 'I can hand the

Ineke van der Wal

responsibility to her, that the family was better off without him, that he was not a good father'. Wink observes: 'What I believe has been the worst of all, is that he could do nothing about the situation. We had to wait. Maybe it was the intent of the Japanese to kill us in order to keep things secret and that we wouldn't learn anything until the very end.'

Tineke asks years later if Beb was scared during her stay in Japan. 'No, not at all,' Beb replied, 'Because it doesn't help and would not have been useful.' Beb was all alone at that time and all scenarios were feasible. Tineke is sometimes afraid of the unknown. 'If I want to do something about my fear, I ask what will happen, what's next but here no one would have responded to a question you posed.' Instead Beb is sometimes angry even though her upbringing taught her not to show her anger but she isn't always successful.

At that time everyone is so nice to Wink because they understand how he misses his father. Every evening he reads English with the Lels family and two evenings in the week he does industrial arts with the Leunis family; Jan Leunis is very handy and he helps Wink with some aircraft models and a drawbridge made out of very light balsa wood. Together they make telescopes from the set of lenses that Wink received at the Saint Nicholas celebrations. Before he died, Wim had taught Wink how to design the telescopes. In Dutch East Indies Wim had earlier shown the planets to the children, Jupiter and Saturn with its beautiful rings and now Wink tries to do it himself. Later, Geo Levenbach in his physics lessons, lets Wink do experiments with the telescope and make some calculations with the results. During the day Wink is busy making briquettes and firing up the furnace. The first three months there is so much distraction that Wink does not despair. Beb writes: 'Wink has enough good memories of his father. With Tineke I just have to emphasize Wim's nice qualities so she also will have good memories of her father. For the girls it will not be easy to forget Wim's unpleasant behavior at the end. That memory has to fade before it can be replaced with good memories.'

The winter is still very cold and on the night of February 23, 1945, they are surprised by 40 cm (16 in) of snow and they wake up in a sheer fairy tale world. The landscape looks enchanting, everything is motionless and still, the sun is shining and the trees are heavily laden with snow. As there is no wind, the snow stays on the branches of the trees. Soon there is a happy group of children outside making snowmen and throwing snowballs. 'We were overjoyed,' writes Kate. The men stay home, because the trams are not in service today. The beautiful pine tree in the garden is covered in snow, but some parts are black from the soot and ash from all the bombings.

The day after Wim's passing they experience the first major bombing of Tokyo starting at 6:30 in the morning and lasting until 5 o'clock in the afternoon. After that the attacks become more frequent, usually at night and the families develop a fixed routine. They are all in bed when they hear the siren for an air raid. At the first alarm, they don't get out of bed because everything is ready in case they have to leave. At the second alarm, they also stay in bed, but the tiny hallway light must be switched off. Then they can open all the curtains and watch the spectacle outside. Tanaka, the Kempe Tai guard, is already up then and fully dressed with his helmet and identity card. The rest of the Japanese staff together with Takesan and the maids are up and wearing their *mompès,* their long baggy pants made of kimono fabric, and their capes with hoods which are thickly padded to protect them from shards falling on their heads. If it gets worse, the families go down to the dining room, and sometimes the children are laid down on the ground while the adults sit on chairs far from the windows. Tanaka always listens to the radio and tells them what is happening. These bombings last about four hours; you're awake, you see and hear the planes, you often see red sky from far away fires and finally after four hours you are allowed to go back to bed. This repeats itself just about every other night. These attacks on Tokyo are due to a change of tactics by the Allies.

Ineke van der Wal

Previously the bombings were carried out against military targets such as refineries, ports and aircraft and rubber factories, with bombs that explode to cause a lot of damage. The new bombings target cities, where much of the war industry is hidden in hundreds of small businesses in residential areas. They are carried out with incendiary fire bombs to create havoc in a city largely built with wooden structures that can be badly damaged by fire. On March 9 there is another attack at night. That night the news at first was 'Too many coming'. That was Tanaka's expression for 'a lot', but it sounded alarming. Soon after he says: '150 coming to Tokyo'. In the distance, they already see a huge fire burning and decide to get up. The fire comes in spurts and when sparks drift down into the garden, the women and children decide to go down into the shelter while the men (including Wink, after having first asked Beb for permission), help by checking outside around the house and immediately putting out any fires that have started. Suddenly a bomb falls into the garden, covered with pieces of sticky, burning material that is difficult to extinguish, but thankfully does not explode. They realize that this is not a regular fire but a large blaze. The fires blow over them and the heat is so fierce that it causes a huge wind. The wooden house behind them is on fire and all the sparks and small pieces of burning wood blow into their garden. They are terrified that their own house will catch fire. The water supply still works and they quickly put out any new fires that start up.

Beside the house is a dead tree covered with ivy and the top of the tree catches fire. There is a bright flash about three meters high (9 feet), which sways with the wind. If the wind changes, the flame could touch the house they are in and then the whole house could burn down. Geo Levenbach organizes a chain of men with buckets, which he throws onto the tree from the balcony on the second floor, and is able to eventually extinguish the fire. Meanwhile, the cook has put a ladder against the tree that's on fire and tries to beat out the fire with a fire whip. It is a somewhat desperate but brave attempt by the cook, who is standing under the fire. Consequently the water that Geo Levenbach throws at the tree and sometimes misses, lands on the cook. The cook is kind enough not to complain that he has been doused by a despised prisoner. They stop the fire in the tree and continue putting out any other small fires.

The women and children are still in the shelter. They see that the whole sky is filled with fireballs and they almost choke on the smoke. They cough and keep their clothes over their faces to breathe through. Then some firemen come from the street and go through their garden to the neighbor's burning house to help extinguish the fire and to ensure that it does not spread. During the last hour, when the fire is so close, the Japanese determine that the shelter is no longer safe and take the women and children to a corner of the yard in front of the garages. Each person carries a suitcase and a hand bag that contains the barest necessities and valuables. Sometimes ash rains down on them, even some glowing embers, which they quickly put out by stepping on them. The garden is completely illuminated by the burning house although it wasn't dark earlier either because of the fires in the distance. Throughout all this activity they hear the roar of aircraft. 'Quite impressive,' writes Beb.

Finally, after four hours, the planes depart and the fires subside. They gather in the main house and Tanaka thanks all the men for their help and is very relieved that it is over. Takesan quickly makes some hot tea and they eat half of their sandwich, which they usually save for the morning, but take with them when there is an alarm. Now they all crawl into bed again, with the promise that they will get breakfast somewhat later together with the men, who cannot go to work because the trams will not run as a result of all the fires.

The next morning they hear wailing outside the gate of the court, along with the sound of carts. It is the screaming of people evacuating the area and it goes on for several days. They discover that the house behind them has burned down and in the garden they find the core of

Ineke van der Wal

a firebomb that sunk into the ground. It is an L-shaped piece of iron with hooks on it. On the hooks hang incendiary devices. Because of the heat the holder swirls around, and the bombs spiral downwards. Fortunately it did not hit anybody, but it sticks out 16 inches above the ground and Henk Lels has hurt himself on it when he was outside during the darkness of the night. Because of his poor health, this tropical ulcer will not heal for years.

The pieces of sticky, burning material which Beb writes about are napalm, a new weapon in the fight against Japan. Invented by a professor of chemistry at Harvard, Louis Fieser. He names his brainchild after the first few letters of the essential ingredients: naphthenate and palmitate. Napalm is first deployed in Sicily in August 1943 against German forces; later it is also used in German cities. However, this is only a prelude to the bombing of Tokyo on March 9, 1945, a hellish inferno later repeated at 64 other Japanese cities. The total death toll among the civilian population is in the millions. As the author sums it up: 'The atomic bomb got the attention, but napalm did the job.' It was, according to an article in Harper's, a military magazine, 'by far the cheapest way to bring Japan to its knees. It would shorten the war by months or even years and save the lives of tens of thousands of American and allied soldiers.' In the battle of the islands in the Pacific it proves to be an effective weapon, along with mobile flamethrowers, to kill the Japanese soldiers who were hiding in tunnels. Although its use is welcomed as confirmation of America's superiority, napalm is also not without controversy. The question is whether the burning of citizens falls within the limits of 'civilized warfare'. (Neer, napalm)

On March 11, 1945 a remarkable opinion piece is published in the *Asahi* newspaper:

'Our capital suffered from damage on an unprecedented scale… an air raid of this terrible sort could well have been prepared for. We cannot deny the fact that our side was completely unprepared and unforgivably ill-equipped for such a contingency. We must give the most serious reflection …..'

Tokyo after the bombardment in the night of March 9/10, 1945. Only concrete buildings remain intact but the inside is devastated. Source: A Torch to the Enemy, Martin Caidin.

Ineke van der Wal

Until now, the national newspaper has never criticized the armed forces or the course of the conquests and this can only mean one thing: the war is not going well. Military leaders have always said that the 'sacred soil of Japan' would never know the impact of enemy bombs. Travel into Tokyo was restricted, for a single look at the ash-choked wasteland was enough to strike the lie to the insistent claims of 'negligible damage'. Nearly seventeen square miles in the heart of the city were burned, and only some concrete buildings are still standing. The authorities do not dare to write about the numbers of the dead, the burned and maimed. They did not write that within twenty-four hours the Japanese knew that at least eighty-four thousand people had died, that possibly another fifty to one hundred thousand also were no longer among the living.   City officials who knew the slum area better than most confided that there was every chance that the final death toll would reach a quarter of a million. People who took shelter in concrete buildings were roasted. People who tried to escape the fire by jumping into rivers were trampled to death by people who jumped on top of them. The water in shallow channels became so hot, that people were cooked. The firestorms that ran through the streets caused tremendous heat and a lack of oxygen that caused people to be cremated alive. All these scenarios took place in less than six hours. (Caidin, pp. 9, 10, 15)

Every Japanese city by the very nature of its flimsy, wooden structures has always been a potential firetrap; thickly populated, weak on water supply and fire-fighting equipment, the cities have often been gutted by unquenchable flames. Every home and building has buckets and an oil drum or bathtub filled with water and the Japanese government believed that was sufficient to put out any fires. The Allies began to set fire to the major cities of Tokyo, Nagoya, Yokohama, Osaka and Kobe. The fire blitz then turned against more than sixty of the smaller Japanese cities. On June 17th, cities with a population ranging from 100,000 to 350,000 went to the top of the target list. In thirty days, twenty three of these cities felt the terrible fire lash of the B-29 Superfortresses. On July 12th, the campaign began against the final group of city targets – those with populations of less than one hundred thousand. The devastation was beyond belief. (Caidin, pp. 152-157)

Three days after the big fire, Tanaka orders all the palm trees in the front yard to be cut down. Their hairy stems prove extremely flammable and the garden has to be made more fireproof. When there are only 3 palms left, Hirahata, the interpreter, comes and is furious because he thinks every palm tree is worth 1000 yen. The Dutch group feels the garden is so beautiful, its beauty gives you comfort, and so no one wants to destroy it. It is the oldest son Reinier Hasenstab, who finally cuts down the palm trees. This way he alienates himself again from the group.

Fourteen days later, the night takes a strange turn. Some unknown Sumitomo Japanese arrive and all the men are convened in the dining room. Wink too is ordered to be present. They don't know what it is about and find it strange that Wink now represents the Einthoven family. In a little while, they all come back looking confused and each carrying an envelope. They listened to a nice speech thanking them for their brave and courageous effort in that fire night and all eight of them receive 50 yen each (at that time by Japanese standards worth 50 guilders) as a reward. Tanaka, the cooks, and Wink too are rewarded. Wink, the only son of Wim and Beb, is so proud to have just earned his own money. Wink was never able to do anything with the money, but this reward has raised his self-esteem. Wink says: 'I was of two minds. We were not supposed to help the enemy, but of course we wanted to help put out the fires. If we didn't help, it would have been worse for us than for the Japanese. And yes, it was money, but what could I do with it? We couldn't go out of the court, but it was a nice ceremony, where we were asked to accept the rewards in the Japanese way with two hands. And so we did.'

On April 9, the men return to Ikuta in cold, inclement weather. There is an even greater lack of tram cars and people are pushed harder into the remaining wagons. Once the pressure in the wagon is so great that someone inside is pushed through a window. They also have to get off at an earlier stop and walk the rest of the way to the laboratory because the tram rails are gone. Although the journey to the laboratory is long and tiring, it's still better than staying at home. Twenty one people packed together all day in two houses in a small closed courtyard, is sometimes very hard on each other. There are problems of boredom, the friction between spouses, disagreement between the families, the distance between adults and children, children who feel that they are 'being babied', the cold, the hopelessness, the feeling of total seclusion, and the feeling of being abandoned. For a Westerner it is impossible to escape because he cannot disguise himself, his white skin and his height betray him right away. And escape where to? The nearest benevolent Westerners are thousands of miles away. Sometimes they have the feeling of being buried alive. When the men go to work, there is distraction, a chance to buy something and also an opportunity to pick up news. This time Geo reads that a new ministry is being formed. It appears that the war is not going as the Japanese thought it would.

As of the arrival in Tokyo, Beb has said that she hoped that she would not celebrate her fiftieth birthday in Japan but it happens on April 13, 1945 in worse circumstances than imagined. The children go out of their way to make something nice for Beb. Loukie builds a beautiful sewing box with all sorts of compartments, so neat and sturdy and practical and so much work. Kate creates a folder for loose papers. Wink builds a shelf that can be placed in front of the window for plants, and Tineke, with Loukie's help, makes a calendar with drawings. All the others work hard too to make something special. Henk Lels gives Beb a nice electric toaster made from extra parts he found in the lab. Jan Leunis used a copper plate, also from the lab, to make a beautiful candlestick to place next to Wim's box. The candle holder is in a special shape based on an instrument Wim had been working on when he was in the lab in Bandung: a double walled spherical tank for storing liquid gases.

The Allies return on the 13th and 15th of April to bomb Tokyo with fire bombs. Fire bombs are less noisy than exploding bombs and soon they begin to recognize the difference. After these bombings the supply of bread stops, because the bakery is burned down. The quality of the bread had deteriorated lately - sawdust was added to it to give it some substance – but Henk's homemade toaster cannot be put to use. Everyone is happy with the bombings: it is finally a sign that something is happening. Beb writes: 'We sit for hours in the shelter, but I see it as a gift for my birthday.' It is unfortunate that Wim cannot experience these bombings. They know that the chance of being hit by such a bomb is real, but their life chances are already slim, so when a bomb hits, at least it will all be over. The bombings have an unpleasant side effect: the food situation quickly deteriorates. They guess that supply lines are probably cut off or the men who work the land are drafted into the army or maybe the black market is no longer functioning. The food that was already without variation and not abundant, is now even simpler and there is less of it. Food supplies they brought from Bandung are now gone, and if the men do not go to work, there is no opportunity to buy anything, provided that they find something. They are and they stay hungry. And not only they, but the Japanese too.

After the war, a journalist writes about Tokyo:

In Tokyo conditions have long been dismal. Rationing is strict and there is little for sale. Only night workers, miners and Navy personnel are permitted to buy vitamins. Health conditions are wretched. All diseases of malnutrition like beri, beri (vitamin B1 deficiency) are rampant, but also tuberculosis, typhoid and malaria are a scourge, probably because of stagnant water in the bomb craters. Almost no one manages to find enough food to use up his ration points. Beef and fish were sometimes obtainable until the end of 1944. Since then people have been eating dog and horse meat. Chickens and eggs are only for children, expectant mothers and hospital patients. There has been no beer or sake since last February. Everybody raises vegetables, even in window boxes or in boxes inside houses or in air-raid trenches. In March 1945 the cabbage ration was one cabbage leaf per person every three days. Children are allowed 370 grams of (cooked) rice per day, adults (above 18 years) get 330 grams, workers get 540 grams and soldiers get 830 grams. By comparison, in peacetime a soldier would have gotten 2000 grams of rice per day. The fuel situation is tight. Last winter Tokyo shivered. Each family is allowed eight 60 lbs sacks of coal or charcoal a year. Cooking gas is limited to seven liters a month, which is too little to cook food and to keep warm. (Time, August 20, 1945)

The shortages undermine the morale of the Japanese population, but the government will have none of it. They believe in their own doctrine that the Japanese spirit will prevail, material things do not signify. The Japanese spirit is pure, ascetic and invincible. Western materialism is gross, overblown and corrupt. The Japanese philosophy is that health follows the will and being ill is a weakness of the spirit and the will.

In May 1945 the United States demand from the Japanese authorities, via the Swiss embassy in Tokyo, to immediately transfer the prisoners of war to safer areas. Sumitomo realizes that it is no longer able to guarantee the safety of the Dutch group and decides to transfer the group to the Ministry of the Interior. In early May, Hirata visits the Dutch group to pass on this message, and he uses the occasion to tell them openly that Holland is truly liberated and adds: 'Don't worry, it will not last long.' The desire to return to their families in The Netherlands is sometimes unbearable.

May 15 is the day of their departure from Tokyo. Upon request, seven trunks are delivered to pack their things because they have acquired some extras like warm clothes, vases, carafes, drinking glasses, toys and other items that take up space, such as the hibachi charcoal warmers. The basket-type suitcases they used were so packed that several of the belts, straps and handles broke. Moreover, these suitcases allow easy access for moths. They have been ordered to bring their blankets and quilts, so they conclude that they will have to sleep on the floor at their next location. When they ask how to transport the blankets and quilts, the interpreter tells them that a little while ago new bags of coal were delivered. They can empty these bags in a pile on the porch and then use them. What strange ways the Japanese have! Anyway, all the quilts are made of silk, so the coal dust does not really stick. They place the cushions and blankets in the middle and use the silk quilts as a protective outside layer. Altogether the Einthoven family has a total of 32 pieces of luggage and the whole group has well over 100 pieces. Beb makes Wink responsible for the urn. As the only son, it's his job to transport the box containing the urn. He carries it by holding the knot of the silk cloth that is wrapped around the box. Sometimes it is too heavy and Henk Lels helps him.

At seven o'clock in the evening they are supposed to leave but they are ready by four o'clock, because with the Japanese you never know whether they will come early or late, but for once they are surprisingly on time. The journey starts with yet another ceremony in which the group is transferred from Sumitomo to the Ministry of the Interior, which places them under the authority of the military. Several of the Sumitomo people come by and they all get tea and little fish. Two soldiers will accompany them; one of the soldiers speaks pretty good English and is not impolite. The baggage goes first and then a bus arrives for the group. In the station it turns out that the train doesn't leave until nine o'clock and they are allowed to wait in the waiting room with proper benches and to their surprise, amongst the public. One of the chefs accompanies them to the station. The maids, Sumidja and Mitsuko, are in tears when the families leave the big house.

There's a whole train wagon reserved for the group, one section for the luggage and one for them to sit in. The train travels through the night and they try as best as possible to sleep on top of the luggage. The next morning the sun rises early, but they are not allowed to open the curtains until a quarter of an hour after sunrise. Shortly thereafter they reach their destination. They have no idea where they are. All the men, including Wink, have to help with unloading and then reloading the luggage on to three large trucks. They group the bedding together in one truck so the group can sit on it. It takes almost two hours before they get started and drive away into the Japanese countryside. It looks poor and full of people, but the natural countryside is quite beautiful,

Ineke van der Wal

and full of variety. Imagine, there are masses of flowering azaleas, tall with lots of pink-lilac blossoms, growing like wild plants along the road.

After about two-and-a-half hours of driving, they know they are near their destination when they hear Japanese youth calling: *Oranda, Oranda* (Holland, Holland). Along the way it had started to rain, but it is dry again when they arrive. They stop at a country road and are told to start unloading. They see a small footpath, about one hundred meters long, surrounded by fields, with a beautiful old entrance gate – Tori in Japanese - at the end on an elevated piece of land. When they walk through the gate, they see a temple. The ends of all the roof tiles of this temple are imprinted with a chrysanthemum, the imperial flower. Inside they see doors made of very fine slats with strange gilded carvings above. These doors shield a large Buddha statue, which they get to see later on. All of this makes evident that a dignified temple has been assigned to them as prison.

Drawing of the temple in the fields outside Nagoya. Taken from the booklet that Beb makes in 1946.

Also in Kotakuji, the village where the temple is located, the guards start with a kind of ceremony. The children are put to bed, because they are so tired after the overnight train trip that they can continue sleeping, but the adults have to listen to a long speech about everything that is not allowed, with emphasis on the rule that it is forbidden to walk more than one hundred meters away from the temple. All this is read to them in Japanese by the Kempe Tai guard and to their surprise it is translated into English by an Italian who was quickly brought to the gathering. He is part of a group of Italians and is housed in a temple a bit further down. During the afternoon, all the Italians, in spite of the rain, appear and introduce themselves. It is a group of fifteen Italians who were imprisoned in Nagoya during the war and have now been living for a month in the Japanese countryside. The only woman of the group, Ms. Topazia Maraini, comes by with her three girls Dacia (nine years old), Yuki (Japanese for snow, and five years old), and Toni (3 years old). Topazia is a very kind, delicate, blond woman that does not look Italian at all but comes from Sicily. She is married to Fosco and they lived in Japan before the war and speak Japanese, like the rest of the group. Edoardo Dentici, the interpreter, was born in Japan and lived there most of his life, and he is more than furious that he has been captured.

The front porch of the temple, the space allotted to them, is only about twenty by forty feet; that is all. Later they get another small room that the Hasenstab family claims for themselves. They soon agree how to divide the space. The Leunis family gets the small extension, the Lels family one side of the front porch and the Levenbach family the other side. The Einthovens get the middle part and Beb sleeps in the middle, with the girls on one side, Wink and Tineke on the other. So, Beb actually lies at the feet of the Buddha.

The mattresses are *tatami mats,* a Japanese floor mat of about 3 by 6 feet, made from thick quilted straw that are full of fleas. After a few nights they become quite sore, their whole body hurts, especially their backs. You have to get used to sleeping on the ground and it does not become any easier because they are so skinny. They no longer have any fat, which can act like padding. Before going to sleep, you try to eliminate as many fleas as possible. If the weather is good, they can sleep outside. There is one hammock that is relatively free of fleas.

Ineke van der Wal

The priest of the Temple, the hōjō, is a nice man and he does his best to learn English. At breakfast they usually enjoy the lilting, never-ending prayer of the priest, accompanied by gongs. He shows them his relics, the typical red lacquered priest's chair, his beautiful robe made of gold brocade quilted with purple thread and the Buddha statue hidden behind the screens. He is responsible for the temple, but to support himself, he is a farmer. After the morning ceremony he dresses up and goes to till the land with his family. The locals, all farmers, are surprised by this invasion of foreigners. The passage of the seasons has for years been the only news here, so everyone wants to know about them.

Tineke fell down the stairs in Tokyo. Her arm hurts, and she cannot use it. Beb wanted to see a doctor but in Tokyo there is no opportunity to visit one because their departure has been announced. Now there is time and it is decided that a guard will take Tineke with him. No other adult may accompany her but after much insistence Paulien is allowed to go. Paulien does not like it but reluctantly agrees out of solidarity. The girls get up early and go with the guide. At six o'clock in the evening they are not yet back and Beb and Annie are so anxious that they do not know what to do with themselves. What can happen with two girls aged seven and eleven in a foreign country, which language they do not speak, accompanied by a guard, they just met? At half past nine they finally come home full of stories about a slice of bread with sugar that they ate. Everyone is so exhausted, that the girls have to wait till the next day before anyone listens to them.

The girls and the guard took a long train ride through several villages before they visit a Chinese doctor who treats Tineke in a Chinese manner with electricity. He will simply hold her wrist and diagnose her with electricity. If Tineke's body is in good order the current will flow but if the body is not in good order, the current will not flow and the doctor is aware of that. The treatment is also performed with electricity. 'I remember this very well' says Tineke 'because the brain works normal but you have no control over your muscles. It was terrible.' Paulien has to wait in a separate room, but it takes so long that she asks whether she can see Tineke. 'How are you?' she asks, but Tineke cannot answer. After the treatment, Tineke can use her arm normally again, so it does help. On the way back, the guard decides to show his unusual detainees to his family and so they get off the train halfway through the journey. After a short walk they are welcomed by a friendly Japanese family and they are treated to a slice of bread with sugar. Perhaps this is the most European treat that the Japanese know or it is the only treat that they can offer their visitors. The girls love it and cannot stop talking about it when they come home.

Now that Sumitomo is no longer responsible for this group of prisoners, they become 'ordinary' prisoners of war, and that means that the representative of the Swedish Red Cross, Mr. Genwell, can visit them, which he does at the end of May. He tells them that the Red Cross knew that they were detained in Tokyo because the Red Cross representation was also located in the same embassy district, but the Japanese authorities never allowed them to visit. The whole embassy district was bombed and destroyed on May 25, so just ten days after their departure.

He cannot do much for them, because there is nothing left, no better housing, no food, no soap, no clothes, nothing whatsoever. The only gift he brings is coffee which they roast and ground themselves and still tastes good even without milk or sugar. He promises them a food parcel, the last the US government has delivered, or rather that has arrived. Japan has refused to forward any more Red Cross parcels and these are now stored somewhere outside of Japan. The Japanese government does not want to deal with the International Red Cross, only with organizations from countries that have remained independent such as Sweden or Switzerland.

Through this representative, they can send a telegram to The Netherlands, but they have to pay for it. The Einthoven family sends a telegram to Gus and Rick Clevering Einthoven in Amsterdam:

'After one year altogether at Tokyo Wim died calmly February fifteenth in 1945 of acute pneumonia in our presence stop cremated stop we five healthy now interned with sixteen others Japan country stop how family and mother stop answer through Red Cross thirty words reply prepaid Beb Einthoven Zeeman.'

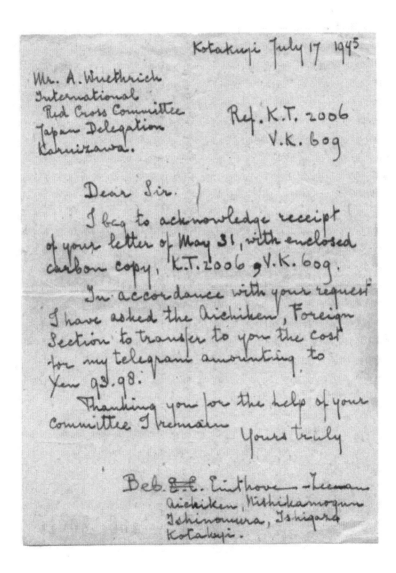

The Red Cross offers to send a telegram to family in The Netherlands. This is very laborious and not for free. The telegram does not arrive.

This telegram never arrives in The Netherlands. The project starts out wrong and that is a precursor for this miscommunication. The Red Cross writes on June 25, 1945, that only then have they received a letter dated May 31.

We beg to acknowledge receipt of your letter of May 31 which reached us only today. We have at once dispatched the therein mentioned telegram to the International Red Cross Committee in Geneva, as evidenced by the enclosed carbon copy. Your share of the cost for the above telegram amounts to Yen 93,98 which amount we shall thank you to pay to this Delegation (delegation in Japan) at your convenience.'

The other families are allowed to send a telegram too, but they don't get an answer either. Beb asks Hirata to pay the cost.

The temple has no running water and no sanitary equipment. There is one well available that only gives water early in the morning for about an hour and has to be used by the priest and his family, the guards and the whole group. After the arrival of the group, this one well is no longer sufficient and the Japanese guard decides that a second well needs to be dug and that the prisoners have to help digging. Wink does not mind, 'then at least you have something to do' and they even receive a little extra food.

The water is not suitable for drinking, so it must be boiled. There are bowls and pots to store the water and they make a stove out of clay fit for a large pot. This way they can make enough water for drinking and cooking, but there is nothing left to wash yourself with. On Saturday, a bath is prepared, it is very primitive but wonderful. There is only one bath and only one supply of hot water, so if you are the last one in line you might not get clean, also because they haven't seen soap for months already, but you have a little respite from the cold. A toilet is also missing at the temple. There is a hole in the ground and that's it.

Ineke van der Wal

The men have made a kind of outhouse from a box on which you can sit and a little deck attached. It is surrounded by a small wall to create some privacy but the guard just comes looking when you are sitting there, very uncomfortable.

In early June the weather changes and the temperature rises and this is good for everybody. Now that all kinds of practical matters are settled, they become more aware of their environment and they realize that they have arrived in an exceptional beautiful place. All the extraordinary features of the Japanese countryside seem united in this valley. 'I have made lots of drawings inside and in front of the temple' writes Beb. If the night is warm and they leave the large sliding doors in the middle open, Beb is able to see the entry gate from her sleeping place.

A drawing from the access gateway to the temple made by Beb and exchanged for food. The drawing still hangs in the temple and has been photographed there during a visit after the war.

This entry gate is a typical small building with a peculiar, tall undulating roof, with two fish on top and a tall tree next to it with a thick trunk that creates a very romantic scene in the moonlight. On the wall outside the ancient symbol, a swastika, is painted, still unaware of the horrible role it will play in history. Mulberry trees and fields extend to the wall of the temple, a little further away are rice-fields with frogs croaking in the night. Behind the temple, where the slope is too steep for rice-fields, is a small forest, with a group of old, twisted, high pine trees along the side, and in the middle are groups of cypresses interspersed by deciduous trees. The wind rustles through the trees and when it has rained, you can smell the cypress trees. There are a few tombstones, some old walls and a gate with a stone arch; a place where they are not allowed to go at first, but later they can walk there and gather lots of big red berries. From there you have a beautiful view of the river, where they can swim occasionally.

On the slopes you will see farmhouses with thatched roofs, connected by paths that meander casually as if no one is in a hurry. It is wonderful to be back in nature and have more freedom of movement. But the best is that they are no longer isolated. There are other Europeans with whom they can talk. They realize only now what all those months of confinement in the small courtyard in Tokyo have meant to them, how bad loneliness and isolation are for human beings.

After a few weeks, they are allowed to walk freely between the two temples; a walk of about ten minutes. It is a pleasure to walk through a field without a guard and with nothing but air and nature around you. The children can also walk freely, which means that they can play with the Italian girls and the Japanese children. They are also assigned a piece of land that they can cultivate but the men have to till it first to remove the roots.

In this part of Japan there are no bombings, no air raids, and no stays in a shelter or fear of fire. They see some bombers occasionally in the distance and they hear some noise but it is all far away above Nagoya.

Ineke van der Wal

They are still hungry, and they are still belittled - Henk Lels has been beaten several times right on his face - but it's easier to supplement their meager food portions and they feel that the allied forces are getting closer.

The Italians are a mixed group with a diplomat, a chemist, silk merchants, an engineer and an anthropologist and none of them are supporters of Mussolini. They were living and working in Japan when the war broke out and they feel much more at home than the Dutch; they do not feel so lost. At the beginning of the war the Italians remained free; the Italians were allies of Germany then. After Italy sided with the Allies, they were first interned in Nagoya and were moved to the countryside about a month ago. They are already acquainted with the surroundings and have made contact with several farmers in the neighborhood. The locals are much more afraid of the Kempe Tai than the European prisoners so they need not fear that the farmers will betray them to the Kempe Tai. The local farmers are actually glad that there are additional workers because so many men are called up for military service. The farmers are friendly and they like to trade because the economy has fallen into a barter economy; Money has no value anymore.

There are no servants in the temple so they have to prepare their own meals. The temple of the Italians is the central place for the food preparation and everyone has to help with chopping wood and carrying water. There is a small fireplace where they make a thin flour soup with an occasional vegetable three times a day. The soup is transported to their own temple in small buckets. There is not enough soup to satisfy their hunger, the soup has no nutritional value and it 'flows straight through you' causing everyone to get stomach aches.

The hunger, they already experienced earlier, begins to totally control their days. Food is on their minds day and night, when they dream, they dream about food, when the children play, food is the basis of their game. They use paint to give bricks the color of food, brown for bread, green for vegetables, red for meat and yellow for fruit and Murk Lels teaches himself how to tell the time. After breakfast he starts to calculate how long it takes before it will be lunchtime. The parents save a little food for the children, no matter how difficult it is, so that the little ones can have something to eat between meals and that is how Murk lives by the clock from meal to in between snack. Fosco Maraini later writes:

> 'The chemist and the engineer put their heads together and calculated that we might perhaps be getting about 800 calories per day. An inactive adult requires at least 2000. The human body reacts by using up its reserves. We all got incredibly thin. On Saturdays, the day of the weekly bath, we amused ourselves by studying each other's skeletons. For all of us hunger had previously been something we had read about in books, in Canto XXXIII of the Inferno, for instance. We had little thought that we should ever become experts in this, one of the most terrible of human ordeals.'

Hunger sometimes manifests itself in the form of pain, sometimes as a feeling of immense emptiness or sometimes as a feeling of extreme weakness. If you take your pulse, you realize that your heart rate is 50 beats per minute, sometimes even less. Life flows slowly out of you. Adults age rapidly and start to see black spots in front of their eyes. Annie writes: 'Yesterday evening the food was two hours later than usual. We did not know how to distract the children. Suddenly Paulien was in a quiet corner in tears. When I asked her what was the matter she said: 'Oh Mommy, I'm so upset that we have so little to eat. I am always hungry and now I'm jittery.' I can't do anything for her! Even though I give her some of my share, it is still far too little.'

They quickly realize that the guards are not very active. There are three Kempe Tai guards assigned to them, but they cannot escape anyhow, so the guards take it easy. As long as the guards don't see what they are doing, they are fine. There are always people on the lookout in case the guards need to be distracted or to invent an excuse if someone is absent. This way, everybody can work to find more food.

Ineke van der Wal

The children collect anything they can find: red currants, wild blackberries, watercress, bamboo shoots, dandelions, sorrel and something resembling wild purslane, which is a type of succulent plant that spreads along the ground and suffocates all other plants. The Japanese are happy when they take the purslane away, and then eat it. Mulberries are not consumed by Japanese, so they gather endless pots with mulberries and as long as they are careful with the plants and the silkworms, the farmers do not mind them picking the mulberries. You can eat the interior of cherry pits too, but they contain hydrocyanic acid; therefore you mustn't eat too many. Henk eats snails from the bushes. Sometimes they grab the offerings that have been placed next to the Buddha. Fosco works for a farmer who wants to plant a vegetable garden. The farmer puts an agreed amount of food outside very early in the morning before the guards wake up. Dacia becomes the benjamin of a family of farmers and she helps them take care of the silkworms. For this she gets a bowl of rice.

The Italians have discovered that Japanese farmers have a shortage of clothes, because the farmers themselves do not sew. Therefore, the farmers gladly exchange food for clothing. First they exchange the children's clothing that have become too small for the children to wear. In Tokyo they once had the opportunity to buy fabric to make larger clothes for the children. From the leftover materials, Loukie sews a neat pair of short trousers with a front fly and pockets, and these are exchanged for no less than 50 *go mamè* – soybeans, a real gain. A *go* is a Japanese measurement, it's about a cup. A *'go'* always concerns cooked rice, often boiled for a long time to increase the volume. Mrs. Maraini makes shirts from sheets. Annie makes shoes and slippers and gets some potatoes and salt in return. Beb draws the temple, the entrance gate and the house of the priest and earns some money that way. Jack Leunis repairs radios and other electrical appliances for the locals.

Not all attempts to get more food are successful. They try to turn inferior material into food, such as straw, which is readily available, but how do you make it edible, how do you get rid of the cellulose? They beat it, knead it, boil it, and roast it, all in secret as if they are making a bomb, but they are unsuccessful. They try acorns, again all kinds of experiments, but it is impossible to get rid of the tannin. After a downpour of rain they discover mushrooms. First they eat only one to test whether they are toxic. They are not, but they work like a laxative if you eat too many.

Wink sometimes helps out in the fields or grinds soybeans, coffee beans or corn. This is done with a small hand-mill made of two large stones on top of each other, each about 40 cm in diameter and 10 cm high with a wooden handle. One day Wink earns a fish for the work he's done for the farmers, but the guard catches him. Wink knows that it is strictly forbidden to work for the farmers, so he claims that he caught the fish with his bare hands in the river. Incredible, of course, but the guard lets him go.

Paulien and Wink capture snakes to eat. Fosco teaches them how to do it. If you see a snake, you pick it up with a stick and drop it on the ground. That way you can see exactly what the front of the snake is and what is the tail. Then you skewer it on the ground with a stick, just behind his head and then beat with a boulder on his head until it is dead. These snakes are a bit slow and neither Paulien nor Wink are ever bitten. You cut the head and tail off and then you skin it with a long stroke (if all goes well) and remove the innards. The snakes are cooked and then you gobble them up. Wink says: " Oh, yeah, that was very nice but it was an awful lot of work; you picked at the little bit of meat for hours and hours and chew on the ribs, but yes, we had plenty of time and therefore we had no objection to a whole lot of work for very little meat.'

Once some Japanese children come to Wink for help, because there is a snake in the attic of one of the farms and they ask him to remove it. Wink succeeds and takes the snake home to cook. Snake tastes like chicken. They always share the meat between the Lels and Einthoven

Ineke van der Wal

families. Even when the snakes are dead, their bodies still squirm and this sometimes causes problems. Wink says:

'I remember one of the snakes I captured; I turned it upside down to cut it and I wanted to skin it, but just then my knife broke. I have another knife at home that I can get and bring here, but what should I do with the snake in the meantime? I decide to tie him into a square knot on to a tree branch. When I return I can just see that the snake has fallen from the tree and he is writhing on the ground. How do I know for sure that it is the headless snake, and not another snake that was nearby? With my stick, I again pick him up and yes, this is the snake without a head, so I can continue to remove the skin. '

Paulien catches a snake one day that twists around her arm. She quickly runs back to the camp and asks for help from the adults. However, the adults are so weak that they are not able to get the snake off her arm. Meanwhile her hand is turning blue. After some anxious moments they manage to loosen the snake.

Kate tells that Wink's knife is very valuable for all of them. One day he loses his knife and so they all invoke St. Anthony: 'Holy St. Anthony, best friend; help Wink find his knife again.' It works, the next day he finds his knife.

Everyone realizes that if they are caught with extra food, it could end badly. But they have gradually become convinced that they will not survive this imprisonment. Perhaps it is also the intention of the Japanese to make that happen. If you accept that fact you become very calm and at the same time extremely brave. That is why the one time that Kate is caught, she is very calm and is waiting for whatever will come, but it turns out quite differently than expected. The Japanese farmer takes her to his house and gives her something to eat. He takes out his dictionary and says in English: 'We will lose this war, which everyone can see. Then the Americans come here. What will they do to us? 'To which Kate says, 'Nothing. They won't do anything to you.'

Well, that was not the right answer. It did not seem to make sense, and therefore it could not be true. The Japanese people are so indoctrinated that they are convinced that when they become the losers, the Americans will murder them. Kate leaves the farmer behind in disbelief.

The period in the temple is a difficult time for Wink. Kate and Loukie have contact with the Italian men and therefore have less time for Wink. Jack Leunis has been secretly working on radios which doesn't leave any time for tinkering nor for reading in the overcrowded temple. Geo Levenbach still teaches chemistry and physics; Annie Lels teaches English and Ms. Maraini gives drawing lessons. Wink doesn't sleep well and feels tired, annoyed and despondent. Beb often walks with Wink to give him some attention and keep the circulation in his legs going. In the beginning they walk in the woods behind the temple, and later they also go to the river, the Johanji. Swimming is good for Wink; in the river there are tiny fish that nibble at your legs. 'I had all these flea bites and they were inflamed. The largest spot was 2 x 2 cm and then the fish took the scabs off.' During this period of time Wink does not have a friend or someone of the same age.

Tineke plays with the Italian girls. 'We are trying to find out if we have the same words. We take a stone and then they say the Italian word for stone and I say the Dutch word for stone. On and on we compare words and then we find out that we both call macaroni 'macaroni'. I come home tell Mom, about macaroni. Of course, says Beb, it is an Italian word that we use in the Dutch language, and I am deeply disappointed.' Tineke also plays with the daughter of the Hōjō, jumping in the sanctuary, only a few rice paper doors down from the sermon with gongs and prayers. Beb makes up math problems for Tineke. The Japanese children are a bit more advanced in their math skills than Tineke. Japanese children cannot read the letters, but they can read the numbers. So, Tineke runs to the Japanese children and they do the sums for her. It takes a long time before Beb realizes what is happening but eventually figures it out and Tineke has to stay until her work is completed.

Kate's first boyfriend is in the Italian camp and has a beautiful name - Bruno Giordani - and has the face of a hero tenor in a colorful Italian opera. He is very handy and has many ways to get food and often shares it with Kate. She then donates it for the general pot for the five of them. Nothing can happen because the women haven't menstruated for many months.

In the temple Beb really has to keep the family together. She tells the children to keep faith and not to give up. You have to keep busy, if you remain idle, dark thoughts take the upper hand and you end up in deep despair and you resign yourself to death. Unanswered questions linger in your mind: what will the Japanese do with us when they lose? Will they leave us to starve? When will this misery be over? How long can I keep this up? Will the children have permanent damage from this period of starvation especially now that they should be growing?

With malnourishment, comes deterioration of the mind. You cannot remember names, you cannot do complicated math problems, you cannot reason, you cannot make conversation. One more reason to stay busy and continue to exercise the brain. You sleep poorly, you're hungry, you're in a bad mood and you get angry and you argue about everything under the sun. For example, Annie Lels tells that the Leunis family, who have no children of their own, do not want to save any food for the children, which causes friction. The families have agreed that each family takes a turn at scraping out the buckets of flour soup. One day they discover that Mrs. Leunis scrapes out the buckets before she passes it on. 'It was hell being prisoners together. When you later heard about the solidarity in women's camps in Java, you were jealous.' The members of this small group reveal their true nature in countless ways, and there is very little of themselves that they can hide from each other.

Birthdays are always celebrated and everybody does their best to do something special. For instance, for Villa's birthday, one of the Italians, they have a picnic in the woods. They feast on a banquet! Mysteriously, they are able to gather all kinds of food: sweet potato, mixed salad, peanuts and tea. Everything is prepared almost under the eyes of the guards. Yuki Maraini's sixth birthday is celebrated in the same way. On July 17, Wim would have turned 52. As a distraction Annie suggests to go to the river with the children. This is of course strictly forbidden, but they do more things that are forbidden. However, it rains that day and they are not able to go. On a rainy day it is even more difficult to be stuck inside with 16 people. Fortunately, they receive news that this summer a raid is expected on the main island. A few days ago, the headline in the paper was: *The curtain opens for the decisive battle for the main island.* The allies gave the Japanese an ultimatum on July 26: either surrender now or the country will be totally destroyed.

At gatherings, such as birthdays, there is an opportunity to talk with the Italians about the Japanese. You don't understand them; the Japanese are so different and they remain total strangers to the Dutch. In Japan, the empire is the most important of all, elevated above all people. You have to give everything for Japan, everything for the emperor; the individual is of secondary importance. Honor is the highest virtue. In everything you do you must aim to preserve honor for yourself, for your family and for Japan. A Japanese will not surrender, because then his honor is besmirched. He will fight to the bitter end or he will commit suicide. The instruction to the Japanese is, 'Don't let the shame of becoming a prisoner of war come over you as long as you are alive.' On the islands that the Americans conquer, Japanese commit mass suicide by jumping into the sea from the rocks, just because they do not want to fall into enemy hands. In Japanese philosophy, prisoners of war don't exist and they are despised because they surrendered and did not abide by the social code. Prisoners of war

Ineke van der Wal

belong to a very low social class and these people don't deserve any care.

They noticed that Fosco was missing part of his little finger and that it was always bandaged. He explains why. In the social pecking order there is an extra low place for the Italian prisoners of war, who were originally allies of the Germans and later became allies of the Americans. This was the reason the Japanese treated the Italians extra badly during their captivity in Nagoya. Fosco Maraini managed to change this situation by chopping off his finger. He stages a tantrum and chops off his finger with a large knife while the Japanese are watching. Through this deed he earns the respect of the Japanese and then their conditions improve. For the Dutch, this is unnatural, but this group of Italians understands some of the morals and customs of Japan; they know who they are up against and have a good sense of the situations in which they can talk back and do so cool headedly and with incredible success. Geo says:

'I feel a huge responsibility to my family and after the death of Wim for the whole group. The families have come along as hostages for the fathers and that creates extra pressure. You just could not die, you had to survive. Fosco, and all his knowledge of Japan and the Japanese, is a gift to us, the best help we can get in those last difficult months.'

Beb keeps telling herself, that the Japanese must have some good qualities because she often sees examples of refined architecture around her. Drawing the temple gives her an opportunity to create her own beautiful world, if only for a moment and to be away from the hitting and the screaming. Japanese people are not nice to each other either; they beat each other as well and yell at each other. They see this as a form of discipline.

The Italians all speak Japanese and so have access to news. They set up an efficient but dangerous system to 'borrow' the newspaper from the guards. They take the newspaper before the guards wake up or during the time that the guards wash themselves and the office is empty. For a little while they even have their own newspaper because 'Baron' Sato, a sad individual, who lives with his sister and nephew in an outbuilding of their temple, was persuaded by them to pass his newspaper on to the prisoners. Mr. Sato has been disowned by his family and his noble title is taken away from him, but his family still pays for things like a newspaper subscription. The family is not able to properly take care of themselves and Mr. Sato dies in July. After that the Italians again have to find the news secretly.

Jack Leunis earns food by making a radio for the brother of the priest. Jack draws parts and the brother buys these parts on the black market. That's how they gradually build a radio. The brother, Watanabe, lives with his family in an annex of the temple, because he and his family were bombarded out of Nagoya, where he owned a laundry. This brother is so nice that he alerts the Italians when news is being broadcast. One of the Italians crawls under the building and there he can listen to the news, which of course he shares with the Dutch. It is clear that the war is not going well for the Japanese, but the Japanese do not surrender and persevere to the end. How long will it still take, they wonder? Everyone realizes that they will not survive the winter in these circumstances.

In early August, it is terribly hot and it is decided to give the children vacation from their lessons. Everybody is hanging around, but they become excited when they hear a report on the seventh of August about the bombing of Hiroshima. The newspapers are not able to give a clear explanation of the event but from the description, it is readily apparent that Hiroshima was hit by a very powerful bomb. Leone, the Italian diplomat, predicts that the Russians will now declare war on Japan and that the war will be over soon. He is right: on the 9th of August Russia invades Manchuria and now Japan is also at war with the Russians. One day later the second special bomb is dropped on Nagasaki but it remains unclear what has actually happened. On August 10, Japan starts negotiations with the Allies to surrender,

Ineke van der Wal

although they continue to talk on the radio about 'One Hundred Years of Opposition'.

The vice-minister of war in Tokyo instructed the commanding general, the Kempe Tai and all POW camp commanders in the occupied territories and home islands that all prisoners should be executed if the Americans land in Japan. In any case it is the aim not to allow the escape of a single one, to annihilate them all, and not to leave any traces. No prisoners – or civilian internees – were to be retrieved by the enemy. However, one of the conditions set by General MacArthur before accepting a surrender, is that the Emperor should command the Japanese commanders not to harm the prisoners. (Goetz, p. 118)

On August 15, Villa, one of the Italian engineers, comes to tell them that Emperor Hirohito will give a speech over the radio at noon. It is the first time in the history of Japan that such an event will take place and everyone is excited about it. 'Maybe he will tell us that we must fight to the death,' says one of the guards, but it is clear that he only declares this to make a good impression.

Then something remarkable happens. The Emperor reads his speech but neither the Japanese nor the Italians understand what he says. The speech is written in 'noble language' that is so different from the normal spoken language, that you need to be a linguist to understand its meaning. The result is that the guards order everyone to stay at the temple until there is more clarity. That comes when the newspaper appears with the speech written in understandable Japanese:

To our good and loyal subjects: After pondering deeply the general trends of the world and the actual conditions pertaining in our empire today, we have decided to effect a settlement of the present situation by resorting to an extraordinary measure. We have ordered our government to communicate to the Governments of the United States, Great Britain, China and the Soviet Union that our empire accepts the provisions of their joint declaration.

To strive for the common prosperity and happiness of all nations as well as the security and well-being of our subjects is the solemn obligation which has been handed down by our imperial ancestors and which we keep close to our heart. Indeed, we declared war on America and Britain out of our sincere desire to ensure Japan's self-preservation and the stabilization of East Asia, it being far from our thought either to infringe upon the sovereignty of other nations or to embark upon territorial aggrandizement. But now the war has lasted for nearly four years. Despite the best that has been done by everyone — the gallant fighting of our military and naval forces, the diligence and assiduity of our servants of the State and the devoted service of our 100,000,000 people — the war situation has developed not necessarily to Japan's advantage, while the general trends of the world have all turned against her interest. Moreover, the enemy has begun to employ a new and most cruel bomb, the power of which to do damage is, indeed incalculable, taking the toll of many innocent lives. Should we continue to fight, it would not only result in an ultimate collapse and obliteration of the Japanese nation, but also it would lead to the total extinction of human civilization. Such being the case, how are we to save the millions of our subjects, or to atone ourselves before the hallowed spirits of our imperial ancestors? This is the reason why we have ordered the acceptance of the provisions of the joint declaration of the powers. We cannot but express the deepest sense of regret to our allied nations of East Asia, who have consistently cooperated with the Empire toward the emancipation of East Asia. The thought of those officers and men as well as others who have fallen in the fields of battle, those who died at their posts of duty, or those who met death, and all their bereaved families, pains our heart night and day. The welfare of the wounded and the war sufferers and of those who lost their homes and livelihoods is the object of our profound solicitude. The hardships and sufferings to which our nation is to be subjected hereafter will certainly be great. We are keenly aware of the innermost feelings of all of you, our subjects. However, it is according to the dictates of time and fate that we have resolved to pave the way for a grand peace for all the generations to come by enduring the unendurable and the suffering that is insufferable. Having been able to save and maintain the structure of the Imperial State, we are always with you, our good and loyal

Ineke van der Wal

subjects, relying upon your sincerity and integrity. Beware most strictly of any outbursts of emotion that may engender needless complications, of any fraternal contention and strife that may create confusion, that lead you astray and cause you to lose the confidence of the world. Let the entire nation continue as one family from generation to generation, ever firm in its faith of the survivability of its divine land and mindful of its heavy burden of responsibilities, and the long road before it. Unite your total strength to be devoted to the construction of the future. Cultivate the ways of rectitude, nobility of spirit and work with resolution so that you may enhance the innate glory of the Imperial State and keep pace with the progress of the world.'

Japan surrendered to the Allies. Topazia Maraini hastens to the temple and says *'Senso Owari,* the war is over - the war is over.' The next morning, the Italians walk to the guards and start shouting in Japanese that they want to talk to them. Something you could not do a day before. The guard comes out, and the Italians shout that the emperor of Japan surrendered to the allies.

The allies are now the highest authorities and the allies in this community are the Italians and the Dutch, so the guards are to regard them as the boss. In Japanese philosophy it is apparently all very logical because the Japanese guard doesn't shoot, but wants to discuss this matter with his superior. Moments later, he comes out and says that it's okay and asks what they want. As far as the Westerners are concerned this is a completely improbable event, but the Italians know that the Japanese thinking is black and white. If the emperor says that Japan has lost, then the allies are the winners and the changing of the hierarchy is effective immediate.

What do they want? First, more food and especially better food. That is possible. They want more freedom, they want to see the area and they want to go to Nagoya, the only major city in the area. Well, their enthusiasm is boundless. They decide that night to organize a party, where the poor baby goat that Corrie Leunis 'found' becomes a victim.

They have received additional food from the guards and the farmers around them. The priest donates 'purple rice' which is only eaten on special occasions. In the camp of the Italians they sit around the rough wooden table outside in the moonlight with a small lamp in the most diverse clothing, young and old together. This morning, the Italian priest has ordered a mass for all casualties of the war, and Benci and Collessi sing. At night after dinner the two chant. It is wonderful to hear all these musical voices.

It is not only joy. Some people experience a backlash after the Japanese surrender. They keep up appearances, but after the liberation they collapse. They had made peace with the fact that they would die but then suddenly the war is over. At that time they cannot cope with the situation. The transition from death to living again, is more difficult than the other way around. After so many years of bad and insufficient food, the stomach is unable to digest more and better food.

Paulien is very feverish and Beb is so ill that she doesn't come out of the hammock. The wife of the brother of the priest takes pity on her and for a few days feeds her little bits of food with a teaspoon. Meanwhile she talks to Beb as you would talk to a sick baby, in Japanese, very sweet and with a tone of voice that seems like you fully understand what she says. This way she keeps Beb among the living.
About a week after the surrender the Italians tell that they have heard on the radio that the allies will drop food from planes for all the prisoners. On the mountain behind the temple is an open area where they place the letters PW and 36 (21 Dutch and 15 Italians) using long strips of fabric so that it is visible from the air. On August 26, the representative of the Swedish Red Cross comes and he confirms that there will indeed be allied food drops. Everyone wants to hear what else is going to happen, but he does not know. No Americans have landed yet on the Japanese mainland and they are still negotiating the terms of the Japanese surrender. A thorny issue here is a list of the prisoner-of-war camps that the Japanese have to provide. Japan has

never reported during the war how many camps exist and where they are located.

Meanwhile, a group of Italians went to Nagoya with a Japanese guard. The city is completely destroyed, nothing but ruins, here and there a fragment of a house or a building, but a wing of the Kanko Hotel has been spared for some strange reason. There are some cracked windows and destroyed plaster but there are real beds, a sofa and armchairs and running cold water. They all agree that they want to go there. The Lels family leaves right away, while the others decide to wait for the food droppings.

They wait a whole day but nothing happens. They wait a second day, again nothing. The men take turns, each waiting an hour on top of the mountain, ready to call the others if a plane appears. On the 29th, on a gray, overcast afternoon they see a big plane that flies low over the mountains. It looks like it touches the treetops and is flying very slowly. They call the others and Beb comes with Dutch flags, she had sewn into the hem of various coats and now dares to show again. Beb knew all along that the flags were in the seams and Wim knew as well. When Wim died, she did not want to burden anyone with this knowledge. 'But if something happens to me, no one will know anymore.'

The end of the war also ends this concern. When everyone is on the hill, the plane is no longer visible. They've already given up hope when it reappears, they wave the flags like crazy. The aircraft continues to fly around the mountaintop and sometimes disappears from sight. Then it flies twice very low over the PW letters and they can observe it very well. It is a huge plane with four engines, a 'B29 Superfortress' they are told later. When the plane flies over the hill for the third time, the doors in the body of the plane open and what looks like a lot of small parcels tied to small parachutes slowly float down towards them. When the packets come closer, they see that these are steel oil drums more than three feet tall, with wooden lids. Not all the parachutes open and some drums come sailing down very quickly. They flee from the mountain top and get out of the way while they hear the drums crashing to the ground.

The plane flies around once more to make sure that their work is done and then flies away. When they dare to look again, they cannot believe their eyes. The mountains and the woods are full of drums with everything inside you can imagine: a whole supermarket is spread before them. They see a tree, which is completely covered with shoes, it seems like a weird kind of fruit growing on the branches. In the dry bed of a small stream are cigarettes, Lucky Strike, Camel, Philip Morris, hundreds of packets. There is a big red stain on the mountain which is a tree on which a drum with cans of tomato juice has fallen. The wooden lid is cracked and several of the cans are damaged. If you stand under the tree in the right place and open your mouth, the tomato juice drips into your mouth. The children find chocolate bars and dance around, crazy with happiness.

They do not know where to begin: do you stop and take a can of pineapple and open it, or do you first go and gather up some of the food and enjoy it later? Since it will be dark soon, they decide to set up a chain brigade to transport as much as they can off the mountain. The Japanese help and they behave themselves; nothing is stolen. That night they all eat until their bellies are full. They surround themselves with cans of every conceivable content, meat, fruit, fish, salad and sweets. They open them up, eat the contents in random order, after which they start on the next can. This evening they will not be hungry when they go to bed. However, you have to be careful not to overeat. Inside the drums are pamphlets, that warn you about overeating, but for the last few days they have been getting more food already, so no one becomes seriously ill. Wink finds cans of flea powder, which he spreads on his tatami mat. That night he can sleep without being disturbed by the fleas. Kate puts on some shoes so she finally can take off the 'camp boot' - a wooden board with a strap nailed over it.

Ineke van der Wal

The next morning they find a severely damaged drum in a pine grove. It turns out that the drum is filled with condensed milk, sugar and packets of chocolate powder. The drum is wedged into the ground and only the smaller children are able to get inside to extract the contents. Wink says: 'I eventually discovered that there was a whole pool of chocolate milk on the bottom of the drum. I had not had breakfast yet and I licked up the chocolate milk like a cat.'

The view from a B-29 plane at the moment of the food airdrop. The parachutes are visible. These prisoners of war have laid down a beautiful text. Source: Daws, Prisoners or the Japanese.

They take inventory of the goods and realize that they are really well taken care of. There is not only food, but also soap, vitamins, medicines, bandages, socks and clothes, beautiful suits, raincoats, and shirts. After months of starvation, counting grains and storing a single sweet potato for a special occasion, they have arrived in the land of Cockaigne. The liberation begins with the secure feeling that they will have enough to eat in the coming weeks. They not only see the fabulous wealth of the Americans, but also their desire to share it with them. Everyone is impressed.

On August 30, nearly all the Italians and the Dutch are transported to the Kanko Hotel in Nagoya. Only Fosco and Geo stay behind to pack up the supplies. Everything is evenly distributed and each family receives a parachute filled with supplies. The drums are packed for 100 persons. Because this group consists of only 36 people, everything is in triplicate. The farmers in the vicinity of the temples and the hōjō-families, can also benefit from this abundance.

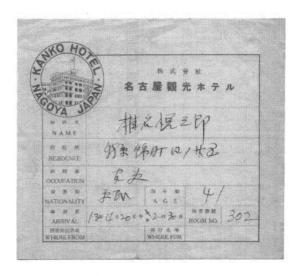

At the Kanko Hotel Beb receives a telegram of condolences from a friend. The friend is sorry for Beb's loss of Wim so now the news has become public knowledge. This is the first contact with other Dutch people, since their transport to Japan. She sends back a telegram and invites him to lunch at the hotel.

On August 31 all Dutch people lunch in the Kanko Hotel to celebrate the birthday of Queen Wilhelmina of The Netherlands. It's a very special Queen's Day. They send her a telegram as well.

Ineke van der Wal

CHAPTER IX

Going Home

On September 2, the Japanese sign their unconditional surrender aboard the American battleship USS Missouri in Tokyo Bay. The ceremony has been postponed for two days because of typhoons circling around Japan. General MacArthur and Admiral Nimitz sign on behalf of the United States and the Minister of Foreign Affairs, Mamoru Shigemitsu, and Commander-in-Chief of the Imperial Army Staff, General Yashijiro Umezu sign for Japan. Finally, representatives for China, the United Kingdom, Russia, Australia, Canada, France, The Netherlands and New Zealand also sign the document. The war is over. General MacArthur goes ashore and decides to set up his headquarters in Tokyo, at the Imperial Hotel that was designed by the American architect Frank Lloyd Wright. President Truman declares September 2 as VJ Day and says on the radio: 'This is a victory of more than arms alone. This is a victory of liberty over tyranny.'

For the fanatical nationalist Japan, the final clause of the surrender agreement represents the essence of defeat: 'The authority of the Emperor and the Japanese Government to rule the state shall be subject to the Supreme Commander for the Allied Powers who will take such steps as he deems proper to carry out the terms of surrender.' This is the first time in 2000 years that this proud country has been defeated and occupied, and to make matters even more humiliating: Japan has been defeated from the air combined with blockades without even one allied soldier setting foot on the land.

According to the conditions of surrender, Emperor Hirohito can stay on as emperor and he will not be charged as a war criminal, but Prime Minister Suziki steps down. The new Prime Minister, Prince Naruhiko Higashi-Kuni, demands discipline and order from the Japanese people in a radio speech on August 16th and that speech achieves its goal as the Japanese turn like a leaf on a tree, and sadistic rulers suddenly become servile servants. There is no protest anywhere, and not one American is killed after the surrender. The Americans call this change of attitude a 'flip flop'.

The Japanese population suffered greatly during this eight-year war. On the Japanese main island 44 cities have been razed, over two million houses have been destroyed and more than nine million people have no roof over their heads. There is a huge food shortage, only 40% of the necessary amount of food is available. Despite the conquest of Korea, Malaysia, Formosa and Indonesia - all four food-exporting countries - Japan was unable to feed its own population this past winter, let alone their prisoners of war. There is no penicillin available, only sulfa drugs, but only one of these, mainly known for its effect on intestinal infections, is available.

The Americans take on the task of removing all former prisoners of war - 32,000 in total, consisting of American, British, Australian and Dutch citizens - from Japan as quickly as possible. The RAPWI (*Recovery of Allied Prisoners of War and Internees*) has been given the responsibility and in order to speed up this exodus, as much transport as possible will take place by plane. The American Navy and Air Force are used for this purpose and at Manila in the Philippines an army camp is set up as a transit camp for evacuees.

On September 3, the Swedish ambassador visits the Kanko Hotel in Nagoya. He instructs army commander Helfrich to get all Dutch people to go to Java as soon as possible, as they are very much in demand there, especially the technicians. The next morning there will be a train that will take the group to the coast. This all goes against their plans - they prefer to enjoy the peace and to get some rest - but this order has to be obeyed, so they quickly pack their belongings until 2 o'clock in the morning. They have not unpacked much, but all the items from the food drop, the cans, the clothes and the parachutes - made from fine material - have to be packed. Many helping hands tie ropes, put names on the bundles, and together they keep up their spirits.

At 9 o'clock the next morning they say goodbye to the Italians, whose help was so crucial, and then cars come to take them to the station. There is a whole train car ready for them and their luggage. They arrive at 1PM in Hamamatsu where there are many more white people on the platform. They look the same as the Dutch group: all terribly thin, with faces like masks of stretched, gray skin, their eyes deep in their sockets and walking slowly. These people did not receive Red Cross packages either and also slept on tatami mats with fleas. The American soldiers are pretty enthusiastic because they have just been told that their salary is being paid from the beginning of their imprisonment.

Here the small Dutch group realizes how special their situation is. All the other former prisoners are men who have left their families behind. You see no women and no children, which is why the few Dutch children are now showered with treats and attention everywhere. The American press hounds them: Families with women and children who also speak English, it does not stop. Geo Levenbach later describes them as '*American Press Mosquitoes*' (like today's Papparazzi).

After half an hour a flotilla of landing boats, which were used to make landings during the war, enters the harbor with American flags gaily waving on the masts. They are fairly small boats with very high sides and front that can hold one tank. The front of the boat is lowered

VOOR DEZE DRIE KLEINE NEDERLANDERS VAN JAVA is het leven weer zoet, nu ze, bevrijd uit het Japansche interneerings- kamp in Nagoya, van de Ameri- kanen het eerste lekkers sedert jaren hebben gekregen, waarvan zij met ernstige gezichtjes ge- nieten.

This picture of Hans and Marijke Levenbach and Murk Lels appeared in the Dutch newspaper *Het Parool* on 26 September 1945. 'For the three little Java Dutch, life is sweet again. They are freed from the Japanese internment camp. In Nagoya, the Americans gave them their first treats in years, which they enjoy with serious faces'.

Ineke van der Wal

completely and forms a kind of gangplank, so the tank drives on and off by itself. Beb writes:

> *'Our group goes on a boat and is waved off by the Japanese Police, who has guided us nicely up to now. This way we sail away from that beautiful country with its cursed people, where we have lived through such a very, very difficult time.'*

First, they leave the long harbor, actually a sea-inlet between very low land. Then they pass under a large railway bridge, and suddenly they are out in the open sea, with many American warships. They are taken to one of the nine white hospital ships, the *Rescue,* where they are welcomed by kind nurses.

The men are separated from the women and they first undergo a thorough cleaning process: a hot shower followed by spraying with DDT to get rid of any lice. Kate says: 'The shower was so wonderful. It was the first time in a year and a half that I got soap and could wash myself so thoroughly.' All their clothes are completely sanitized, but all the men's clothes are burned, which is disappointing because they were new American suits from the food drop.

But that is how the Americans behave, being overly generous because immediately everyone gets new clothes again. They did not expect to have women and children on board, so the ladies each get a dress from the nurses and for the children something is quickly gathered together. Medical care is also provided. Wink's legs are cleaned and covered with dressings. A doctor removes Kate's dead skin from a tropical ulcer with a sharp instrument that resembles a spoon. On board they sleep in real, clean beds, which they enjoy very much. In the morning the staff brings them food in bed on a neat little table that fits exactly on the bed. It all is an amusing experience.

The next day, the doctor declares that they are healthy enough to continue traveling. The seriously ill are being kept on the hospital ship, but they have had better food for some time now and they feel so free and so happy that everyone wants to continue on and the doctors take this into account.

In the middle of the night they are informed that they will be transferred early the next morning to a destroyer, again using landing

boats. They are taken to the destroyer USS. *Lardner*, named after a US civil war admiral. The whole crew is going wild. Women and children on board, that has never happened before! They are surrounded and pampered, only the seasickness sometimes causes small interruptions.

They are put in the officers' huts and are allowed to use the pantry where they finish the entire supply of cheese in a short time. Great food, sandwiches thick with butter, and anything else they ask for. Kate writes: 'Stuffed with goodies, I become as sick as a dog. All the cute sailors come with goodies. Do I want to have this, or that? And I was so sick. There is a black sailor who arrives with toast. That works better for me. He is the only one I take something from.' The crew shows them the whole ship; they love to keep the children busy as much as possible. They see radar in action there for the first time and hear more about the special bombs that were dropped in early August and about which the Japanese newspapers gave inaccurate news. Hiroshima was

Ineke van der Wal

hit by a parachute bomb, nicknamed 'little boy', with a head of uranium 235. Nagasaki is hit by 'fat man' with a head of plutonium 239. They are called atomic bombs.

The Lardner sails them to the bay of Tokyo. They are still together and their luggage - a hundred pieces - mysteriously also came along. It is a glorious day. All along you can see the coast of Japan with the soft silhouette of the Fuji as it appears in thousands of prints. You are surrounded by people that are happy and the sea is wide open as far as you can see. The whole bay is full of American ships with waving stars and stripes; a colossal and impressive sight. The sailors proudly point out the USS Missouri, the battleship on which the peace treaty was signed and chosen because Missouri is the state where President Truman was born.

The port of Yokohama is the next stop. You don't see any Japanese, only Americans. The group waves from the quay to all friendly faces on board of the slow moving Lardner. Then somebody sighs and says: 'I would like to sit down now' and right away, a jeep full of folding chairs is driven up and quickly they are having a pleasant picnic on the waterfront. 'Maybe they will bring us ice cream too' they laugh at each other and, then indeed, ice cream does arrive, large servings in neat cardboard cups. That is how the American troops live.

A few hours later dinner is set out for them. After dinner camp beds are set up so that the children and those people who are very tired can get some rest while they wait for trucks to take them to *Atsugi*, the Tokyo airport. The road between the port and the airport still has to be cleared with bulldozers; they will soon be the first to ride over it.

On board another ship they are allowed to quickly go to the toilet and this causes a big commotion, because the whole crew – only men of course – is scarcely dressed. When it is completely dark four trucks appear, two for the luggage and two for the passengers. They see how badly Yokohama has been bombed with bomb craters everywhere, that are now used as living space. Occasionally you see fires where people huddle around. Strangely enough, there are still buildings standing close to the road, but further away in the distance nothing is left for miles at end. Atsugi is quickly put into operation and is being used extensively. At about midnight, the air traffic is so busy that they see 19 aircraft land within ten minutes. It is a fantastic vision of the future with all those shiny aircraft lined up in a row and with jeeps scurrying between them, plus rattling trucks and a search light that scans the sky and illuminates a layer of clouds.

Long tables are set up in a large Red Cross hall, where everyone can take whatever they need. Soap, coffee, towels, all kind of cans, goodies, toothpaste, toothbrushes, combs, washcloths, notebooks, pencils, etc, etc. As much as you want, for free. Imagine such a land of plenty. It is really fantastic, it seems like a dream.

They stay for about an hour and then they go with trucks to a beautiful DC4 plane. The most modern transport plane in existence, with wonderful soft seats and reclining backrests that turn into comfortable sleeping places. The seats even have soft headrests and the children fall asleep immediately. For many it is the first time they have ever flown and then in such a beautiful plane. They watch the lights disappear quickly, go to sleep, and sleep soundly after such a triumphant liberation. When they wake up they see a beautiful sunrise over the clouds and then soon Okinawa, *the large string island*. The large string island is the literal translation of Okinawa and they used this name among themselves so that the Japanese would not understand what they were talking about.

Early in the morning they arrive and are immediately taken by truck to a few tents where the evacuees register. Papers have to be filled out and they get real American breakfast with hot coffee, cold Coca-Cola and lots of donuts, á kind of non-greasy dutch 'oliebol'. They can eat as much as they like and they eat a lot, because it is the abundance that is so wonderful. In Okinawa they stay only one night before traveling

Ineke van der Wal

on to Manila, but Okinawa leaves a very special impression with them.

A whole new road network was created by the Americans on Okinawa and that is how they drive past many bomb craters to the camps, where there are clean cabins with wooden floors, each capable of housing ten people. Beb writes: 'We have seen Okinawa and again we think we are dreaming. In two months' time, the Americans have set up a camp in an enormously vast area. It is beautiful and clean! Several airstrips. Magnificent! Beautiful roads, just created. No one can withstand such an organization. It makes you feel that you are far better than the Japanese.'

Nice nurses take care of them, another great shower and the best food. No matter how they try, they cannot eat everything, it is too much. You cannot control the tendency to save something after so many months of hunger, but of course it is not necessary. In the afternoon they come with ice-cream bowls for everyone and if you want you can have a second one. There is powder, rouge, lipstick and eyebrow pencils and they organize a movie night, their first in years and it is all wonderful and happy and nice - an abundance of goodwill. The film is about the life of George Gershwin, but none of the children know who he is. Then Beb realizes how devoid they have been of news and how much the children will have to learn to get up to date again. The only thing that reminds them of war is the harbor full of warships and the paper they had to sign that they will never give out details about this.

Wink is immediately taken to a doctor, who puts new bandages on his legs. He tells the doctor that he is assigned to the women's camp and then it is quickly decided that he belongs with the men and he is assigned to his own private barrack. When he gets to the men's camp, the American soldiers want to hear what happened to him. Wink also asks about their experiences, but they've heard each other's experiences many times before so Wink, being the newcomer, has to tell his story. He hardly sleeps. It is wonderful, yes, way too much fun

R E S T R I C T E D

GENERAL HEADQUARTERS
UNITED STATES ARMY FORCES, PACIFIC

APO 500
15 July 1945

CIRCULAR)
:
: NO....28)

PUBLICITY IN CONNECTION WITH ESCAPED, LIBERATED, OR REPATRIATED
PRISONERS OF WAR, TO INCLUDE EVADERS OF CAPTURE IN ENEMY OR ENEMY
OCCUPIED TERRITORY AND INTERNEES IN NEUTRAL COUNTRIES

1. Publication or communication to any unauthorized persons of experiences of escape, release, or evasion from enemy or enemy-occupied territory,
activities or equipment in connection therewith, internment in a neutral
country, or release from internment, furnishes useful information to the
enemy, jeopardizes future escapes, evasions and releases, and under Army
Regulations, must not be disclosed to anyone except to military officials
specifically designated.

2. a. Personnel who have evaded, escaped, or have been released from
LIBERATED AREAS may relate stories of their experiences, after clearance
with Public Relations Officer, this headquarters, or War Department Bureau
of Public Relations, but no reference may be made to:
(1) Existence of unannounced organizations established to
assist evaders, escapers or to methods employed by the organization.
(2) Names, pictures, or any other means of identification of
helpers of escapers or evaders.
(3) Treacherous actions of Allied Prisoners of War or evaders.
(4) Sabotage activities of Allied Prisoners of War whether
escaped or detained.
(5) Briefings and equipment for evasion and escape, and other
intelligence activities within the camps which constitute intelligence
information.
b. All other personnel will not publish in any form whatever, or
communicate either directly or indirectly to the press, radio, or any
unauthorized person any account of escape, release, or evasion of capture
from enemy or enemy-occupied territory or internment in a neutral country
before or after repatriation, unless authorized by the Assistant Chief of
Staff, G-2, WDGS.

3. Subject personnel shall not be interrogated on the circumstances
of their experiences in escape, evasion, release or internment, except by
authorized intelligence agencies. In allied or neutral countries, American
Military Attaches are authorized to interrogate on escape, evasion, release
and internment matters.

4. Requests for the services of subject personnel, deemed necessary
for lecturing and briefing, will be cleared by the Chief of Counter-
Intelligence, this headquarters.

- 1 -

R E S T R I C T E D

The American armed forces control information that becomes public
concerning the stay in Japan and particularly information concerning
escapes or attempts to this end.

Ineke van der Wal

Early the next morning they continue their journey after a delicious breakfast with coffee and donuts and after being signed out at the evacuees' tent. This time a less luxurious plane - a DC3 - takes them to Manila. Again, the Americans are surprised by the presence of children and do their utmost to please them. Tineke can come into the cockpit; she is allowed to sit in the co-pilot's seat and she may even steer the plane. In Manila it is pouring rain and they cannot land right away, but the arrival is cheerful anyway because of all the friendly faces around them. Of course again coffee and donuts and as a surprise a cheerful 'brass band'. *'Oh, that American kindness. Never, never, will we forget how we have been received by them everywhere.'*

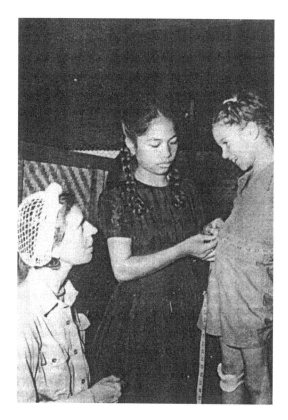

Beb and Tineke on the Philippines. Clothing for Tineke has to be made because nobody reckoned with women and children as prisoners of war in Japan. Beb wears military clothing.

At the airport a truck takes them to the Manila-camp. They are the first to be taken care of because women and children have priority. Right away they get a medical checkup. Winks legs have not improved enough. The doctor decides to do something new and gives Wink three penicillin injections hoping he will get better faster. That does help rapidly. Wink has not grown as much as he should have - he is not even five feet tall at age 15 - and the doctors are a bit concerned about that. They do not know what to do about it or whether it's okay to do anything about it.

Several members of the group receive a ticket with instructions that they can eat something small every hour; that way their body can slowly get used to eating again. You see food, but you get sick of it, you do not want to touch it. In the beginning they get a biscuit from a large strong soldier once an hour; later on they are given small portions of fruit and vegetables and so on. The canteens in the camp are open 24 hours a day because there are many people on this diet. Tineke follows her own diet: she only drinks milk. Beb is worried, but the doctor thinks that she will know what's good for her and she can always ask for a milkshake. In short, a very pleasant doctor. Tineke gets interested in solid food after a long period of only milk. It looks as though her intestines seem to have skipped a period: from children's food to survival food. There has been no time to develop a normal intestinal flora.

In Manila they stay three weeks; it's a busy time. Next to the women's camp is a men's camp that gradually fills with Dutch people. These men would like to receive news about their families who have stayed behind in the Dutch East Indies. They cling to you to hear if you know something. The last two weeks they have a visit every day from a bunch of Dutchmen. Beb writes:

The men find female company after all these years so pleasant that some come to us almost every evening and not especially for the girls, but just to be part of the group. We really do not have a minute's rest, but it's fun.'

Ineke van der Wal

They answer questions from reporters, they meet all kinds of important people, Dutch and Americans. Annie writes:

'Yesterday we were picked up by a car from the Dutch consulate in Manila, to drink tea and eat dinner with Mr. Hendrik Bos. There is so much to talk about during such a visit'

Besides the wonderful care and concern, every evacuee is given more clothing: four dresses, a pair of khaki pants with a shirt, two sets of underwear, a pair of shoes, a coat and a 'ditty bag'. The ditty bag is a cotton bag with a Red Cross sign on it and the text: 'Convalescent kit' with, according to Beb, 'a truly delightful collection of all sorts of trifles, which you so terribly miss during the war years: a nice piece of soap, a new toothbrush and toothpaste, a razor, a comb, a detective novel, writing paper and a pencil, some sweets, mostly chocolate, and not to be forgotten, chewing gum.' Beb has to get used to the habit of chewing gum. 'We heard a soldiers' orchestra, mainly brass, so the horn players could not possibly chew gum, but the pianist chewed gum from start to finish.'

The barracks in the camp are for fourteen people and are neatly arranged in rows of five or eight next to each other; they have turned into entire streets. On the side are the latrines, long buildings with a bench, on which 26 people can do their 'business' at the same time with small screens between the seats. There are also bathhouses, first a long bin with 24 taps and then a corridor with lots of shower stalls. There is a funny lack of embarrassment and it is understandable that men cannot come in. It can rain very hard here and then it is quite a trip through the mud to get to the showers. That is especially annoying at night, because:

'After all these wondrous war diets I cannot go a whole night without a trip to the bathroom. We have big round bellies, and sometimes we even look so pregnant that we might deliver at any time; then it is suddenly gone for a few days. You never can tell.'

Tineke and Beb sleep with the other families in one barrack. Loukie and Kate are with Corrie Leunis in another barrack. The older girls like to be independent and there are too many to sleep together in one barrack. The dining room for more than a thousand people is outside the fence and there they see each other again, in the midst of all the nurses and Red Cross workers. The food is delicious: breakfast with fruits, often an egg, milk for the children (made of milk powder, because almost everything comes from America), something hot at lunch and a warm dinner. There is always fruit juice to drink, with tea or coffee or hot chocolate. Next to the dining room is the cafeteria, which is open 24 hours a day where you can get Coca-Cola, tomato or grapefruit juices and beer, packages of cookies, cans of nuts, cigarettes and some daily necessities, morning, afternoon and evening, and it is all free, imagine that! Even late at night they can go there to drink something because with the heat everybody needs a lot of liquids, and the tap water is unsafe to drink.

Not to be forgotten is the view over the bay, the famous *Manila Bay*. They are so far from Manila, that they can't see any signs of the destruction, but if you were familiar with the city from a past visit, you would of course miss seeing many high buildings. The city is beautifully illuminated and the ships in the bay are all lit up at night too. It is truly unique and on many days they enjoy sitting on the beach with guests from the men's camp and talking endlessly. Unfortunately, the stories they share with each other are often sad.

There is also a Red Cross reading room in the camp, where they spend many hours. There are newspapers, American magazines and also Dutch magazines such as *Oranje (Orange)* and *Vrij Nederland (Liberated Netherlands)*. There are also three books entitled *Je Maintiendrai (I will not give up, the motto in the Dutch national crest)* about the first, second and third years of the war, with all sorts of information so that they can learn something about all those years of occupation and oppression.

Brief I

Manilla 14 September 1945

Brief I

Lieve Moeder, Gus, Wies, Rik en Arnold.
Zijn jullie er nog allemaal en allen goed en gezond na deze lange moeilijke jaren? Ons rijtje is geschonden, voorgoed. Wim stierf, 15 Febr. '45 aan acute pneumonia en uit gebrek aan dokterszorg. Wij zaten toen al bijna een jaar met de heele familie en nog 4 andere families in Tokyo gevangen; we hadden het daar volgens Japansche begrippen goed, maar én de geestelijke zorg én het toch zeer schrale rantsoen hadden Wim dusdanig verslapt, dat alle weerstand verdwenen was en hij na een ziekte van slechts 6½ dag van ons heenging, heel rustig, volkomen buiten bewustzijn, zonder iets te beseffen, dat we allen bij hem waren, zonder van iemand afscheid te hebben genomen of iets te hebben geregeld. Hij had zich dat jaar heel erg ongelukkig gevoeld, weg van zijn werk, en het is goed dat hem die laatste oorlogsmaanden, die voor ons veel erger gebrek brachten, dan we ooit in Tokyo hadden, bespaard zijn gebleven. Naar Tokyo waren wij geforceerd gevoerd, opdat de mannen der werken konden, maar dat werk beteekende niets, ook al kregen ze er salaris voor en woonden we in een net huis met een aardige tuin, maar gevangen waren we daar toch. In Mei werd het in Tokyo zoo gevaarlijk dat ze ons naar buiten brachten, in een Buddhistische tempel, 1½ uur rijden van Nagoya, waar we met ons zestienen, mannen, vrouwen en kinderen in één ruimte, huisden en sliepen, alles op den grond, zooals Jappen gewoonte. En bar slecht voedsel, wat meelpap 's morgens, wat meelpap aan de lunch en wat meelpap voor het avondeten. Binnen 3 maanden hadden alle ouderen dan ook beri-beri en Wink had de echte kampziekte van wonden, die niet overgingen. Maar toen kwam goddenk op eens het eind. En nu zijn we geëvacueerd door de Amerikanen, en worden door hen in hun reuzenkampen opgekweekt en verzorgd op zoo'n royale manier, dat de kinderen zienderoogen opzwellen en nu al volkomen zijn bijgegeten. Met ons ouderen gaat het niet zoo vlug omdat bij ons het leed niet alleen lichamelijk heeft ingevreten en al de droeve berichten, die we nu moeten inhalen én over Holland én over Indië ons iederen dag weer voor oogen brengen hoe vreeselijk deze oorlog toch is geweest en hoevelen wij moeten missen bij het verdergaan –
Ik dacht met de kinders naar Indië te gaan; Wim en ik hadden samen al eens besproken dat het wederopvatten van schoolwerkzaamheden voor ons viertal daar waarschijnlijk makkelijker zou zijn dan in Holland. Want daar zijn de scholen toch nog altdoor doorgegaan, terwijl in Indië na de capitulatie geen enkele school meer voor Europeesche kinderen geopend is geweest, we moesten alles thuis doen, in groepjes en ongemerkt. Na deze prachtorganisatie hier gezien te hebben en al die jonge soldaten en sailors en nurses gesproken te hebben, denken we nu voor de meisjes ook over Amerika. Maar Wink, Tineke en ik gaan zeker naar Bandoeng. Bereikt deze brief jullie vlug, schrijf dan naar het adres op de envelop, anders naar Hoofdbureau P.T.T. Bandoeng, Java. O, wat verlang ik naar bericht het was zoo eenzaam. Dag lieverds allemaal

Beb.

Het adres op de envelop is
Women's Replacement
and disposition center
A P. O 354
Manilla Philip. Isles

The first letter which Beb's mother receives from Beb at the end of September 1945. The mother copies this letter on her typewriter with 5 carbon copies. This way she can distribute the copies to everybody longing for news.

When they read about The Netherlands, the need for news about the family becomes even stronger. The first letter from Beb that arrives in The Netherlands, is addressed to her mother and all members of the Einthoven family. It is dated September 14, 1945 and is sent from the *Women's Replacement and Disposition Center* in Manila, Philippines. Beb gives a rough overview of what happened, describes the death of Wim - 'Our family is incomplete, permanently' - and she indicates that she wants to return to the Dutch East Indies as soon as possible. She concludes with: 'Oh, how I long for a message, it was so lonely.'

Beb's mother re-types the letter with carbon copy paper between the pages so that anyone who craves news can be informed. Beb's mother already knows that Wim did not survive the war. Gus and Wies visit Beb's mother on September 10 and tell her that they read in *Het Vrije Volk (The Free People)* that Beb and her four children have been liberated from a Japanese camp and all five are healthy, but that Wim has died.

> *'(September 8, 1945, Het Vrije Volk) Dutch people are free! In the Japanese village of Aria, 21 Dutch nationals and about 300 British have been liberated after a long period of imprisonment since the fall of Hong Kong and Java. Among the Dutch are Ms. Elisabeth Einthoven from Bandung with her four children. She said that her husband had died from beriberi in Tokyo. Ms. Einthoven first wants to return to Java and then travel to The Netherlands. Furthermore, Mr. and Mrs. H. Lels were freed with two children, Paulien and Murk. Mrs. Lels said that she had been transferred from Java to Japan in a convoy, four of the ships that escorted them were torpedoed along the way by American submarines. The Japanese feared the American submarines more than anything else in the world. The twelve Dutch children, who were liberated, were dressed in home-made clothes. They were happy and danced hand in hand around their liberators, who gave them treats. (United Press)'*

Beb's mother writes in her diary: 'Poor, poor Beb, so young and already a widow, just like her mother.' At the beginning of October, the families place an advertisement in the newspaper: 'We are saddened by the death of our only brother and son-in-law Willem Frederik Einthoven who died in Tokyo on February 15, 1945 while interned'.

Klaas Dijkstra, the author of the book *Radio Malabar*, also learns about the passing. He writes:

> *When I heard of Mr. Einthoven's death, I had to stand still and couldn't utter a word. The highly skilled radio technician, whom I would like to consider to be the second radio pioneer of the Dutch East Indies after the late De Groot (the first pioneer), and by whose side I had worked for many*

years, was no longer alive and, like so many others, had not survived the occupation. His wish to immediately start rebuilding after the capitulation of Japan would therefore not be fulfilled. Just like the late De Groot, Mr. Einthoven passed away far too soon. He only worked for fifteen years at the Dutch East Indies Radio Service, but much has been achieved in this short span of time.'

Beb's letter to her mother is answered on the 23rd of September by a telegram from the family: all are alive and healthy. This is the beginning of an intensive correspondence between mother and daughter, which lasts until August 1946, when the families are reunited. Beb describes for her mother and Wim's family all the events from the time that there was no contact, from May 10, 1940 to mid-September 1945. Her mother writes back about her experiences and tells about many, many family members, friends and acquaintances. Beb replies to her mother on September 24. 'We are well, our health improves every day, our only desire now is to get information on what will happen, but that too will come. We now want to move forward, we can already get back to work, there is such chaos in the Dutch East Indies; so much work has to be done. Write back to Bandung, Head Office PTT.'

In the camp all kinds of things are organized to make it as pleasant as possible for the evacuees. They visit a devastated Manila, where the concrete skeletons of buildings lean over the road and the totally ruined Spanish old town. They make a trip to caves and an old Spanish church, where to their surprise they find Flemish nuns, who have been stuck there throughout the war and are happy to speak their own language again. Then they drive to a beautiful lake with a volcano in the middle of it. Classical concerts are organized and so are performances by Deanne Durbin and Gracie Fields.

They also visit the island Corregidor. It played a major role in the attack by the Japanese. They sail for two hours across the water between the many American ships. The only drawback is that all their transport always goes by truck, and as they are still very skinny and have no padding on their behinds the rides are not always appreciated. Every evening there is a free film performance in the dining room. Such performances always start with a preview about the war under the title 'Lest we forget', followed by a modern American film. In the beginning they were able to enjoy this, but now they are becoming more critical again, 'civilized life also has its drawbacks'. The children speak reasonable English thanks to the lessons of their parents and translate during the film for other children, because luckily they have all made new acquaintances. Wink asks his sisters after the film to explain the part he did not fully understand. There is also dancing. Wink says: 'The children have a large degree of freedom, which they are not quite used to. The Japanese authority is gone, but the parental authority is also gone for a while.'

The Manila camp is intended as a transit camp and the Americans want to transfer the families to the Dutch authorities. Beb wants nothing more than to go to Java, but because of the unrest there this is not possible. It is decided that they will go to Camp Columbia in Brisbane, Australia, a Dutch camp. This is the camp where during the war the Dutch lived, who fled the Dutch East Indies before the surrender to the Japanese and where now the civil servants and soldiers ready to re-establish Dutch authority in the Dutch East Indies are waiting.

'We hoped that we could wait in Manila for news about our luggage. It travelled from Yokohama to Okinawa on the plane, but then disappeared without a trace', Beb writes. While they were interned by the Japanese the families always kept their possessions with them and so everything always came along. The Americans constantly insisted that they should not carry anything themselves, and that is why even all the backpacks and the violin in its case were transported separately in a cargo plane, and now everything is gone:

The linen with our monogram, the drawings I made in and near the temple and of the houses in Tokyo, the candlestick made of material from the laboratory, all the sweet gifts we made for each other on birthdays and holidays, the little book with Dickens' stories, the photos taken in Tokyo after Wim's death, all Wim's personal belongings, the generous donations from the food drops, it is all gone. The box with Wim's ashes that Wink and I kept was saved, and I also have my sewing kit because it is always in my handbag.'

The luggage was probably lost during a typhoon. They have to fear that they will not find anything in Bandung either. 'After all the stories about the riots in Java, I fear that our belongings in Bandung are completely gone. You can buy a lot of things again, but Father's portrait, which was drawn by Grips, paintings by grandfather, the films and the photographs of the children, what a loss.'

They receive an official order in General MacArthur's name that on September 25, 1945, their entire group will travel to Brisbane, in Queensland, Australia and that there is a plane at their disposal. There is no other option but to follow this order.

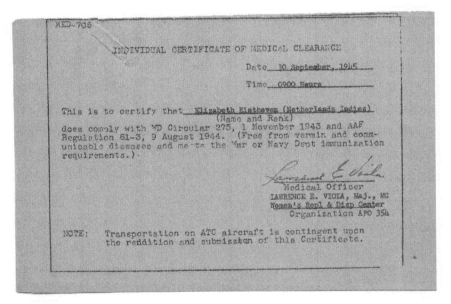

The medical clearance necessary to enter Australia. They are free from vermin, contagious diseases and they have been vaccinated.

Ineke van der Wal

GENERAL HEADQUARTERS
UNITED STATES ARMY FORCES, PACIFIC   3831
                                            AGPO

AG 370.5 AGPO   APO 500
                                            25 Sep 1945

SUBJECT: Invitational Travel Order.

TO   : Individuals concerned.

    1. Following-named Netherlands Indies Government personnel are hereby authorized and invited to proceed by air transportation from Manila to Brisbane, Queensland, Australia.

Alexander Hasenstab	Reinier G Hasenstab
George J Levenbach	Hans N Hasenstab
Hendrik Lals	Frieda E Kelling
Jack Leunis	Frits Levenbach
Cornelia Leunis	Hendrika J Levenbach
Katy E Einthoven	Marijke M Levenbach
Louise J Einthoven	Hans Levenbach
Elizabeth Einthoven	Annie Lals
Tineke N Einthoven	Murk Lals
William C Einthoven	Paulina Lals
Irene A Hasenstab	

    2. Travel by military or naval aircraft is directed as necessary for the accomplishment of an emergency war mission. Transportation Corps will furnish necessary transportation. Travel expenses are to be borne by the individual.

    3. Baggage to accompany the individuals will be marked with the owner's full name and will be limited to sixty-five (65) pounds.

    4. Prior to departure from this headquarters, each individual will require physical inspection as prescribed by Section III, USAFFE Circular No 26, 1945.

    5. Expenses incident to this travel chargeable to Netherlands East Indies, Government.

    By command of General MacARTHUR:

                                     J. H. LOWELL
                                     Lt Col   AGD
                                     Asst Adj Gen

DISTRIBUTION:
  Individuals concerned (10 each)
  G-4 (1)
  AG Adv Ech (1)
  AG Rear Ech (1)
  Dir AG Div AGO (1)
  Dir Control Br (2)
  AG Records (22)

With this document, the American armed forces transfer the group to the Dutch authorities in Australia. The group is then still together.

Everyone must first be declared healthy. On September 30, 1945, 0900 hours they receive a *'Certificate of medical clearance. Free from vermin and communicable diseases and meets the War or Navy Depot immunization requirements. Transportation with* ATC *aircraft is now possible.'*

Also a *promissory note* must be signed, that 'I, Elizabeth Einthoven promise to pay on demand to the government of Netherlands East Indies in the currency of the realm, the cost of my repatriation, and that of members listed below (the four children are mentioned here). It is understood that the cost per person by water transportation from the Philippine Islands to the Port of Debarkation in Australia shall not exceed the equivalent of $275.00.' Beb wonders how she will repay all these cost, but she decides to worry about that later. On September 30, at 3 o'clock, two trucks arrive. They have all bought a suitcase again, you can buy them in the PX (camp store) and every evacuee was given a duffle bag. The new baggage will go with them in the trucks and then to the Nicholsfield airport, where they arrived a few weeks ago.

A new chapter starts: Australia. The month of September has flown by, the evacuation by the Americans was so overwhelming and generous that they feel blessed again and again. What strikes them constantly is that the American soldiers are so comfortable with each other. They show great mutual goodwill, much nicer than the Dutch or Australians.

After an hour in the waiting room the plane arrives. It is a C54, a four-engine aircraft with long sideways seats, which are not nearly as pleasant as the adjustable seats of the DC4. The plane taxis briefly and climbs very quickly. You then get a brief view of the seas, bays, land and colorful lakes below you, but soon there are white cotton wool clouds and you see nothing more of mother earth. The sunset above the clouds is fantastic, for ten minutes it is like the clearest glow of the Alps as far as you can see, then it gets dark and it all fades away. A steward distributes nice boxes with dinner: large sandwiches with some

—COPY—

PROMISSORY NOTE

1. *ELIZABETH EINTHOVEN* .... of
...*DUTCH*.......... nationality, promise to pay on demand to the government of *NETHERLANDEAST INDIES*
in the currency of the realm, the cost of my repatriation, and that of below listed members of my family. It is under-
stood that the cost per person by water transportation from the Philippine Islands to the Port of Debarkation in the
AUSTRALIA
United States shall not exceed the equivalent of $275.00.

Members of Family	Age
1. *KATY E EINTHOVEN (DAUGH)*	*19*
2. *LOUISE J EINTHOVEN (DAUGH)*	*12*
3. *WILLIAM C EINTHOVEN (SON)*	*19*
4. *TINEKE M EINTHOVEN (DAUGH)*	*7*
5.	
6.	
7.	

E. C. Einthoven
Signed

(To be prepared in quadruplicate. One copy to individual
concerned. Original and 3 copies to EF. OHQ, AFPAC)

The IOU, which Beb signs to pay for the transport from the
Philippines to Australia for the children and herself. The Dutch
government wants to receive payment for everything.

savory on it, some fruit, a paper cup, and a wooden spoon. Large
thermos flasks with hot coffee are passed around and they get sugar as
well. Then everyone puts on his coat and wraps himself in blankets,
because it becomes quite cool. You read a book or nod off for a while.
Soon the plane starts to dance, however, and poor Beb and Tineke

The Temple with the Chrysanthemums

become air sick. They sit still, close to each other for the rest of the trip till they land at Biak north of New Guinea at about 1 o'clock in the morning. There is no American canteen in the arrivals hall, nothing to buy and only hard benches to sit on or stretch out on. At first, nobody knows what has to happen; then, at about three o'clock some cars pick them up and drive them over this surprising coral island to a warehouse where they quickly set up some camp beds.

Biak is beautiful, its nature is overwhelming. Again, Wink immediately has contact with soldiers who want to hear what has happened to him. That night they show Wink the three airfields of Biak using the headlights of a jeep to illuminate the aircraft. All planes that the Americans can no longer use have been taken there and they are packed so closely together that, at two of the airports, no more planes can land. Furthermore, the jungle is slowly starting to overrun the planes. One of the soldiers has been carrying a letter for two weeks. He received it from a wounded Dutch person whom he met in a hospital. Wink can finally translate the letter into English for him.

They have to sleep in their clothes because they are woken up at half past six. After a lavishly improvised breakfast they go back to the airport to wait and wait while young airmen entertain them to pass the time. By chance they meet the son of one of Beb's friends. He gives Beb several school books and a notebook with excerpts. Just when he wants to show her his camp, they are called to board the plane. The next island they see is New Guinea and then finally Australia. They land at eight PM, nine o'clock local time. The checks take an hour, so it is ten o'clock before they are outside, where they have to find their own bus. It is clear that they are no longer in American hands. Camp Columbia is their final destination, a camp run by NIWOE which stands for *Netherlands Indies Welfare Organization of Evacuees*. The bus drives for half an hour and then they search for a long time where they are supposed to go. A woman corporal takes them to a dining room where they enjoy a nice sandwich with cheese. Barracks are assigned

Ineke van der Wal

to them and at 1AM they sleep like logs until nine the next morning. They almost miss breakfast.

Camp Columbia is huge. It is more than an hour's walk from one end to the other. It used to be an American army camp which the Dutch government bought and modernized to accommodate the Dutch East Indies government together with Dutch citizens during the Japanese occupation of Dutch East Indies. The camp consists of houses made of wood in the shape of a bungalow with three rooms off a hallway and a bathroom with shower, a sink and a toilet. There is electric light and running hot and cold water, so what more could they wish for after all the primitive camp conditions that they experienced during imprisonment.

Drawing of the cabin in Camp Columbia by Beb Einthoven-Zeeman.

The Einthoven family has two rooms, Kate and Loukie sleep in the front room where there is also a small seating area; Wink, Tineke and Beb have the middle room and then there are two ladies, an Australian and an Indonesian in the third room. They also have an electric heater, because nights and days vary in temperature here. All the cottages are detached from each other at a distance of more than twenty meters, in an Australian forest of *gumtrees*:

> *(...) narrow, bare trees, that do not lose their leaves, but in the summer they lose their bark, so that the trunk reminds them of a newly-sheared sheep. A*

large part of this country looks like this, not necessarily ugly but rather boring. The land is never flat but gradually undulating, high and low. Very little grows in our forest, but it is nicely quiet, which is greatly appreciated after the extremely busy Manila camp. Being together again is wonderful, although Wim's open space is now more obvious. In a dining room for a thousand people, just one is scarcely missed.'

You get plenty of food here. The camp is divided up into 20 parts and each area has its own dining room, in their case at the top of a rather steep slope. At first they were served by the local 'djongos' (Indonesian servants), but because of the trouble with the indigenous people, this has changed, now there are Australian girls. If you want something in between meals, and that is what ex-prisoners still want, you have to take care of that yourself. You take a sandwich or an apple from the dining room or you can buy something from the PX. There you can buy a package of cookies, lemonade, ice creams, some household items, a sewing kit, powder and make-up. Every evacuee aged 17 and over are given 250 guilders, the youngsters receive 180 guilders. After a lot of walking, photographing, visits to the police, the consul and the rationing board, interspersed with long periods of waiting, they finally receive their distribution cards and additional clothing coupons. 'And then comes the wonderful moment that you can choose something yourself and buy it.' writes Beb.

The camp is opposite a station from which you can take a train to Brisbane. The trip takes half an hour. Brisbane is a big city which has not seen war, so everything is normal and functions well. Kate writes:

'In Brisbane we did not feel at home at first. It is all so fancy and luxurious, all ladies are always well dressed, they are even overdressed, but the men are mostly just gentleman farmers. We drink tea in the city, there are very large tearooms and we gradually get used to it. You see Australian houses from the train on the way in. Australians live in detached bungalows, in the middle of a private garden, usually having an abundance of flowers.'

ABCDEFGHIJKLMNOPQRSTUVWXYZ

REGISTRATIEKAART KRIJGSGEVANGENEN EN GEÏNTERNEERDEN

Blokletters a.v.p.
NAAM _EINTHOVEN — ZEEMAN_   NICA
VOORNAMEN _ELIZABETH_   Registratie
ADRES _C.C._   No.
LAATSTE WOON-ADRES: _KROMHOUT WEG 2 — BNG_
Landaard: _NED_ Geboren te: _DELFT_ dd. _13-4-95_ Godsdienst: _—_
Beroep: _BOUWK. IR_
Werkgever: _LYCEUM BNG Emad. '41 - '42_
Rang: _—_   Stamboeknummer: _—_
In militairen dienst sedert: _—_   Sgt. (2e kl.) sedert
~~Ongehuwd~~ Gehuwd ~~Gescheiden Weduwnaar Weduwe~~ (het niet toepasselijke doorhalen)
Naam en voornamen (~~vroegere~~) echtgenoot(e): _WILLEM FREDERIK_
~~Zijn, haar~~ laatst bekend adres:
Voornamen, geboortedata en laatstbekende adressen kinderen: _KATY_   _14-6-26_
     LOUISE   _23-3-28_
     WILLEM   _C.C._   _20-1-30_
     TINEKE   _31-10-37_
Van wanneer laatste gegevens over gezinsleden: _SAMEN GEÏNTERNEERD_
Familiebetrekking aan wie(n) bij ongeval of overlijden kennis dient te worden gegeven:
1. Naam en voorletters: _A. CLEVERING_ Graad van verwantschap _SCHOONZUSTER_
Adres: _BALLE I PLS. S B ATDAM EINTHOVEN_
2. Naam en voorletters: _____ Graad van verwantschap
Adres:
Laatstgenoten salaris (c.q. van echtgenoot): _f 950.— ± toelage_
Indien geïnterneerd geweest, waar en voor welke perioden? _ADA '43 — JAN. '44_
BNG JAN '44 — SEPT '45 JAPAN
Genoten onderwijs (diploma's en scholen vermelden): _HBS TH DELFT B.I_

AANGETROFFEN TE: _HAMA MATSU_   dd. _4-9-45_
Verstrekte kleeding: _2 SHIRTS 2 SLIPS 2 JURKEN 1 JAS_
1 PR SCHOENEN 2 STEL ONDERGOED 2 KINDER
W.2 _2 SHIRTS 2 BROEKEN 1 OVERALL 1 JURKEN 1_ Roode Kruis pakket: _3_
Maandelijksch voorschot: _OVER ALLS 1 TRUITJES 1 PR SCHOENEN_
Afgeschreven wegens vertrek naar/overlijden:
Opgenomen in hospitaal:
Handteekening of afdruk rechterduim van den geregistreerde:
Gesteld te _C.C._ dd. _9-20-45_   _E. C. Einthoven_
in tegenwoordigheid van: _[handtekening]_ _Zee_

GEZONDHEIDSTOESTAND (door officier van gezondheid in te vullen): a. gezondheidscertifica
verstrekt dd. _____ b. geschikt tot werken _ja_ ; _____ uren per dag; soo
    neen
werk _____ c. op te nemen in herstellingsoord _ja_ d. komt in aanme
    neen
       spoed
king voor evacuatie naar het buitenland, _ja_ e. op te nemen in hospitaal geen spoed
    neen   neen
       dd.

Bijzonderheden: _gehuwd te Manilla_

(Handteekening Officier van Gezondheid)

N.I.C.—1643/3.45.

X GALILEÏ PLANTSOEN

2) OMBERGOED

Registration card of Camp Columbia with detailed information about
the received clothing.

Beb is not impressed by the architecture and speaks of 'wooden monstrosities'. They are lucky and have good weather. In Japan they had two seasons of Spring, now in the southern hemisphere they find yet another Spring. Some streets have trees that are blooming with pink and red blossoms.

The family is in Australia now and will stay there for the time being, because at the moment women and children are more often taken away from Java rather than sent there. What has happened in Indonesia in the meantime and why can the families not return to their former lives?

The British forces are responsible for the liberation of the Dutch East Indies under the direction of Lord Mountbatten. However, they give preference to the British colonies and the SEAC (*South East Asia Command*) is mockingly called *Save England's Ancient Colonies*. This policy means that there is a period of several weeks between the Japanese capitulation and the arrival of the British troops in the Dutch East Indies. The Allies have instructed the Japanese High Command that during the capitulation they are to maintain the status quo in the occupied territories. Nobody worries, but the Indonesian freedom movement seizes its chance. On August 17, 1945 Kusno Sukarno declares Indonesia independent. 'We do not like Japanese oppression and we do not want a Dutch one either' and 'We prefer to live in hell rather than being colonized again' A day later, eight provinces are created and on August 22nd the 137 member *Komite Nasional Indonesia Poesat* is formed, which serves as a parliament. Kusno Sukarno becomes president and Mohammed Hatta vice president and director of propaganda.

Sukarno and Hatta, the real force behind the well-organized independence movement, feel emboldened by the prediction in the book of Jayabaya, the Hindu king, who ruled a large Javanese empire eight centuries ago. This book states that one day a white man will come to Indonesia. He will stay and rule the islands for many years. After that, a yellow man will rule Indonesia for a period of three years.

Ineke van der Wal

At the end of these three years there will be self-government. The indigenous freedom fighters, who call themselves *Pamudas*, are determined to prevent the Dutch from returning, if necessary by using force. The liberation of Dutch East Indies comes soon after the Dutch liberation and the Dutch are insufficiently prepared. Not until September 15, 1945, one month after the armistice, do two Allied cruisers arrive at Tandjong Priok. One of them is the 'HM Tromp' with commander-in-chief Van de Plas. He observes 'a constant build-up of acts of violence, a Japanese authority, which can stand up less and less frequently against the actions of extremists, a Dutch population in poor condition / health and a destroyed infrastructure'.

A more serious problem than the creation of the Republic of Indonesia is sheltering the prisoners of war and internees in Indonesia, which is to be carried out by RAPWI (*Recovery of Allied Prisoners of War and Internees*), an organization that did not reckon with Java and Sumatra. Lord Mountbatten, responsible for RAPWI, quickly concludes that there is a powerful nationalist movement in Indonesia and that large-scale military operations will lead to a bloody colonial war, which could jeopardize aid to the internees and prisoners of war. He therefore decides that relief is the primary task of the English, in addition to the evacuation of the Japanese occupying power. The Netherlands are on their own when it comes to the restoration of colonial authority. With this, Mountbatten acts in the spirit of the Americans, who believe that the colonial system has been in existence long enough. In the Atlantic Charter between Roosevelt and Churchill, signed in August 1941, it has already been explicitly stipulated that every national group has the right to choose the government under which it wants to live.

Soon after the capitulation of Japan, all over Java, Dutch and Indonesian Dutch are kidnapped and murdered. In Bandung the Japanese lose all control and they hand over their weapons and armored vehicles to the Pamudas, who plunder the areas from Depok to Bandung and from Semarang to Surabaya. The red and white flag of the 'Republic' waves on many a plundered house. Beb writes: 'We hear stories about the natives, who really get out of hand, and love to ride on the cannons and shoot whenever they feel like it.'

An economic boycott against the Dutch is announced on October 13. The Dutch no longer have access to food. This means that if you are assigned to an organization such as an army group or a department, you can still get food, but if you are on your own you have to take care of yourself, which is dangerous and incredibly expensive. For instance, one bunch of bananas, formerly 15 cents, is now suddenly three guilders (300 cents).

On October 15, 3500 male (Indonesian) Europeans are deported to among others the prison in the Werfstraat, Surabaya where forty people die and several hundred are seriously injured. In the *Simpang* Club in Surabaya, a tribunal takes place where (Indonesian) Europeans are tortured and murdered. People's anger in this *Bersiap* (Malayan for 'be vigilant') period prevails and Europeans, and sympathizers, are unsure of the safety of their lives.

Mail to The Netherlands on Red Cross stationery.

Ineke van der Wal

As a result of the violence, the leadership of the Republic of Indonesia decides to intern the Dutch again. Eventually 220 protection camps are set up in Java, where almost 35,000 Dutch (Indonesian) people are brought together. In view of the fierceness of those who want to defend the revolution and the limited military means available to the Allies, it is a small miracle that at the end of 1945 more than 200,000 Dutch (Indonesian) people can find a safe haven in the archipelago itself, or in Australia.

To prepare for the return of the Dutch rule over Dutch East Indies, a Council of seven department heads was formed in April 1944 under the leadership of Deputy Governor General Van Mook with their headquarters at Camp Columbia in Brisbane. Now that the war has ended, the Council wants to start its work. People and equipment are needed for this endeavor but there is a gross shortage of both. All hope is placed on the prisoners of war and the internees, such as the PTT families gathered in Camp Columbia, who have to be deployed quickly in order to establish authority and start the reconstruction.

Ship space is also needed to bring in materials. Neither seems to be successful: the troubled situation makes it impossible to transport civilians to Indonesia and at the end of September the Australian dock workers go on strike and refuse to load Dutch ships as long as The Netherlands does not recognize the Republic of Indonesia. This means that relief supplies and installations remain on the quay. Ultimately, it is decided to call for the help of Dutch army units and military transports from The Netherlands are started. They are needed to get a foothold back in Indonesia to restore order. After that, it must be made as attractive as possible for the Indonesian population to voluntarily opt for a bond with The Netherlands.

The Dutch government is divided over the future of the Dutch East Indies. Do they want to re-capture this colony and once again exploit it as one large plantation for pepper, coffee, rubber, tin, oil and quinoa? Products that can be sold well on the world market and bring profit to the Dutch. Or does The Netherlands have a debt to pay and do they need to improve education and strengthen the economic position of the indigenous population, must they help the archipelago grow up - 'we have to raise the child into an adult' - and then work with her in a United Kingdom? The suggestion for the latter was already made in 1942 when Queen Wilhelmina promised Indonesians by radio that they would become partners of The Netherlands after the war.

The Dutch do not want to follow in the footsteps of the Americans, who tried to make the Philippines self-sufficient and independent as soon as possible. According to The Netherlands this went much too fast and the 'childish' population could not handle it at all. The Philippines were given self-government in 1934, as the conclusion of a decision made in 1912, and in 1944 they became completely independent.

The liberated Governor General Van Starkenborgh refuses to negotiate with the new Indonesian government and he is replaced by Deputy Governor General H.J. van Mook, who will negotiate with President Sukarno himself, if necessary. The Netherlands has always left the traditional Javanese governance structure intact and has strengthened it and this was seen as a successful colonial policy. It is not clear to what extent the native heads of state can be trusted, but it is assumed that the Javanese regents can be counted upon to support the establishing of a new Dutch regime. After all, 'only European civil servants can ensure a good and just administration.'

As long as the situation in Java is unclear, Beb and the children do not have much choice other than to wait and make the best of it in Camp Columbia. So they go to work. They help with the packing of masses and masses of pamphlets, Dutch and Malayan, all for Indonesia. The girls also help. Now it's done and that's a good thing too, because a kind of school has started. Wink and Loukie both participate. They want to obtain their diploma from the HBS (Dutch high school), but Kate is not interested. She starts with shorthand and typing in

Ineke van der Wal

Brisbane, which she likes. 'This week Kate had a test, but they do not get any grades, only percentages. If you get under 80%, you have to repeat that month. She got 91%, so we are very satisfied.' Over Christmas, Kate gets a month of summer vacation. Beb thinks it a shame: 'Kate is so good at her study, and she did it with enthusiasm.' Kate eventually receives her emergency diploma for three-years of HBS from Bandung. They have written to the school and receive a cordial letter in return with the official document from the Department of Education out of Batavia together with a copy. The director says that the lyceum in Bandung already has 800 pupils, but that they are primitively housed, because the building is primarily occupied by evacuees.

Tineke works hard and makes a good impression now that they are finally getting started with normal education. Education had only been play and tinkering because of the considerable age difference, varying education levels combined with a quick turnover of pupils. Some Dutch children try to enter the Australian education system, but that is still using the old English one, with corporal punishment. That almost always goes wrong immediately.

Wink and Loukie receive lessons from, among others, Mr. and Mrs. L'Ecluse. Wim and Beb know them both from the past. They are engineers and both taught at the institute in Surabaya, where the midshipmen were trained. On one of the last days before the fall of Java, they (Mr. and Mrs. L'Ecluse) left for Australia via Tjilatjap, then were in England for a long time and have now been in Camp Columbia for more than a year for the Department of Education. The Math teacher gives Beb 'a feather in her cap' for how well she has taught Loukie and Wink; they understand it well and have such a clear insight, and what they had learned, had been taught well to them. Beb is grateful for the compliments directed to her and Wim. Wink is happy with his lessons, but he thinks he is lagging behind with his Dutch.
Beb helps in the post office, where she has lots of work looking up addresses and forwarding letters to people who have already left Camp

Columbia. A total of five people work there. Beb's work serves two purposes. First, to keep her from worrying and secondly to make it possible for the family to stay here, despite the fact that this is actually a transit camp. Beb prefers to stay in this camp, now that the children are busy with classes and are enjoying themselves, rather than having to start over again in Melbourne or Sydney. However, they hope to be able to visit these cities sometime, especially because the latter is said to be very beautiful.

After the lessons and work, there is still enough time left for entertainment. They buy a violin again for Wink. Tineke develops a love for stamps and they buy an album for her. Wink helps with soaking stamps off envelopes. One teacher has a horse and the older children help with the construction of a paddock, and with cleaning and feeding. When the horse is trained, they will get riding lessons. There is a swimming pool in this camp and Kate goes to swim again. In the Dutch East Indies, she swam almost daily, but here she is halfway through the pool and afraid she won't reach the other end. They are not in shape, but gradually they are making good progress. Wink learns chess and he plays a lot with his friends. Every Sunday they can go to the sea to sunbathe and swim. Beb visits a dentist. The children go to a beautician to cleanse and restore their skin; the bad food situation has left its mark. Wink writes:

'I like it here in the camp. More and more boys are coming and that is what I consider the most important after the loneliness in Japan. One of my friends broke his arm in the previous camp. The arm was not properly set. On Wednesday he was operated on and I went to see him in the hospital together with two other friends. He moves to another city on Monday and then I have to find other friends. That is a shame, but I will not get bored here.'

Beb is happy about what her son writes: 'Wink enjoys the many friends, he is a leader of his group because he is the only one who speaks English which offers an advantage when going to the city, shopping in the afternoon or looking for car rides'. About 25 children in the upper

Ineke van der Wal

classes of the school visit an English warship, which is moored in the dock. They were received with honors but afterwards had more words for the sweets and treats than about the ship, although that was also very interesting. Beb goes to the movies in the open-air theater, and also to a concert where classical music is played on a record player. Concerts are held in a nice wooden building, called the *Princess Irene Hut,* where you can get tea. You can also go to concerts in Brisbane: 'It is not a big orchestra but a good one that always keeps a good tempo,' according to Beb.

Camp Columbia is slowly filling up with Dutch people who return, or who travel on to other places. The adults especially are interested in catching up with the news and hearing what is going on in the Dutch East Indies. They meet people who have witnessed the atomic bomb explosion up close; the pigment in their skin has disappeared. They see acquaintances and friends again. Beb says:

'A good acquaintance arrived, the wife of a radio engineer from Batavia. She came up to me with outstretched hands. Beb, are you really here! And I did not recognize her; she was so thin and had become so pale and gray. We all use rouge and lipstick here, all Americans do it and all Australians too and so you yourself don't want to be so unkempt. When the girlfriend was made up with a little rouge and lipstick, I did not understand how it was possible that I had not recognized her right away. These days such a long journey by air is terribly tiring; often in a very uncomfortable troop-transport plane with stops in places where they are not yet totally geared to transporting women. We cannot remember names properly, a memory loss that we all suffer from, due to a lack of vitamins, according to the doctor. For all Dutch people it is a time to gain one's strength, do nothing and talk a lot. It takes a long time before you are back to normal, before your stomach can digest normal food again and you start to recover, before your hair and nails start to grow again, before you start to menstruate again and become interested in your surroundings.'

There are bad reports from Bandung and Beb writes to her mother:

'I just heard from Bandung that our neighborhood was completely abandoned by Europeans. They all went to the protected area and had to leave their homes. Everything has been looted there, many of the houses have been set on fire. Now there is little chance that we will still see some of our dearest possessions. You are attached to so many things, that it makes you sad to know that everything is lost. But when you hear that one of your friends from Bandung has been in a prison, (not a POW camp), for three and a half years and that after two months of freedom, was kidnapped with many others and probably chopped up, while on his trip by train to Batavia, you accept your loss and are thankful that Wim died so calmly. Of course he would not have stayed in the camp, but would have returned to the lab. The southern part of Bandung, where the lab was located, has also been abandoned. In between is a protected neighborhood, where it is safe, but Wim would certainly have wanted to go to our house and even preferred to go to his lab. And if he had done so, he would have been sad about all the vandalism and destruction, and he would have wanted to save some of it, but certainly then he would have been slaughtered by the extremists in their usual gruesome manner.'

In Camp Columbia Beb finally receives news about all sorts of friends and family. Gus writes about Beb's mother: She is quite well, she has a heart condition and walks with a cane but looks good although she has to be careful. She now lives in Baarn with the Bosschieter family, nice people, who take care of everything to make it pleasant and who are extremely cordial and compassionate. Financially, it all went well and that is a relief for Beb: 'The fact that you managed, mother, even if you had to sell something that gives me comfort. I often worried about that.'

Wies and Arnold had a hard time. Hilvarenbeek was bombarded every day with grenades by the Germans, although the Allies had already liberated it. They got ten direct hits in their garden, pieces of wall were knocked down and the roof was so broken that it rained inside as hard as it did outside. They had to live in the basement for three weeks. Wies with a broken arm, which could only be set, after Tilburg was liberated and an X-ray could be taken. Everything is all right now and

Ineke van der Wal

Gus has already visited and Wies has been with Rik and Gus. Arnold, a reverend, wants to go to Indonesia to help, but because he is 64 and the age limit is 60, he isn't allowed to go. Rik has become very old and retired due to his illness. He has Parkinson's disease, which is an early symptom of old age. He trembles a lot, has difficulty walking and is easily tired and extremely slow. There is nothing one can do to cure this illness. It is unfortunate.

There also is news about Tip Carpentier Alting. He unexpectedly visits Beb's mother in June and she writes: 'It really moved me to suddenly see Loukie's boy. He has her eyes and her friendly smile.' In 1942 he was drafted and went to Semarang and England and trained in the Navy there. He received a high school diploma from the Dutch East Indies and is now a first lieutenant in the naval flight service. 'He has something very civilized, benevolent and funny about him.' His father Albert is still in a camp on Java, his second wife Pia has died.

It takes a long time before they receive any news about Koos. 'We are so afraid for her, because she was not that strong.' Koos was interned in a women's camp, where she, as a doctor, fiercely opposed the Japanese. That resulted in her imprisonment and she had a very bad time. She first went back to Bandung where she quickly retrieved her instruments, but Bandung had become so dangerous that she decided to go to The Netherlands instead and arrived there in April 1946 on the MS Sommelsdijk.

Gerrit van der Veen was with the underground movement and led the *Persoonsbewijzen Centrale*, where false ID's were made. He had once participated in a competition for a design of a new ten-guilder bill and had already experimented with the paper for these notes. The step to false ID's was made easily, according to him. He did a great job, but unfortunately he was caught and shot on June 10, 1944. Loukie became a widow and Loukietje and Gerda, their two little girls, no longer have a father. Word has it that Gerrit fathered a son. Loukie and the girls have had a lot of financial worries throughout the war. Lou Einthoven,

Wim Einthoven's first cousin, is still alive. He was part of the triumvirate '*De Nederlandsche Unie*' (The Dutch Union) founded in the middle of 1940. As a result they were imprisoned from 1942 in camp '*Sint Michielsgestel*'. The family had to go into hiding according to Beb.

'He can do some good in Holland now, even though I do not know what Holland thinks of him. We heard so little about the Union at the time. Two of our acquaintances claimed to have heard on the radio that he was shot with five other people from Rotterdam after a train accident that the Germans knew to be sabotaged. Among the victims was a Mr. Ruys, a Mr. Van der Bilt and also someone named Einthoven, a former police chief.'

Various uncles and aunts have died, nieces and nephews are married and had children. Other family members lost everything in the bombing of The Hague and stay with their family. Maria and Willem Hofker were interned in the prison of *Den Pasar*, but after a few weeks were allowed to work in relative freedom again. In December 1943 they were finally taken prisoner and deported to Celebes. Willem could still work there, but a lot of work was taken by Japanese officers. Only few pieces were left. They later move to Amsterdam, because they have not been allowed to settle in Bali again.

The news about family from The Netherlands is not too bad, but the news about friends from Indonesia is often not good. The women coming from Java to Camp Columbia, always bring bits of news. Of the men, especially of Bebs and Wim's generation, many died. From an announcement concerning war victims, Beb knows six people very well. Claus and Too Süverkropp are dead. Lous Hillen is no longer; her husband, the former director of the PTT passed away on November 6, 1945 after the end of the war. He had a hard time with the Kempe Tai, made it to the end of the war, but died anyway. Early on in the war, Corrie Weitner-Ballego, Beb's primary school friend from Leiden, lost her husband, who was also from Leiden. He was shot down by the Japanese while he was on a flight.

Ineke van der Wal

Tineke is burdened by various diseases and needs constant care. She has a wound on her knee, so her groin gets swollen. They try to treat it by applying a wet bandage, made from a strip that Beb cuts off a skirt but that does not help enough and Tineke gets a fever. They don't know how bad the fever is, because they do not have a thermometer. She spends several days at home in bed. Another unfortunate incident that Tineke experiences is that she ends up stuck for a few minutes to an electric wire. A man wraps a rubber cloak around her and is then able to pull her away. One of her fingers is burnt, but it quickly heals. She again gets a fever and that turns out to be malaria. She is admitted to the hospital at the camp. Beb is at work and she feels guilty every time she has to leave Tineke alone for a long time.

Passport photos are made for the various necessary documents and Beb sends copies to her mother but she is not sending the one of herself, because she thinks it ugly and she looks so awful that her mother would certainly think that she is on the verge of death, but that is not the case at all. She is well again and the children are too. They don't live under a black cloud, although they are a little tougher than the youth in Beb's time. They don't mind about something so easily.

Beb and the children decide to send two boxes with gifts to The Netherlands as a Christmas present for the family. They mainly send woolen clothing, fabric and yarn. It is of good quality and cheap in Australia and they don't need a coupon to buy it. They send everything in triplicate so that it can be divided. They also send soles for shoes, and some food. Beb writes: 'The chocolate powder 'Milo' is also for Loukietje and Gerda (the children of cousin Loukie van der Chijs) because I cannot find anything appropriate for children to send. One tin for each child and the third for you, Mother. We loved it so much, even when mixed with water only. I hope very much that it all arrives by Christmas time and that all of you can use the warm materials.' Sending a letter via the mail goes fast: a letter from The Netherlands dated November 18 arrives in Brisbane on November 26, but parcels are in transit for a very long time.

For them a happier new year

For these sons and daughters of Dutch evacuees from Java 1946 will be a happier year. At Wacol staging camp they are finding a new freedom, far removed from Japanese internment camps. The sand pit and toys are part of the elaborate nursery school and kindergarten equipment provided for their rehabilitation.

Below, Warrant-Officer Toni Reelandschap, in charge of the kindergarten, watches some of her charges drinking their afternoon milk ration. Without proper feeding for years, the children are now being given a well-balanced diet, tasting food they have never seen before.

A newspaper clipping from an Australian newspaper at the end of 1945. Tineke sits at the back row.

Sinterklaas 1945 is celebrated on December 5 with a party in the Dutch club in Brisbane. The children go in big buses. One of the teachers from the camp school will be Saint Nicholas and Wink is asked to play Black Pete, which he thinks is a great honor. Tineke does not recognize him and, although she does not believe in 'Saint Nicholas and Black Pete', she is still a little afraid of him. 'Wim and I always did our best to spoil the children so terribly on this 'holiday' so I did not want to leave our little one empty-handed. She was allowed to put out her shoe from December 1, as was always the rule in our family. And imagine: one evening, one of the other women in our house put something into it. Wasn't that nice?' Beb writes to her mother. Beb and the children are doing their best to make a fun 'Sinterklaas' evening. Everyone has bought presents and Tineke has to search the house for her package. There is also a box that is passed from person to person that has chocolate letters in it (one for each). Beb made them from chocolate bars, because these Dutch kind of chocolate letters do not exist in

Ineke van der Wal

Australia. Wink bought some nice warm slippers for Loukie and Beb, who are always cold, but it is precisely on such an evening that Wim is missed a lot.

A big Christmas play is organized in the camp and as many children and adults as possible are involved. Katy and Tineke do not want to participate - those two have not inherited Beb's love of dancing at all - but Loukie and Wink do. The others are busy making the costumes. On New Year's Eve Beb writes to her mother:

> *'I wanted to tell you that I understand that you had so much faith in Wim. He would have managed to find a safe place for us all no matter where or how. If the Dutch East Indies would be lost, then we would go to America. If the Dutch East Indies had been saved, but totally destroyed, he would have rebuilt it to be better and state of the art. And then he would also have become the old pleasant Wim, with whom I had so many good years. And now Mother, have a wonderful New Year, this year seems to have lasted a century. We enjoy being free, in spite of how the peace has evolved so far.'*

On January 10, 1946, Ir. Hendrik Lels and Ir. George Joseph Levenbach officially state that on February 15, 1945 Willem Frederik Einthoven, electrical engineer, officer in the order of Oranje Nassau, died in captivity in Tokyo, Japan from acute pneumonia and due to the lack of proper medical care. A notary takes this statement and together with the Japanese deed of death they prepare a Dutch deed, so that various formalities can be set in motion.

Via the Dutch consul in Brisbane, who has to visit Batavia and is kind enough to take one of the deeds with him, Beb finally acquires an official death certificate. With this document she seeks arrear pension payments. One can buy so much more in Australia than in Holland. Beb sends Rik a copy of the certificate so that Rik can try to gain access to Wim's bank accounts. Beb asks Rik to find out something about the state of Wim's account at the Amsterdam Bank, Leiden office, and

NETHERLANDS INDIES GOVERNMENT

DEPARTMENT:

DIVISION: POST BOX:

REF No.   TELEPHONE:

                                                  TELEGRAM:

TOUR No.:

SUBJECT:

ENCL.:

Hierbij verklaren ondergeteekenden:

Ir. Hendrik Lels, electrotechnisch ingenieur, geboren te
Vlaardingen Holland, 9 October 1904, ingenieur bij de
Gouvernements Post, Telegraaf en Telefoon dienst in
Nederlandsch Indie, Nederlandsch onderdaan
en
Ir. George Joseph Levenbach, electrotechnisch ingenieur,
geboren te Philadelphia U.S.A., 20 Juni 1912, idem,
eveneens Nederlandsch onderdaan,

dat op den 15° Februari 1945 is overleden in gevangenschap te
Tokyo Japan, adres: Sumitomo Electrical Communications Company,
Shirokane-Daimachi Dormitory, n° 7 - 1 Chome Shirokane-Daimachi,
Shiba-ku aan acute pneumonia en door gebrek aan goede dokters-
hulp

Ir. Willem Frederik Einthoven, electrotechnisch ingenieur,
Officier in de Orde van Oranje Nassau, geboren te
Zoeterwoude Holland, 17 Juni 1893, in leven Hoofdingenieur
bij de Gouvernements Post, Telegraaf en Telefoondienst in
Nederlandsch Indië, chef van het Radiolaboratorium te
Bandoeng,

zoon van Willem Einthoven, in leven Hoogleeraar aan de Universi-
teit te Leiden Holland en van Jeanne Wilhelmina Louise Einthoven-
de Vogel, beiden overleden,
echtgenoot van Ir. Elisabeth Cornelia Einthoven-Zeeman,
bouwkundig ingenieur, geboren te Delft Holland, 13 April 1895,
Nederlandsch onderdaan
en vader van vier kinderen:
Kate Lisbeth, geboren te Leiden Holland, 14 Juni 1926
Louise Jeanne,   "   " Bandoeng Java, 23 Maart 1929
Willem Frederik   "   "   "   "   20 Januari 1930
Tine Marlene   "   "   "   "   31 October 1937

Brisbane, 10 Januari 1945.

Henk Lels and Geo Levenbach testify to the Dutch Government in
Brisbane that Wim Einthoven passed away in Japan. This declaration
is considered as death certificate.

what kind of official documents are required to make it available to
her. Similarly for the 'giro' account, but Beb does not even know
Wim's number nor does she have statements of these accounts. The
money in England at Lloyds Bank in London will hopefully still be
intact. Beb no longer knows the address. Wim had stocks from Lever
Bros more commonly known as the Sunlight Soap Factory. Rik does
not waste any time; Beb's mother appears to have kept all the papers
from the year of leave and he finds deposits for Wim and Beb,

everything blocked since May 22, 1940. 'Fortunately, Beb is well taken care of.' writes Beb's mother. The Dutch family members offer to send money to Australia, but that is not necessary. The children and Beb receive a monthly allowance from which they can pay camp costs and keep some for purchases, although it disappears quickly because they need so much. Beb writes: 'Just this week I bought a clock, and the ticking really helps to make us feel at home.'

Camp Columbia is slowly closing down. The entire camp must be empty by April 15 because the Dutch government wants to sell it. Riek Levenbach leaves with the children to go to Wellington, New Zealand, where some of her family lives. The Lels family moves to Sydney. The Frank family, their neighbors from Bandung, have also moved to Sydney, where they have family. What will the Einthoven family do? It is clear that they cannot return to Java and that there soon will be no room for them anymore in Australia. Wies and Arnold have kindly offered their house in Hilvarenbeek, The Netherlands as a place to stay. They live in a large rectory with enough room for the whole family. 'Wies, thank you very much for your invitation and for opening up your home,' Beb writes, but she remains indecisive for a long time.

Tineke tells years later that Beb did not discuss this problem with anyone. She was alone, she did not want to ask for help and she felt that she had to make up her mind by herself, even in case of this very difficult decision. The idea of asking for help did not occur to her; she felt that she had to do it on her own, she wanted to reach a conclusion and did not want to show any weakness. She could have asked Kate and Loukie: 'You are still young, but I want to discuss it with you, what do you think?' or she could have discussed it with one of the other adults. In the end Beb decides that it is best to go to The Netherlands. The family registers for the crossing; they are all still entitled to a first class trip to their home country, but that is very unlikely to happen. They are assigned to the MS *Bloemfontein*, but it is unclear when this ship will sail.

The passages below come from Beb's letters to her mother.

April 13, 1946: Beb's birthday. *We are still in Camp Columbia. Wink is better, he had mumps, but on the day he was declared free of contamination Tineke fell ill again and the doctor insisted that she returns to the hospital because she has a terrible case of bronchitis, presumably whooping cough and perhaps a recurrence of malaria. We have no news about the ship yet but traveling with a sick child would be completely impossible and I doubt whether we would be admitted on board. I am very downhearted. It is so wretched that the little one cannot even recover in her own time and that we will have to leave before she is completely healthy again. This persistent fever remains the same every day. Now I will not write any more here, you do not have to worry about Tineke, she will soon get better, but it makes me so upset. Goodbye until next time, when hopefully the news will be better.*

April 28, 1946. *We are out of Camp Columbia, but unfortunately Tineke is back in the hospital because she got mumps this week. She was not allowed to go into one of the city hotels, nor was she allowed to go to Sydney. She is admitted to* NEI, The Netherlands East Indies *hospital in New Farm (part of Brisbane). We are lodged in New Farm Camp, where normally only workers and other personnel can go to. The three children go their own way. They make sure that Camp Columbia's luggage goes to New Farm by stopping trucks and loading their baggage. It is better for Tineke to be here rather than in Camp Columbia, because she is in a children's ward. But it is too bad that the child does not have a home where she can recover, even when she is sick with such a minor illness as the mumps. At the same time we heard that the MS Bloemfontein is still in Holland and that the sailors manning it are on strike. So it will be seven weeks plus the length of time of the strike before we can leave here. A departure in May is out of the question and June is doubtful. I am terribly upset because that means we will arrive after the schools have started for the New Year. The camp school closed, so the children are idle and we do not have money to buy any courses. They do sew quite a lot, because the ready made goods still have to be altered, reinforced or nicely finished, but this does not compare to a real job. So I*

Ineke van der Wal

decided to ask if I could go to the ocean, for example to Coolangatta, because it is friendlier there and will be better for our health.

Lo and behold, Friday morning I asked and after a few hours I was told that it was possible, but that I had to leave the next day with the 10 AM bus, together with the other children. So that afternoon I had to do a lot of shopping and I went with Tineke and Wink to the city. When I got home, I was given a wonderful opportunity. In Broadbeach, between Southport and Coolangatta, lives a Dutch lady, a mother of a girl aged 11 and a boy of 15 together with two horses. She has to go to Sydney for two to three weeks and she is looking for someone who can do housekeeping for her during that time. I immediately accepted the 'job' and 20 minutes later everything was arranged. I met the lady, Mrs. Klei-Van Dam. She also comes from Leiden, where she was at the same high school, but one class lower than Koos. Can you still remember her Koos, Tine van Dam, from a family of eight children? She gave me a list full of information and an address from another Dutch person in the neighborhood, who could help me if necessary. Within 24 hours I was dropped off by the bus at the nicest little house, where two nice, polite and not the least bit shy children waited for Tineke and me. I have to do everything myself, but it is a very simple house to take care of, comfortable and neatly arranged. The owner is very untidy; it makes me look like a saint. The horses are an important part of the household, so I also have to feed them, because the children leave early in the morning and don't come home until 4 o'clock. The whole garage is full of food for the horses; it has a nice earthy smell, just like on an actual farm. The horses are in a paddock close to the house, both during the day and at night. The cottage is near the ocean and most people who walk by are barefoot and in a bathing suit. The sea is beautiful. Because the sun does not set over the ocean but over the land, the waves are lit up just the other way around as in Holland. It is a wonderful sight to look at all afternoon. During the day it is lovely, sunny and warm, but in the evening and at night it gets cold so you always have to have a sweater or a jacket handy. In the morning – we have to get up at six o'clock - I shiver in the cold and I enjoy a cup of hot coffee. We always eat in the kitchen, straight out of the pan, and after that the children help to *wash the dishes. The children are both in English schools. During the war they were in South Africa, England and America but speak fluent Dutch, although with a distinct accent.*

Tineke tells later: 'I believe this interlude was very much needed for my mother.' The tone of the letters was very negative in recent months. Beb has difficulty staying positive because of the lack of structure in their lives and the uncertainty about their departure. Now Beb has a household for herself and more time for Tineke, she is busy and she feels useful. Wink, Kate and Loukie are already in Greenmount-Camp in Coolangatta. There is hardly any public transport so Beb and Tineke see little of them during this time.

When Mrs Klei-Van Dam returns, she invites the entire Dutch community to celebrate her birthday at the beach with a barbecue. They make skewers to weave the cubes of pork onto. The skewers are held over the fire and then you eat the meat from that stick - it is like a giant satay. There is bread and butter and tomatoes and everyone brings their own plates, forks and spoons. People here often cook and eat outside. Beb has to get used to eating while sitting on the grass and roasting meat over a fire. In Holland it is usually forbidden to walk on the grass in a park. Australians use their parks: on Sundays many families sit down in the grass to eat.

Tineke and Beb move to Camp Coolangatta at the beginning of June 1946 and are again united with Kate, Loukie and Wink. The camp is beautifully located by the sea where they see dolphins jump, whales spouting or a shark chasing its food. Because of the sharks, you cannot swim every day, then the alarm sounds all the time. Tineke goes to school, Loukie works as a waitress, and Kate works in a restaurant.

Ineke van der Wal

The Greenmount Camp in Coolangatta is used as a gathering place for the refugees who have to leave Camp Columbia but cannot yet travel to The Netherlands.

In Coolangatta, a picture is taken with koala bears, a long cherished wish. From left to right: Wink, Kate, Tineke and Loukie.

Ineke van der Wal

In the camp they also meet the Van Katwijk family, with whom they spend a lot of time. They see a koala bear, a wish they cherished for a long time and they have their picture taken with the little bear. On these photos everyone looks healthy, well-fed and they all have a nice tan. They celebrate Katy's 20th birthday with the Van Katwijk family with a tea from four to five o'clock. A girl from the Goudkade family comes by unexpectedly. Fortunately Beb has a lot of cakes. She writes about it:

'We still enjoy so much to be able to buy delicious things again; a tray filled with colorful jelly rolls or cupcakes in paper cups sprinkled with powdered sugar on top and a scoop of artificial cream inside and then best of all, cups of filo dough, filled with apple and artificial whipped cream. They are delicious, but the Dutch and Dutch Indies cakes were even more refined, with real whipped cream. Just seeing all these delicacies is a pleasure in itself.'

The twentieth birthday of Kate on June 14, 1946 in Coolangatta with from left to right: Kate, a Goudkade girl, a boy Van Katwijk, Loukie, another Van Katwijk boy and Wink.

Beb and the children try to pass the time as best as possible, because the departure date and the route of the MS *Bloemfontein* remain unclear. 'June 17 on board the MS *Bloemfontein*? Now, that is a date full of happy memories in my life, so maybe that will bring us some good luck this year.' Then the news is that the MS *Bloemfontein* will be in Batavia on June 20th and then sail straight to Brisbane. That would mean that they will travel past Sydney, where they will enter the harbor with the famous bridge, past Melbourne, and past Fremantle-Perth. In this way they still get to see a lot of Australia. *That will be exciting!*, Beb writes.

Before they leave, they receive extra coupons to buy warm clothes and there is extensive correspondence about the purchases. Because there is still a lack of stockings in Holland, women wear pants, so they buy these with matching jackets. Also shorts. 'Can I wear that in Holland?' Beb asks. Rik and Gus have sent money and Beb decides to buy two bikes - a very valuable possession. Beb buys an English book as a birthday present for Wies and writes the following:

'I started reading it and it seemed very good to me. I will read more of the book on board the ship. (Shameful actually, since I want to give it to you as a present, but yes, we have become so practical)."

Beb is slowly becoming impatient and the Australian authorities are too. More and more they turn into *only* evacuees and are slowly being treated like undesirable aliens.

'We hear that no one is allowed on the ship or even allowed on the quay when they see us off. Neither in Sydney nor Melbourne are we allowed to disembark nor can no one visit us or meet us there. Upon arrival in Holland we will have to wait a whole day before we can disembark. We will first be taken to a sort of immigration office where we will be given all our coupons, our first money and all our other papers. We will probably have to stay an extra night to complete the processing. Whether we can receive visitors then remains to be seen, opinions differ. We will be brought home and our luggage

Ineke van der Wal

will be taken care of, which is of course very pleasant again. The journey is expected to last more than six weeks and it could even be that we arrive exactly one year after the armistice. During that year we've become disillusioned and hopes for the future have been unfulfilled.'

The MS *Bloemfontein* is a cargo ship with passenger accommodation.

July 6, 1946. *'Yes, we're actually on board!! I am on the deck in the sun and everything went very smoothly and quickly. On Tuesday, the heads of the families had to go to Brisbane to clear their luggage and with seven women and a single man crammed into a station wagon, we drove straight to New Farm Camp, where all the crates and suitcases were neatly arranged by family and where the Australian Custom Officers were generous and accommodating. Out of my 14 pieces I only had to open two trunks, which was easily done with a key. None of all the other boxes or trunks that were nailed or screwed shut had to be opened. Within five minutes everything was approved and marked with chalk. There are three trunks, three duffle bags, two boxes with camp beds and deckchairs and six crates, one of which is a huge crate with two bikes inside. You'll be shocked, Wies, when you see it all.'*

It is only a small ship and it immediately rocks back and forth. The older children do not suffer at all, but Beb has to take it easy and Tineke is seasick immediately. The first four days they are assigned to nice cabins. They feel lucky because they have a cabin with its own conveniences such as a nice toilet and a neat solid bathtub, filled only with cold seawater but in the afternoon they get warm water for an hour. The beds are comfortable, but they're stacked on top of each other at the two sides, so that it has become a cabin for six. This means that you can't sit on the beds and have to slide sideways in and out of your bed while partially lying down. They are delighted with their two cabin mates - two young females. Mrs. Briët lost her husband and had only been married for half a year when he had to leave. Mrs. Bos lost her little son, but she is expecting another baby now. Her husband was stationed at Biak and she was allowed to join him, but considering her condition going to Holland seemed much better.

The ship first sails from Brisbane to Melbourne, where the English people are dropped off and then they continue on to Sydney. Many more come on board and then they leave for Perth to pick up the last passengers to go Holland. When the large group of people arrives on board, Beb and Tineke will have to leave the cabin, which is then only for the sick, the elderly and women with babies or women who are expecting. Regular passengers then go into the hold and Beb says:

'That's terrible, just like a transport for prisoners. There are at least 100 people in the hold, with open toilets in a row, open showers in a row, no storage space at all, only berths, 5 high on top of each other, and 2 abreast each other in long, long rows. All of this deep down in the ship so windows cannot be opened and all depends on the mechanical ventilation. First they travel across the Indian Ocean, which is very rough at this time of year, and then through the Red Sea, which is so uncomfortably hot. The outlook is horrible, but at least we can count down the days. We know there is an end to the journey and that we won't have to wait indefinitely.'

IVAL WILL CUT

1200 DUTCH TO LEAVE ON CARGO VESSEL

FIVE TIERS OF BUNKS in one of the holds in the ship Bloemfontein, which sails from Melbourne today with 1200 Dutch refugees. These young passengers volunteered to sweep out the hold and make everything ship-shape.

Loukie and Kate in the middle at the back in the hold of the MS *Bloemfontein*. There are five beds stacked on top of each other. The ship is overcrowded and there is absolutely no privacy. Source: *The Herald* from Melbourne, Australia, July 15, 1946.

The girls and Wink have signed up for work during the journey and earn four guilders a day each. At the beginning of the journey they enjoy eating in the lounge in proper chairs, in pleasant surroundings. Later on this also takes place in the hold below.

Food is distributed at three different seatings; Wink, who sleeps in a completely different part, is assigned to the first seating, the women to the third seating, one and a half hours later. They hardly ever see each other, but Wink has discovered several old friends and makes many new ones, just like the girls. With all those volunteers on board, the interaction is very different, much more amical and more jovial than in the past with the crew. The food times are: 8.30, 1.00 and 7.00 and it is completely American. In the hallway in front of the dining room is a counter with huge baking dishes with food on top. In front of the dishes are several rows of steel bars that form a platform. Everyone takes a metal tray that is divided into differently sized compartments, then slides it over the steel bars. The people behind the counter plop meat, vegetables, potatoes, gravy and dessert in the various compartments and then you take your tray to a table where cups, water and bread are waiting for you. The food is good and plentiful, only the coffee is poor. In between you get nothing, neither at 11 o'clock nor at 4 o'clock, but after Australia the bar will be opened again and you will be able to buy a snack.'

Melbourne, July 12, 1946. *We have been too optimistic in calculating our expected arrival, because the sailors are still on strike. The MS Bloemfontein is also declared 'Black' out of loyalty to the striking boat workers in Holland so that the ship is now handled by volunteers. This makes loading and unloading so amazingly slow, that the departure was first moved from Wednesday to Friday and then on to the following Monday. Their stay in Melbourne will have lasted exactly one week by then. The only advantage of this situation is that they can disembark and they already know the city quite well. It is a much larger city than Brisbane, much higher and more spacious and there is more variety in the stores. Too bad the money and coupons are gone. They visit 'The Shrine', the war memorial for the fallen soldiers from the First World War and the famous St. Kilda Road, which resembles the Maliebaan (a long avenue in Utrecht), but longer and wider. Beb meets an acquaintance from Bandung, who worked at the PTT. He lives here with his wife and daughter in half a house and Tineke and Beb are invited to join them for lunch on Sunday.*

Melbourne, July 16, 1946. *Well, we are on our way again. On Monday at exactly 5 o'clock the first whistle blew and a waving crowd stands on the quay and threw streamers as usual. The 'luxury life' of the first week is over; we are now one of the many who sleep two floors down in the hold* *with hundreds of others. It is very bad, especially the toilets. The girls work in the food serving team and enjoy themselves with all the volunteers and their former friends. Wink is an orderly and brings letters and messages around. Beb has to schedule the various chores; only Tineke is free and has 200 friends and girlfriends here. Fenneke Boterhoven de Haan-Carpentier Alting, Albert's sister, (Albert is Beb's brother-in-law) is aboard with her husband and daughter Karin and many acquaintances from Brisbane. Mrs. Prof. dr. Buisman from Bandung is there and Cor Weidner-Ballego with her two children and then five other families, whom they know from Coolangatta. In Sydney, Annie Lels will come on board with Paulien and Murk; Henk stays in Indonesia. 'Cozy, all those acquaintances, but we will bless the day on which the journey is well and truly over.'*

July 21-28 1946. *After three days in Sydney, we sailed away from that last location and now we really have the idea that the long journey has begun. Together there are now 900 passengers on board, in Fremantle-Perth that number rises to about 1200. There was a lot of crying today when people saw where they were going to have to sleep. It is really very bad. 'Prepare the bath for our homecoming, warm fresh water will be a luxury for us.'*

The ship calls at Fremantle-Perth after a very stormy crossing along the south coast of Australia, a coast that is as notorious as the Bay of Biscay. Tineke and Beb lie in the hold for four days without eating anything and on the first day without drinking anything, until Loukie ventures into the bumpy room to bring them some refreshment. The girls stay well and only suffer from the storm for a short time; Wink doesn't have any problem at all. Tineke and Beb are eventually transferred to cells with 4 other incurably seasick patients and they are very grateful for that. These are some tiny rooms in the middle of the ship each with a control hatch that can only be opened from the outside; it is meant for prisoners. Now that the ship is docked in Sydney, they feel better already. The harbor of Sydney, with all its bays, is filled with nice houses, with beautiful gardens and long walkways and 'the bridge' - the bridge in the background as a great symbol of the

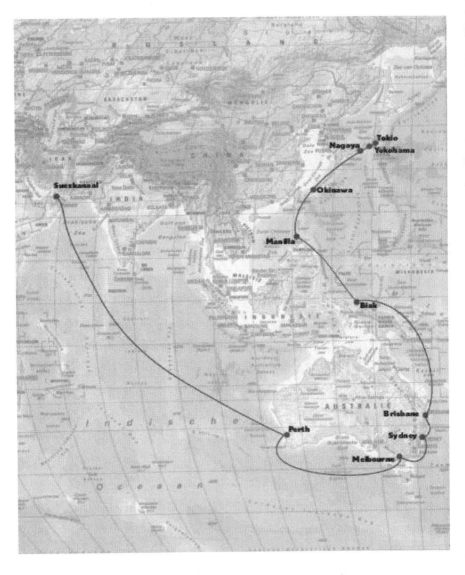

The route to The Netherlands. From Nagoya per train to
Hamamatsu. Per boat to the Bay of Tokyo and then on to
Yokohama harbor. By car to Tokyo airport and per plane to
Okinawa, Manilla, Biak (New Guinea) and Brisbane (Australia).
With a ship to Sydney, Melbourne, Perth and via the Suez-Canal
to the Mediterranean Sea, the Gulf of Biscay and the port of
Rotterdam.

Ineke van der Wal

possibilities of the steel industry. 'Yes, that is impressive and it was nice that we did not miss Sydney after being in Australia for more than half a year.'

The medical service on board protests against taking on more passengers and so the group from Perth is now reduced from almost 300 to 75, actually only those who must to go to Holland. The total number of passengers remains at almost a thousand and Beb and Tineke are told that they can stay in their little cell and are less apprehensive about the coming days. Annie Lels sometimes comes to their area for more privacy. She sees how nicely Wink has matured and has become so masculine, which Beb likes to hear, of course. 'This is my last letter, because we sail directly from Fremantle-Perth to Holland without calling at any ports and we expect it to take about five weeks. We hope to be there for Koos' birthday on August 22nd. How wonderful that we can now say 'see you soon'.

On August 25, 1946, Beb, Kate, Loukie, Wink and Tineke arrive in Rotterdam and travel to Wies and Arnold's house in Hilvarenbeek where the family is reunited. Mother and daughter can embrace each other again after 75 months.

Distribution card for Beb needed in The Netherlands to receive money and clothing.

Ineke van der Wal

CHAPTER X

Back in The Netherlands

The house of Aunt Wies and Uncle Arnold on Markt 286 in Hilvarenbeek is a large minister's house and the family Einthoven is warmly received there in August 1946. Aunt Wies feels it is her duty to welcome her brother's children but she also likes to have a house full of family. Uncle Arnold is a protestant minister in the South of Holland which is mostly Catholic and that can sometimes be lonely. On September 9 their luggage arrives in Hilvarenbeek with their bicycles and some household goods. Kate rides on her Australian bicycle, which is cornflower blue. This is unusual in The Netherlands where bicycles are only made in one color, namely black. A passerby calls after her: 'Allee madammeke, heddege een mooi fietske metgenommen?' (Hey little girl did you bring back a nice bicycle?) The dialect is rather different from the standard Dutch that they were taught in the Dutch East Indies.

They receive a warm welcome from the family, but the rest of The Netherlands is not as friendly. They feel unwelcome; no one has an eye for their needs. Paulien Lels says that 'she was not prepared for living in a cold country, to which you do not feel connected. We were unadjusted to this life. It was so difficult for us. It took us a great deal of trouble, a wall of incomprehension from both sides.

Aunt Wies Terlet-Einthoven and uncle Arnold Terlet at the time of their fiftieth wedding anniversary.

The repatriation not only tells the story of anxious escapes, of sad farewells, of cold receptions, of discrimination, of taking many steps back on the social ladder - it is also the story of carrying on, of persevering, of 'sacrificing everything for the children' of adjusting and yet retaining one's own culture. (Boon, p. 9)

It is not in Beb's nature to despair and she quickly goes to work to get the children back in school. Kate has clearly said that she no longer wants to go to school, and Beb has given up fighting against it. Uncle Arnold, however, thinks that the family should not allow this. Beb agrees with him, but she no longer knows how to handle it. They decide that uncle Arnold will talk to Kate. He is not the first to try, Beb has asked everyone she could think of for help and so he enters an area where many people have failed. Uncle Arnold says one day: 'Kate, I want to talk to you.' Nobody knows what is being discussed, but Kate leaves Uncle Arnold's office and wants to do her final exams.

Shortly after arriving in Hilvarenbeek, a boy suddenly appears at the front door, saying: 'Wink, do you remember me?' Wink looks at him and realizes that it is Willem-Jan Bake. Willem-Jan was always smaller than Wink because he is younger, but he is now a head taller. Willem-Jan has heard that the family has arrived and so he hitchhiked to Hilvarenbeek. The Bake family wanted to leave The Netherlands when the war broke out but were unable to do so and has spent the entire war in The Netherlands. Wink and Willem-Jan hitchhike back together to Voorburg where the Bake family lives. Willem-Jan is at the *VCL* high school in The Hague where Kate went while they were on leave and where Aunt Wiesje Zeeman, a relative of Beb, is an administrator. Wiesje advises the children to try to get into the *VCL*. Uncle Arnold agrees that this is probably a much better solution than traveling from Hilvarenbeek up and down to the Lorentz Lyceum in Tilburg. After consultation, it is decided that Wink and Loukie both belong in the graduating class HBS-Beta and Kate goes to the 'condensed' HBS-Alpha. Wink is in the class where he belongs, Loukie loses a year and Kate loses several years. She is already twenty when she starts this undertaking. Beb sees three of her children leave home within a week's time.

Kate, Loukie and Wink will live in the Bloemstraat in The Hague with Mrs. Eline Kwast, an acquaintance from Beb's. Mrs. Eline's daughter, Floor, goes to the same high school. Kate and Loukie have to work hard, but they manage because they want to move forward, but Beb is not satisfied about Wink. After the long period of loneliness in Japan,

Wink now has to enjoy school, sports and friends. After a consultation with the head of the school, it is decided to hold Wink back a class; he is only sixteen and can afford a year of postponement. He receives an exemption for mathematics, some tutoring for other subjects and the opportunity to be a normal schoolchild. It is also decided that he is allowed to live with Willem-Jan Bake. 'That was a real fun time,' says Wink later. Beb and Tineke remain in Hilvarenbeek and Uncle Arnold recommends that Tineke should not visit the public school, which has only one grade, but to ask permission for her to go to the Catholic school with the Sisters. Tineke is called '*the Chinese one*', because she has been in Japan and the difference between Japan and China has escaped most people, but Tineke is satisfied there.

Kate passes her exam in 1947 and obtains an authentic Dutch diploma, with good grades and Loukie passes her HBS-B exam. Both diplomas do not include German, but nobody cares about that. This is a tremendous achievement for the children, teachers and parents. Kate says: 'I am still very grateful to these teachers for helping us to move on in life.'

Beb prefers to live near her children, which also seems to be better for Tineke, who now relies heavily on Beb and misses her brother and sisters very much. Beb and Tineke are also welcome at the Bake family in Voorburg at Hoge Weidelaan 40 and Tineke can go to school there.

It is in Voorburg, that a box of luggage is delivered by the Red Cross (*Nederlandse Roode Kruis*) on July 23, 1947. This luggage 'was left behind by you in Japan at your departure to the Dutch East Indies and was sent to me by the Dutch Embassy in Washington for further distribution'. This luggage has been on the road for two years. Some of the items that survived the war, but were presumed lost, are returned to them with this box. They have to laugh about the Christmas lights that Tineke once found in the attic of one of the vacant houses.

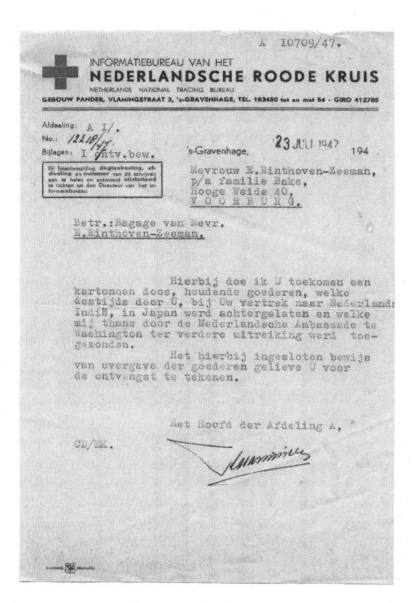

A 10709/47.

INFORMATIEBUREAU VAN HET
NEDERLANDSCHE ROODE KRUIS
NETHERLANDS NATIONAL TRACING BUREAU
GEBOUW PANDER, VLAMINGSTRAAT 2, 's-GRAVENHAGE, TEL. 183450 tot en met 54 - GIRO 412785

Afdeeling: A I/.
No.: 12218/47
Bijlagen: I ontv.bew.

's-Gravenhage, 23 JULI 1947 194

*bij beantwoording dagteekening, af-
deeling en nummer van dit schrijven
aan te halen en antwoord uitsluitend
te richten tot den Directeur van het informatiebureau.*

Mevrouw E.Einthoven-Zeeman,
p/a familie Bake,
Hooge Weide 40,
V O O R B U R G.

Betr.:Bagage van Mevr.
E.Einthoven-Zeeman.

          Hierbij doe ik U toekomen een
kartonnen doos, houdende goederen, welke
destijds door U, bij Uw vertrek naar Nederlands
Indië, in Japan werd achtergelaten en welke
mij thans door de Nederlandsche Ambassade te
Washington ter verdere uitreiking werd toe-
gezonden.
          Het hierbij ingesloten bewijs
van overgave der goederen gelieve U voor
de ontvangst te tekenen.

                    Het Hoofd der Afdeling A,

CD/EK.

Almost two years after the end of the war Beb receives a box in Voorburg, where she then lives. This box contains items belonging to the Einthoven family that were handed over to the Red Cross in Japan. American liberators brought the box to the United States where the Dutch Embassy takes care of transport to The Netherlands.

Due to the housing shortage, it is necessary to share a house with other people, but Beb prefers to have a place for herself and her children. In that case there is basically only one possibility: to build something yourself. That is a difficult project to take on so soon after the war, because there is a shortage of all building materials. Beb gets a chance to buy land in Haarlem in the area Kennemerland. This area is known as open-minded and various family members already live in Haarlem such as Han de Voogt on the Zonnelaan and Uncle Frits and Aunt Jet van Heel on the Van Merlenlaan.

In order to supervise the construction, Beb looks for a place to live close by and in the beginning of 1948 she finds two rooms with an older widower, Mr Schim van der Loeff, and his son. Beb has to prepare meals every day for the two men and her mother has a hard time with this decision, but this address is within walking distance of the construction site. Beb builds a house at the Frederik Hendriklaan 19 in Haarlem that she and Tineke move into in 1949. Tineke goes to school in Haarlem and becomes a member of the rowing and sailing club 'Het Spaarne', where she learns to sail. Beb buys a sailing boat for the children, one of the BM type. She changes the semi-circular sail sign of the boat into a smiling face and they call the boat *the Phantom*. In Haarlem Tineke starts to relax and becomes more independent.

Ineke van der Wal

Beb enjoys her own home, it is furnished simply with various pieces of furniture that Beb designed herself and are crafted by a carpenter, such as a couch, which can also serve as a bed, and some shallow shelves on the wall for books and art in the living room and gloves and hats in the

Frederik Hendriklaan 19 in Haarlem, the house that Beb builds for herself and her family.

hallway. There is a fireplace, hardwood flooring, central heating, a modern kitchen by Piet Zwart and a view of a pond with ducks and a beautiful white house. There is room for all the children and Beb can now also entertain visitors. The architect club 'Kwim Kwam Kwepele' surprises her with a special gesture: each member donates a book from his or her collection so that Beb again has some architectural books of her own again. The house of Gus and Rik in Amsterdam is only a short train ride away and they often go there to visit. When Arnold retires, he and Wies also move to Amsterdam. Kate starts a psychology study in Amsterdam and lives on the Van Baerlestraat in a house with twelve girls; Loukie studies architecture in Delft, and Wink also decides to go to Delft after his final exams. Kate quits her studies in Amsterdam after a year and then moves to Delft, where she becomes the secretary to a professor. She makes good use of her Australian training this way and lives near her brother and sister.

Beb has achieved her goal to give all her children a good education. Their neighbors in Bandung, meet up with them again in The Netherlands and the daughter tells that her mother has not insisted on finishing high school. She is a clever girl, in-between the ages of Kate and Loukie and she later regrets that she did not finish high school. Wink says: 'Yes, here I have to give respect to my mother that she was able to get us this far in spite of the limited means and that she persisted despite criticism.' A friend from Bandung, has doubts about Beb's decision to let Wink repeat a year in school even though it was not strictly necessary. The friend's daughter, quickly finishes her high school and then goes to Delft and is a full year ahead of Wink. A year later she fails her first exam and two years later she fails two exams while Wink passes two exams and then there is no difference between the two anymore, which Beb always sees as confirmation that she had made the right decision.

Beb wants to work to supplement the disappointing pension and she manages to find a position as a math teacher at the *Kennemer Lyceum*. Sister in law Koos also wants to resume work, but does not receive permission to do so. Koos, who carried out all conceivable medical procedures in the Japanese camp with very limited supplies and equipment, is no longer allowed to work as a doctor in her homeland. She decides to study psychiatry and to help ex-internees with her knowledge.

Ineke van der Wal

On February 26, 1947 the following people meet at the district court in Amsterdam:

- Wies Terlet-Einthoven, aunt on the father's side,
- Gus Clevering-Einthoven, aunt on the father's side,
- Kate Zeeman-De Bruijn, maternal grandmother,
- Loukie van der Veen-Van der Chijs, mother's niece, all four as external witness and representative of one child,
- Beb Einthoven-Zeeman, mother.

These five people together appoint Henri Willem de Voogt, shipbuilding master in Haarlem, Zonnelaan 12, as guardian of the minor Einthoven children. Together with the death certificate of Wim Einthoven, various processes can now be set in motion to request the inheritance, distribute ownership and apply for benefits for the widow and the children.

Beb is faced with a multitude of organizations and decisions:

1. The Board for Rehabilitation will determine whether Wim and Beb's securities and bank accounts were already in their possession before the war started, after which the accounts can be released.

2. The Ministry of Overseas Territories, Commissioner for Dutch East Indies Affairs (later the name is crossed out and replaced with Indonesian Affairs) decides on February 27, 1947 that the pension, which Beb and the minor children are entitled to, is reduced by 17% because the war years are not included. This means that the salary during the war years is not paid out and that the pension is correspondingly cut from 1680 guilders per year, to 1400 guilders per year for Beb and for children from 840 to 700 per year.

A listing of the lost paintings from the house in Bandung for which Beb hopes to receive compensation. The name Einthoven on the back of the paintings was changed to *Engelbert van Bevervoorde* because the paintings were hidden there. The paintings have not survived. The table silver, also hidden there, did survive and was eventually returned to The Netherlands.

3. On May 27, 1947, the Widows and Orphans Fund for European Civil Servants in The Netherlands Indies assesses the pension at 214 guilders per month for Beb and 110 guilders for the four minor children, so a total of 324 guilders per month. They do not receive this amount in full, because all advances which they received in Australia are deducted and an Indonesian war tax of 64.97 guilders per month is also collected. In addition, this pension is paid to a bank in Batavia in the Dutch East Indies and the fees for

Ineke van der Wal

transferring funds to The Netherlands are high. Virtually nothing is left. Wim earned 950 guilders per month in Bandung, now Beb does not even get 500 per month.

3. On May 27, 1947, the Widows and Orphans Fund for European Civil Servants in The Netherlands Indies assesses the pension at 214 guilders per month for Beb and 110 guilders for the four minor children, so a total of 324 guilders per month. They do not receive this amount in full, because all advances which they received in Australia are deducted and an Indonesian war tax of 64.97 guilders per month is also collected. In addition, this pension is paid to a bank in Batavia in the Dutch East Indies and the fees for transferring funds to The Netherlands are high. Virtually nothing is left. Wim earned 950 guilders per month in Bandung, now Beb does not even get 500 per month.

4. On July 19, 1956, the Ministry of Foreign Affairs, Department of Rehabilitation of Indonesian War Victims, declares that Wim 'had the opportunity during the Japanese occupation of the Dutch East Indies to earn income and to reasonably provide for the livelihood of himself and his family and because of just that reason, he is not included in the definition of a war victim, as defined in the rehabilitation ordinance; as a consequence of this decision he is not eligible for rehabilitation benefits.' However, the Ministry can grant an allowance for refurbishment cost of 3,450 guilders, but it is stipulated that this amount will have to be reimbursed if the state is obliged to pay the salaries of the former Indonesian Government officials for the years of the Japanese occupation of Dutch East Indies or if the state has to pay compensation for lost salary. Beb started this application in 1949 when she moved into the house at the Frederik Hendriklaan in Haarlem.

5. On October 28, 1957, the Ministry of Foreign Affairs, Directorate of Transitional Affairs Indonesian Bureau Japanese Benefits, announces that Wim is entitled to a benefit under the agreement

concluded between The Netherlands and Japan concerning payments to former civilian internees in Asia, the amount of which has been set at 385.- guilders, about 100 dollars. This benefit is a consequence of the Yashida-Stikker agreement, which was signed in March 1957. It is agreed that Japan pays approximately ten million dollars to The Netherlands as compensation to the Dutch East Indies' prisoners of war.

6. Then there are four other official bodies that deal with compensation for war victims: the **PIG** (*Provisioning Dutch East Indies' evacuees*), the **CBVO** (*Central Bureau for the Care of War Victims*), the **NIBEG** (*the Dutch East Indies Association of former prisoners of war, internees and repatriates*) and finally the **CDWV** (*Central Directorate of Reconstruction and Housing, Department of General Affairs and Settlement of War Damage*). Each of these organizations has its own forms and rules. It is a full-time job to arrange everything adequately. In 1953 Louk, Wink and Tineke finally receive their Indonesian birth certificates. This request has taken 12 months.

The banking system in Indonesia also shows that it can display sparing behavior. When Beb receives dividend on shares that she still holds in Indonesia, the bank ensures that the commission is always the same amount as the payment, so that she receives nothing.

All these slow and laborious procedures give repatriates the feeling they are not very welcome in their own country and that is basically true. The Dutch government does not think that it can properly take care of its subjects and pursues an active policy to encourage Dutch citizens to try their luck in other parts of the world. The German occupation, the repatriation of more than three hundred thousand nationals and the fact that the gross national product drops by thirteen percent after the loss of the Dutch East Indies, all contribute to this idea. Between 1948 and 1965, more than four hundred thousand Dutch people leave their homeland.

Ineke van der Wal

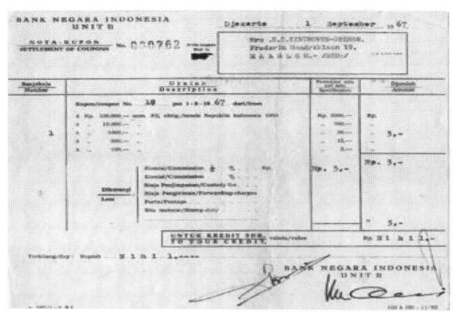

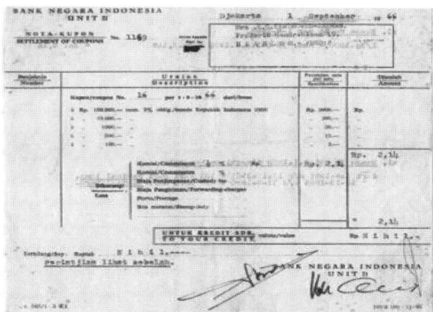

Two copies of statements of the Bank Negara Indonesia. The expenses are always exactly as high as the paid interest as a result of which the payment is always nil.

On April 12, 1951 Beb's mother dies (the day before Beb's 56th birthday). She was 79 years old and lived in Oegstgeest, in a nursing home. She leaves her clothing, jewelry and furniture to Beb while her five grandchildren inherit her assets. This allows Beb's and Loukie's children a good start in life.

Koos Einthoven in 1952

In 1952 Koos receives the *Resistance Star East Asia 1942-1945*. It is awarded to those who 'especially distinguished themselves on Japanese or Japanese-occupied territory in East Asia during the period 1942-1945, in spite of humiliating and grievous treatment by the occupying power, severe privations or ill-treatment.' From the nomination the following quotation:

'Has especially distinguished herself by acts of courage, strength of mind, strength of character and community spirit during the Japanese occupation.

Was interned during the occupation in the Poelan Brayan women's camp (near Medan) on Sumatra's east coast. Has firmly promoted to the Japanese camp command, the medical and hygienic camp interests as well as those in the field of food supply. Firstly, because of clandestine connections and secondly, due to her moral authority over the Japanese, she managed to obtain medicines, food, and special facilities. Was self-conscious and to a large extent fearless in her conduct where her campmates were concerned. She managed to prevent a shooting by the Japanese of camp residents with direct danger to her own life, while on another occasion intervened when an innocent campmate was abused by the Japanese. For this latter act she was taken away in captivity. A completely unselfish, incorruptible woman, for whom any act on behalf of her fellow comrades was never too much.'

Already in 1945, the Amsterdam Euterpestraat, where the German Security Service had its headquarters, is renamed Gerrit van der Veenstraat to honor this resistance hero. The 'Driemanschap' (Triumvirate), of which Lou Einthoven was a member, is scrutinized shortly after the liberation, but Lou is later put in charge of the National Security Office (after 1946 Domestic Security Service).

Now comes the time that Beb only has wishes: she hopes that her children will all get married, that they all have children and if possible at least a son and a daughter. These wishes all come true and Beb is happy to teach her grandchildren their first baby steps in her house.

This is a time in which Beb can leave the hard work and perseverance behind and can finally pick up her former enjoyment of traveling again. She travels regularly to the United States where Wink lives and to Switzerland where Tineke lives, but she also goes to Egypt to view the pyramids.

For company she gets a dog and names it Niki. It is important to Beb to maintain her contacts and she accomplishes this with regular visits, correspondence or by calling them on the phone. She always starts a phone call with: Hello, this is Mrs. Einthoven. She is very independent up to her old age and determines her own course without asking for help or advice.

Dog Niki in the driveway of Beb's house.

On Beb's sixtieth birthday in 1955, Kate organizes a beautiful get together, where all four children recite a verse about a part of their mother's life. This get together ends with the observation that her four children are healthy and well and that Beb can be proud of her achievements. On this birthday there are no grandchildren yet but the first one is already on the way. On Beb's seventieth birthday there are ten grandchildren and eventually there will be twelve. Beb enjoys them and takes her role as a grandmother seriously. She makes a habit of visiting when a grandchild celebrates his or her birthday and everyone regularly comes to stay in the house in Haarlem. She asks Willem Hofker to make a portrait of her oldest granddaughter.

Beb decides to place Wim's ashes in the grave of his parents at the Green Church in Oegstgeest, where Beb's family is also interred. This finally happens in 1955. Beb regularly visits to lay shells on the grave, a family habit. She becomes a member of a book club again, makes drawings of beautiful buildings, or of a beautiful view like the one from the apartment on the Oude Delft in the city of Delft where daughter Kate lives with her husband. She is always interested in architecture and writes, for example, about a visit to Hoog Catharijne (a modern shopping mall) in Utrecht. 'I just appreciate this from an architectural point of view' and 'Through the Dom Tower, that beautiful tower that has something so unique that you can always recognize it immediately. And the old cloister, how well-maintained that is. I'm glad that I was able to show you the stone rope.'

Portrait of granddaughter Ineke van der Wal, by Willem Gerard Hofker for Beb Einthoven-Zeeman.

Water-color drawing of the view from the apartment where daughter Kate lives with her husband. Painted by Beb Einthoven-Zeeman.

What was the purpose of their stay in Japan? A question that the group has posed many times. After the war several attempts are made to answer this question and various theories pass in review. Was the intention to be exchanged for Japanese who were interned in the United States? This is unlikely because the exchange of prisoners of war after mediation by the Swedish or International Red Cross, was halted halfway through 1943. Approximately 2,700 prisoners have been exchanged in this program, including 45 Dutch on Lourenço Marques, an island off the coast of Mozambique. The internees had to be equal in number, gender, education and status.

Henk Lels was in Japan in 1965 for a large conference on electronic issues and then tries to obtain more clarity at Sumitomo, but in the usual polite Japanese manner his request is denied. Geo Levenbach

Ineke van der Wal

went back to the United States where the data on the atomic bomb are made public in the seventies. Was the secret laboratory, which was set up in Bandung part of the study, which was to lead to a US atomic bomb? The work in the laboratory was so secret that the researchers themselves did not know what exactly it encompassed. In the book *'Japan's Secret War. Japan's race against time to build its own atomic bomb'* by Robert K. Wilcox, it is suggested that Japan had almost developed its own atomic bomb at the end of the war and was prepared to use this weapon against the Allies. President Truman knew of this and it was one of the reasons to actually use the American atomic bomb.

The research for the Japanese atomic bomb first took place in the Rikken Laboratories in Tokyo and Sumitomo was an important partner and supplier. These Rikken Laboratories were established by the military after the First World War so that Japan was not dependent on Europe or the US for research. After the Americans bombed Tokyo, work on the Japanese atomic bomb was moved to Konau, the Japanese name for Hungnam, in Korea, the Korean naval headquarters. Here enough electricity was available due to the proximity of the Chosin and Fusen reservoirs, which supplied the 'largest hydroelectric complex in the empire' with water. Was it the intention that the five researchers from Bandung had to cooperate to develop a Japanese atomic bomb? It seems unlikely that the Japanese would involve enemy researchers in such an important war project.

Geo Levenbach tried in 1970 to make direct contact with Sumitomo to find out what the purpose of their stay in Japan was. With his son Frits, Geo had an 'audience' with Baron Sumitomo. It was not the intention to ask questions or get answers. This was considered a courtesy visit. What Baron Sumitomo was able to tell them, however, was that Wim Einthoven's widow had written a letter that his death was not the fault of Sumitomo, while Geo Levenbach knew for certain that such a letter had never been written. They had to leave again, while constantly bending up and down at the waist.

Paulien Lels manages in 2001, through an informal approach, to gain access to NEC (*Nippon Electric Company*), part of the Sumitomo group. She writes: 'In a huge conference room, at the top of the NEC building, a special 'reception committee' of management, archivists, former employees and in their midst a hale and hearty old gentleman over 90 years old, Mr Osawa, who during the war, was the director of the laboratories, where our fathers had been forced to do their work. Standing perfectly erect and with a forceful voice he welcomed us and discussed a number of papers that had been compiled especially for us and discussed the papers together with us. Clear diagrams showed that people were busy setting up a radar system and that is the honest conclusion: the purpose of our stay in Japan was the development of radar.'

The freedom they so longed for does not only bring joy, but also disappointments: not being able to return to the Indies, losing all their belongings as well as all the luggage that they managed to carry with them through the war, the very cool reception in The Netherlands, the long-standing battle for money with many, ever-changing institutions, the visit of Emperor Hirohito, who was received in The Netherlands with honors and then the appearance of Lou de Jong's books on the Kingdom of The Netherlands during WWII, in which it is stated simply that the group of twenty-two Dutch was 'well cared for' in Japan:

'In Japan the engineers of the Radio Laboratory in Bandung and their families were well cared for: a group of 22 people, who, were transferred to Japan by the Sumitomo group as mentioned in chapter five.'

And:

'In early 1942, the Japanese government pledged to the governments of the US, UK and NL that she would treat not only the prisoners of war but also the internees in accordance with the provisions of the Geneva Convention. As far as Japan's internees are concerned, the Japanese

Ineke van der Wal

government has kept this commitment, in fact, it has gone further than the Convention prescribed, by in principle accommodating, feeding and dressing internees according to Western standards. 'All buildings', according to Dr. Van Velden 'used for internment, were built in a Western style and healthy and often very well located.' Often the internment complexes were not even fenced.'

Mr. De Jong relies on a study by Dr. D. van Velden entitled *The Japanese internment camps for civilians during the Second World War*, published in 1963. In it we find this statement:

'The internees were able to speak freely with the representatives of the protective powers every month, and had contact with the delegate of the International Red Cross. In many camps private visits were allowed: also the internees were allowed to leave the camps for visits to the hospital and to the dentist and sometimes also for walking, shopping or visiting their families (The latter in cases where for the family in question only the man was interned). Every month they were able to write a letter of a hundred words to countries outside Japan and usually once a week a letter to a place in Japan. The Japanese commanders and guards generally acted appropriately. The maintenance of the camps and the provision of food, soap, medicines and clothing were sufficient except in the last year.'

The question is how the RIOD (*Dutch National Institute for War Documentation*) reached this conclusion. In 1946, Beb receives a letter from the RIOD requesting information. In 1947 she complies with this request, after which further written questions are posed. In 1958, Wies Terlet-Einthoven donates the copies of the letters she received from Beb and Koos to the RIOD. The diary of Annie Lels is also donated. In other words, there was sufficient information available to come to a different opinion.

Paulien Lels decides in 2000 to add an extra statement to her interview at SMGI (*Foundation Oral History Indonesia*) to contradict the view of Lou de Jong:

Correction concerning Lou de Jong, page 741, The Kingdom of The Netherlands in the Second World War, 11b, Dutch East Indies, 2, second half.

First quotation: In Japan, the engineers of the Radio Laboratory in Bandung and their families were well cared for: a group of 22 people, who were transferred to Japan by the Sumitomo group as mentioned in chapter five.

Second quote: No wonder, according to Dr. Van Velden, that after the Japanese capitulation one could say that the internees looked healthy and in particular the Dutch group had done very well.

These statements must be corrected once and for all on behalf of all those involved. Upon the announcement of the forced deportation to Japan - meaning the taking of women and children as hostages so that something could be done to them if the men did not want to cooperate - a loaded revolver was pushed into the ribs of Mr. Einthoven's eldest daughter. On the way to Japan, twenty-two people were crammed into two hotel rooms for seven weeks in Singapore. The group arrived in Japan so exhausted and famished that the Japanese decided to provide the group with food from a hotel for two weeks. After that, the quality and quantity of food gradually decreased to a bare minimum. Mr. Lels was hit in the face by Sumitomo, Mr. Einthoven died of double pneumonia despite repeated requests for medical care. A doctor only came after his death. They were moved to a Buddhist temple just outside Nagoya, where there was no western housing, no fresh water and no plumbing. But there were lice, fleas and rats. Systematic starvation was applied. Especially the adults were so weakened at the time of liberation that they either could not or could hardly walk or stand. The group was emaciated. They would not have survived another winter. After their liberation, the Americans determined the following: severe malnutrition, beri beri, tropical ulcers. Members of the group received a card to carry around their necks with a prescription for the ex Bergen Belsen diet. They were advised to spread their food intake throughout the day in small quantities. Members of the group suffered for many years from avitaminosis (deficiency

Ineke van der Wal

of vitamins), gastrointestinal complaints, ulcers that did not heal, growth of the children was halted, children did not fully grow, their internal organs were underdeveloped, early osteoarthritis due to captivity, body was not able to make fat, etc., etc. None of the members of the Sumitomo group would have made or confirmed the statements of page 741 as quoted above. The survivors therefore ask themselves which indirect source has been used to proclaim the above quotations as facts. Veenendaal, November 26, 2000, A.P. Greeven-Lels.'

Beb Einthoven-Zeeman in 1985

Beb turns 80 years old in 1975 and she is convinced that she will die that year. All important events in her life take place in a year ending with a five (birth, loss of father, marriage, loss of husband) but it is not her time yet. The house on the Frederik Hendriklaan, however, becomes too much to manage and that is why Beb decides in 1979 to move to *Spaar en Hout* in Haarlem. This retirement home is located on a former country estate that lies between the river *Spaarne* and the *Haarlemmer Hout* (a park), hence the name. This choice is not surprising, because the building is beautiful and will later become a National Monument.

Beb leaves the house that she herself built in 1948. On a Saturday, all the grandchildren come to visit to say goodbye to the house and to distribute the remaining furniture. Beb thinks that there is not much to give away: 'I have so little, because all our possessions were left behind in the Dutch East Indies.'

After a short illness, Beb dies in her own bed on December 23, 1990. She is 95 years old. She acquired flu, which turns into pneumonia and she does not want treatment for it. The mourning card speaks of 'a creative and fascinating life'. It is Beb's wish that the cremation ceremony – on December 28 in Driehuis – will be a nice gathering and that is what it becomes. There are many people present because everyone knows that an era has come to an end, the era of Mrs. Ir. E.C Einthoven-Zeeman.

Acknowledgments

The fact that you write friendly Christmas letters is of course a narrow basis for the creation of an entire book. Many people helped me to turn an idea into reality. I am grateful to Maarten, Bella and Tineke for the management of the family archive, family tree information and photos. Kate for all the books about the Dutch East Indies. Geo and Wim for their warm welcome. The Library of Congress in Washington DC as an inexhaustible source of information available to everybody. Martien, who took in an amateur author. Charles, who inspired me to keep going. Everyone who remained friendlty when I told them that I wanted to write a book. Adriaan and Willem for their fresh views and especially Paul for his constant interest in this project. Thank you.

After publishing The Temple with the Chrysanthemums in The Netherlands, Hans and Maryke wanted to make it available to their families in the United States. Maryke took on the translation, supported by her husband Robin. Hans combined text and illustrations into a book. Hans and Maryke are members of the group that was transported to Japan in 1944; they were 4 and 2 ½ years old then. Working with them was a pleasure and an honor for which I thank them.

Bibliography and Abbreviations

AID-press release concerning the departure to Dutch East Indies of W.F. Einthoven, *Locomotief*, October 3, 1927, KITLV, inventory 288, H-1800, nr. 24.

Akihary, Huib, *Architectuur en stedebouw in Indonesië, 1870-1970*, De Walburg Pers, Zutphen, 1990.

Algemeen Indisch Dagblad, Friday, August 3, nr. 206, p. 4.

Alphen de Veer, Ir. W. van, 'In memoriam Ir. W.F. Einthoven.' *Electrotechniek, economisch-technisch tijdschrift*, January 3, 1946, 24th year, nr. 1, pp. 8-9.

Aneta press release, 'Belangrijke uitvinding op radiogebied', De Zeeuw, *Christelijk Historisch Nieuwsblad voor Zeeland*, July 26, 1930, p. 3 via https://krantenbankzeeland.nl.

Baar, P.J.M. de, *Wonen aan het Galgewater*, 1988, Matrijs Publishers, Utrecht, 1988.

Berlage, H.P., *Mijn Indische Reis, gedachten over cultuur en kunst*, 1931, Rotterdam.

Biografisch woordenboek van Nederland, Visser, J.G. about Cornelius Johannes de Groot.

Blokker, J., 'Kleinkinderen van de thee', *de Volkskrant*, August 12, 1995.

Boon, S., Van Geleuken, E., *Ik wilde eigenlijk niet gaan – de repatriëring van Indische Nederlanders 1946-1964,* Tong Tong Society, Den Haag, 1993.

Braaksma, Tjalling, *Met het SS Nieuw Holland naar de tropen, Amsterdam – Batavia, 30 oktober – 28 november 1947,* via www.boordgeld.nl/index.php/ss-nieuw-holland.

Bruyne, Marnix de, 'We moeten gaan, Nederlandse boeren in Zimbabwe', Podium, bookreview in NRC, June 24, 2016, p. C10.

Buning, Ank, Condolence letter, December 1990.

Ineke van der Wal

Caidin, Martin, *A torch to the enemy – The Fire Raid on Tokyo*. Ballantine Books, New York, 1960.

Christelijk Lyceum Bandoeng, *Mededelingen*. 1939-1940 4, 1937-1938 3, 4, 5 and 7.

Daws, Gavan, *Prisoners of the Japanese – POW's of World War II in the Pacific*, William Morrow and Company Inc, New York, 1994.

Delft, D. van, *Einstein & Friends*, Museum Boerhaave, Leiden, September 2015.

Doel, H.W. van den, *Afscheid van Indië, De val van het Nederlandse imperium in Azië*. Prometheus, Amsterdam, 2000.

Doorn, J.A.A. van, *De laatste eeuw van Indië, Ontwikkeling en ondergang van een koloniaal project*, Bert Bakker, 1994, bookdiscussion in *NRC*, April 8, 1994 from Elsbeth Locher- Scholten.

DSC – Male Student Society in Delft, The Netherlands.

DVSV – Female Student Society in Delft, The Netherlands

Dijkstra, K, *Radio Malabar, herinneringen aan een boeiende tijd 1914-1945*, Emaus, 2005. This book is written by an employee of Radio Malabar and gives an extended and very technical description of the history of Radio Malabar (first part) and Dajeuh Kolot (second part).

Einthoven, J.F.G., *De Einthoven's wie en wat*, Heemstede, 1989.

Einthoven, J.J., *Afschrift voor de Indische dagboeken en egodocumenten van Mw. Drs. J.J. Einthoven*, NIOD, archive 401, inventory number 166.

Einthoven, Prof. Dr. W, Lettters to his son W.F. Einthoven, *1912-1920*. KITLV, inventory 288, H-1800, nr. 3.

Einthoven, W., Einthoven W.F., Horst, W. van der and Hirschfeld, H., Brownsche bewegingen van een gespannen snaar. *Physika* 5, 358 – 360, nr. 11-12, 1925.

Einthoven, Ir. W.F., *De snaargalvanometer ten dienste der radiotelegrafie*. KNAW - Royal Netherlands Institute of Arts and Sciences, Amsterdam, 1922, (www.dwc.knaw.nl/DL/publications/PU00014984.pdf).

Einthoven, Ir. W.F., 'The string galvanometer in wireless telegraphy'.

Proceedings 26, no's 7 and 8, 1923, *Journal of the Optical Society of America*, L. Behr, 1924.

Einthoven, W.F., *Voordracht over de radio-telegrafische verbinding Indië-Holland voor de Nederlandsch-Indische Maatschappij van Nijverheid en Landbouw*. Nederlandsche Afdeling, De Bussy, 1922.

Einthoven, W.F., *Méthode de réception de signaux sans fil*. Patent CA246737A, 1925.

Einthoven, W.F., *De snaargalvanometer en de storingsvrijheid van de ontvangst bij de draadloze telegrafie,* 1925, Tijdschrift van het Nederlandse Elektronika & Radiogenootschap, deel 50, 1985, reprint from 1923.

Einthoven, W.F., 'Rede bij onthulling De Groot monument', *Radio Expres*, KITLV, inventory 288, H-1800, nr. 32.

Einthoven, W.G. 'Wink', interview by Wal, van der, I., November 11, 1991, Trenton, NJ.

Einthoven-Zeeman, Ir. E.C., *Afschrift voor de Indische collectie van brieven van Mw. Ir. E.C. Einthoven-Zeeman,* NIOD, archive number 401, inventory number 167.

EKNJ - Stichting Ex-Krijgsgevangenen en Nabestaanden Japan, Society for ex-prisoners of War and relatives Japan, part of Indisch4Ever.

Goetz Holmes, Linda, *Unjust Enrichment – How Japan's Companies Built Postwar Fortunes Using American POWs*. Stackpole books, Mechanicsburg, PA, USA, 2001.

Greeven-Lels, A.P., 'Deportatie naar Japan: zoektocht naar duidelijkheid', lecture for EKNJ, KITLV, inventory 288, H-1800, number 25.

Greeven-Lels, A.P., *Interview,* by SMGI, September, October and November 2000, nr. 1649.

Greeven-Lels, A.P., 'Wij waren het onderpand voor onze vaders', *Moesson*, January 2007.

Groot, C.J. de, 'Hetgeen op Radiotechnisch gebied in Nederlandsch-Indië is tot stand gebracht en de radiotelegrafische verbinding tusschen Nederland en Indië', *De Ingenieur*, 1925, nrs. 40 and 41, KITLV, inventory 288, H-1800, nr. 30.

Heldersche Courant, 'De telefoonprijs van de Haagsche Post', January 4, 1930, p. 9, via Kranten Regionaal Archief Alkmaar.

Hillen, C., Nieuwjaarsrede, *PTT-Nieuws*, January 1939.

Hillen, Ernest, *The way of a boy. Viking, 1993.* Bookreview in *NRC Handelsblad*, August 27, 1994.

Hofker, Seline, *Willem Gerard Hofker.* Uitgeverij De Kunst, 2013.

Hofker-Rueter, M., *Maria Hofker's Indische impressies*, J.H. Gottmer/H.J.W. Becht bv, Bloemendaal, 1994.

Hogesteeger, Dr.G. (Redactie), Naar de Gordel van Smaragd. De postverbindingen tussen Nederland en Nederlands-Indië 1602 – 1940. Sea Press, PTT Museum, 1995.

Hoogerwerf, Dr. S., *Leven en Werken van Willem Einthoven. Grondlegger van de Electrocardiografie.* U.M. West-Friesland, Hoorn, 1955.

Immerzeel, B.R., *Bandoeng. Een stad met toekomst,* October 26, 2011 via https://javapost.nl.

Immerzeel, B.R., *Berichten uit Japan*, March 13, 2012 via https://javapost.nl.

International Telecommunications Conferences Cairo 1938, *Report to the Secretary of State by the Chairman of the American Delegation,* 1939, Washington DC, USA, Government Printing Office.

Ir. – Master of Engineering Science.

Jong, Frida de, 'Standhouden in Delft', *Gewina/TGGNWT*, nr. 20, 1997.

Jong, Lou de, *Het Koninkrijk der Nederlanden tijdens de Tweede Wereldoorlog,* 11b, Martinus Nijhoff uitgeverij, 's Gravenhage, 1985.

Keilson, H., *Daar staat mijn huis.* Van Gennep, 2011, bookreview in *NRC*, March 31, 2011 by Arnon Grunberg.

KITLV - Royal Netherlands Institute of Southeast Asian and Caribbean Studies, Leiden, inventory 288, H-1800, nrs. 1-36. Gift from W.G. Einthoven and J.N. Vles. Mr. Vles had plans to write a book about Ir.

W.F. Einthoven. That did not happen, but he donated his research documentation to KITLV.

Kluijver, J.C., 'P. Zeeman Gzn, in memoriam', *Leidsch Dagblad*, 1915 and *Eigen Haard*, nr. 22, 1915.

Kunto, Haryoto, *Wajah Bandoeng Tempo Doeloe*, PT Granesia, April 1984.

Lels, Ir. H., *Interview*, by Wal, van der, I., The Hague, November 1976.

Lels, Ir. H., *Rapport betr. MTA Hasenstab* aan Kol. Ir. C.J. Warners, directeur van Verkeer en Waterstaat, November 6, 1945.

Lels-Visser, A., *Deportatie naar Japan, 23 januari 1944 – 30 september 1945*. Diary of Annie Lels-Visser addressed to A. (Gon) Hoeffelman-De Jong, NIOD, archive 401, inventory nr. 406.

Levenbach, Geo, *Verslag van deportatie naar Japan*, January 10, 1990.

Lugt, F, *Oorlogsgraven in Oegstgeest*, Oorlogsgravencomité Oegstgeest, April 2005.

Maraini, Fosco, *Meeting with Japan*. The Viking Press, New York, 1960. Chapter 12, *Red Skies over Nagoya* decribes the inprisonment in Japan.

Ministerie van Koloniën, *brief gedateerd 22 november 1921 gericht aan W.F. Einthoven*, concerning payment of 100.000 guilders and reminder about patent registration, KITLV, inventory 288, H-1800, nr. 3.

Ministerie van Koloniën, *Contract van 18 september 1916 met W. Einthoven*, KITLV, inventory 288, H-1800, nrs. 4 and 5.

Neer, Robert M., *Napalm, an American Biography*, Harvard University Press, 2013, bookreview *NRC*, June 7, 2013 by Jan Donkers.

New York Times, '7,500-Mile Radio Links Holland to Indies as World's Largest Stations Begin Service', May 7, 1923, frontpage.

New York Times, August 15 – September 15, 1945.

New York Times Magazine, September 10, 1945 'First Impressions of Conquered Japan', Frank L. Kluckhohn.

Newsweek, August 13 and November 5, 1945.

Nieuwe Rotterdamsche Courant, 31 oktober 1920, 'Het radiostation op den Malabar, verslag van een lezing door W.F. Einthoven voor de Electrotechnische Vereeniging te Delft', KITLV, inventory 288, H-1800, nr. 16.

NIOD - Netherlands Institute for War, Holocaust and Genocide Studies, Amsterdam. Mrs. L.M.M.C. Terlet - Einthoven *(Wies)* donated several items concerning the internment during WWII of her family members to this institute in 1958.

Nortier, J.J., Kuijt, P., Groen, P.M.H., 'De Japanse aanval op Java', maart 1942. *De Bataafsche Leeuw*, 1994, bookdiscussion by Michiel Hegener, *NRC*, April 9, 1994.

Operatie Berlijn, *De wereld in vlammen 1940-1945, de aanval van Japan op midden en West Java* nr. 31a via https://sites.google.com/site/degrotezoektocht/.

Passchier, Cor, 'Bandung, groei en ontwikkeling van een stad1900-1942' in Berg, H.M. van den (eindredactie), *De stenen droom,* Walburg Pers, Zutphen, 1988.

Preangerbode, Algemeen Indisch Dagblad, Anniversary edition for 25 years of Bandoeng, April 13, 1931.

PTT - Post Telegraph and Telephone.

Raë-Einthoven, T.M. 'Tineke', *Interview,* by Wal, van der, I., October 1992, Monaco.

Reitsma, S.A., [compiled by], *Bandoeng, the Mountain City of the Netherlands India.* G. Kolff & Co, Weltevreden, Batavia (Java), 1935.

Saturday Evening Post, September 8 – October 20, 1945.

Schippers, H.J., *Verslag van de eerste internationale wereld conferentie voor telegraaf, telefoon en radiodienst te Cairo op 1 februari 1938 en de gevolgen tijdens de Japanse bezetting in Nederlands Oost Indië.*

Schuuring, Casper, 'De nieuwe heren van de thee', *NRC*, bijlage wetenschap en onderwijs, March 17, 1994, p. 1.

SMGI - Stichting Mondelinge Geschiedenis Indië, Oral History Archive Indonesia available via KITLV, Leiden

Snellen, H.A., *Willem Einthoven (1860-1927) Father of electrocardiography,* Kluwer Academic Publishers, Dordrecht, 1995.

Stichting Wetenschappelijk Radio-fonds Veder via www.vederfonds.org.

Time Magazine, August 20th – September 24, 1945.

Vles, J.N., *Hallo Bandoeng, Nederlandse Radiopioniers (1900-1945).* Walburg Pers, Zutphen, 2008.

Vles, J.N., 'De hartslag van een langegolf telegrafiezender'. *Radio Historisch Tijdschrift,* nr. 129, 2, 2009.

Vogt, W., *Een leven met radio, de belevenissen van een strijdbaar radioman.* Semper Agendo, Apeldoorn, 1973.

Waart, A. de, *Het levenswerk van Willem Einthoven 1860 -1927,* Erven F. Bohn N.V. Haarlem, 1957.

Wal-Einthoven, van der, K.L., 'Gevangene in Tokio', zoals verschenen in *VEDO, tijdschrift van oud VCL-Bandoeng leerlingen.*

Wal-Einthoven, van der, K.L., 'Ik bleef leven en dat was een moeilijk proces', *Tubantia,* August 14, 1999.

Wal-Einthoven, van der, K.L., 'Toespraak, ter gelegenheid van de herdenking van de overgave van Japan', 15 augustus 1999, Enschede.

Wal-Einthoven, K.L. 'Kate' van der, *Interview,* Wal, van der, I., Munich, Germany and Enschede.

Wilcox, Robert K., *Japan's secret war. Japan's race against time to build its own atomic bomb.* William Morrow and Company Inc, New York, 1985.

Withuis, Jolande, *Juliana's vergeten oorlog,* De Bezige Bij, Amsterdam, 2014, bookdiscussion by Daniëlle Pinedo en Jannetje Koelewijn, *NRC,* March 8, 2014

Woltjer, H.R., 'De ontwikkeling der natuurkunde in Indonesië gedurende de 100 jarige werkzaamheid der Koninklijke Natuurkundige Vereniging'. *Chronica Naturae*, Koninklijke Natuurkundige Vereniging, part 106, nr. 5, May 1950.

Wormser, Dr. C.W., *33 Jaren op Java, deel III*. Uitgeverij W. Ten Have N.V. Amsterdam, ca. 1950.

Woud, A. van der, *Koninkrijk vol sloppen. Achterbuurten en vuil in de negentiende eeuw*, bookdiscussion by Gert J. Peelen, *de Volkskrant*, November 27, 2010.

Wij varen! Op 12 mei 1940 met de Johan de Witt van Amsterdam naar Batavia via Kaap de Goede Hoop, 4e druk, uitgave G. Kolff & Co.

Zeeman-De Bruijn, C. E., various journals of the mother of Beb Einthoven-Zeeman about her children, her journey to Dutch East Indies and the period during WWII without contact with her daughter.

Colofon

This edition of *The Temple with the Chrysanthemums* was published in December 2018. It was originally published in the Dutch language under the title *De Tempel met de Chrysanten, Krijgsgevangene in Tokio* in November 2017.

Design and typesetting: Hans Levenbach and Ineke van der Wal
Translation: Maryke Levenbach and Robin Williams
Editing: Ineke van der Wal
Typeface: Garamond
Cover Design: Rose Tannenbaum

Illustrations were made available by:
Family archives of W.G. Einthoven and E.C. Einthoven-Zeeman
Libraries of K.L. van der Wal–Einthoven and T.M. Raë–Einthoven
Frontcover: Beb Einthoven-Zeeman
Photo page 347: Loukie van der Veen-Van der Chijs
Photo pages 4, 98, 109, 128, 341 and 342: Bas Uterwijk
Geographical maps and pedigrees: Martien Frijns

The publisher, Ineke van der Wal, has made all reasonable efforts to trace all rights holders to any copyrighted material used in this work. In cases where these efforts have not been successful the publisher welcomes communications from copyrights holders, so that the appropriate acknowledgements can be made in future editions, and to settle other permission matters.

TheTemplewiththeChrysanthemums@outlook.com

54364986R00213